MY KINGDOM COME

THE MORMON QUEST FOR GODHOOD

BY ED DECKER

Ed's Final Book on Mormonism

After 50 years of daily involvement with Mormonism, as a member and an Ex-Mormon researcher, I have concluded that there is only so much one can write about the subject. This book is the summation of all that research, study and personal observation. Some portions of this book come from earlier writings that have been updated and revised.

Copyright © 2007 by Ed Decker

My Kingdom Come
The Mormon Quest For Godhood
by Ed Decker

Printed in the United States of America

ISBN 978-1-60477-378-1

All rights reserved solely by the author. The author guarantees all contents are original and do not infringe upon the legal rights of any other person or work. No part of this book may be reproduced in any form without the permission of the author. The views expressed in this book are not necessarily those of the publisher.

Unless otherwise indicated, Bible quotations are taken from the NKJV. Copyright © 1996 by Broadman and Holman.

For more information, please contact Ed Decker/Saints Alive Ministries, PO Box 1347, Issaquah, WA 98027 or visit www.SaintsAlive.com.

www.xulonpress.com

TABLE OF CONTENTS

INTRODUCTION……ix
THE PEOPLE WHO WOULD BE GODS
Setting the stage: The LDS struggle and need to earn godhood

CHAPTER ONE……15
THE LAW OF ETERNAL PROGRESSION
The LDS doctrine of where we came from, where we are going and what we must do to get there

CHAPTER TWO……29
A NEW FACE FOR AN OLD SCAM
How and why the Mormon Church keeps changing as it seeks to be included in the Christian Orthodoxy it privately mocks and rejects

CHAPTER THREE……55
THE BIRTH OF HERESY
Going back to the beginning days of Mormonism and looking at the root heresies

CHAPTER FOUR......73
BEHIND CLOSED DOORS
Looking at the destructive forces of heresy and false faith in the lives of families

CHAPTER FIVE......115
CLEANING UP THE UNCHANGEABLE TEMPLE RITUALS
The unchangeable Temple Ritual that keeps changing with the times

CHAPTER SIX......135
There is nothing new under the sun. The astonishing parallels of Mormonism and Islam.

CHAPTER SEVEN......145
LET'S BE CHRISTIANS ABOUT THIS
The reasons behind the Mormon zeal to convert the world

CHAPTER EIGHT......173
TESTING THE PROPHET JOSEPH SMITH
The core testimony of every Mormon is that Joseph Smith was a holy prophet. But was he a true prophet or a false prophet?

CHAPTER NINE......201
A MASSIVE MESS OF SCRIPTURE
Mormons believe that the Bible is the weakest link in scriptures and place their full faith in three other books that contain their fullness of truth. But do they believe in vain?

CHAPTER TEN......227
FUNDAMENTALLY MORMONS

Why the Mormon Fundamentalists are living out the real LDS Doctrines

Joseph Smith, the self-proclaimed prophet of God and founder of the Mormon Church, used the doctrine of divine revelation to legitimize his polygamous marriages to many wives at the same time. He spiritualized the immorality of his plural marriages and declared it to be "a New and everlasting Covenant; and if ye abide not that covenant then are ye damned; for no one can reject this covenant and be permitted to enter into my glory."

CHAPTER ELEVEN......285
THE DEVIL IS IN THE DETAILS

Satan has his claws entwined throughout the doctrines and practices of Mormonism, especially throughout the temple ritual and even sewn into the temple garments

CHAPTER TWELVE......309
THE MORMON PLAN FOR AMERICA AND THE RISE OF MITT ROMNEY
THE MAN WHO WOULD BE GOD

The very ethos of the Mormon faith is built around the anticipated return of Jesus to Independence, Missouri, for his thousand-year millennial reign. It is here that he will assign godhood to the worthy.

However, it cannot take place until the U.S. Constitution falters and is saved by the LDS church. The nation will become a Mormon theocracy. Mitt Romney has raised Mormon speculation that this may be the time and that he may be the one to lead the way as both U.S. President and LDS high priest.

CHAPTER THIRTEEN......347

THE CASH-COW KINGDOM

The "Kingdom of God" has become a cash-cow kingdom. The where and the why of the great wealth.

CHAPTER FOURTEEN......365

THE BOOK OF MORMON: FOUNDATION OF FAITH

A quick summary of the root heresies of Mormonism and how we are to deal with them

CHAPTER FIFTEEN......397

FINALLY, BRETHREN

INTRODUCTION

The People Who Would Be Gods

**Setting the stage: The LDS struggle and need to earn godhood.
Ed Decker Discusses the Importance of This
Final Book**

You would think that after so many years of dealing with the errors of Mormonism, I would be beyond the task of yet one more book. The title, *My Kingdom Come,* points to the hard-core heretical teaching that the goal of every believing Mormon is to become a god or goddess, just like "Elohim" — the LDS god of this world and his many goddess wives. There is no other reason to be a Mormon.

Yes, to a Mormon, happiness may be Family Home Evening, and *families* may be forever to a Mormon who makes godhood, but becoming an actual god is the ultimate goal of every member of the church. As you will read throughout the coming chapters, Mormons believe the reason for coming to earth from the planet near the great star Kolob is to gain bodies for our spirit beings and to be tested. To become gods, they need to be Mormons, to go through the temple to learn the signs and tokens for entry to the celestial glory and to be obedient unto death to the holy prophet. As you read on, you will see that everything else is tied to, and wraps around, this one goal.

Amazing? Yes, it is! But even more disparate is the position of Christ in all this. Mormonism teaches that when their god decided it was time to populate this earth with his spirit children, a great council of the gods was held to decide the method. The Mormon god asked his two eldest sons, Jesus and Lucifer, to both prepare plans for presentation to the council. They chose the plan of Jesus.

Lucifer rebelled and led one-third of the "children" to revolt against god, and in a great battle he was defeated by Christ and the two-thirds who were "valiant." Lucifer and those one-third of us in that pre-existent world who fought with him were cast to earth without bodies and became the devil and his demons. Those others who were less than valiant became the black race, and the very valiant became the "white and delightsome" race.

Mormonism teaches that if Mormons are faithful, pay their tithes, obey all the laws and ordinances of the (Mormon) gospel, do their genealogy and go to the temple for secret, sacred rituals for both the living and their dead, wear sacred undergarments marked with sacred talismanic sewn into them, they too can become gods and goddesses as "all gods have done before them."

To the Mormon, Jesus is our elder brother who pointed the way, but is not The Way, as we orthodox Christians understand. To the Mormon, Jesus was the god of the Old Testament, but once he took his physical form, he justified his own spiritual salvation through his works while in the flesh, just as each of us must also do.

Mormonism teaches that Jesus suffered for our sins in the Garden of Gethsemane, providing personal salvation (which may lead to exaltation or godhood) conditional upon our obedience to the laws and ordinances of the LDS gospel. His death on the cross provided a general salvation, whereby all mankind, every human being who ever lived, will be resurrected to be judged for their works of obedience to whatever spiritual law or set of ethics by which they lived.

Jesus is the LDS savior only in the sense that his death gives the Mormon the means of *returning* to the god of this world, using the secret keys, hand grips and passwords learned only in the Mormon temple, which will ensure safe passage. At this time, each Mormon will be judged according to his or her obedience to LDS laws and ordinances. The result will send the very worthy to the Celestial Kingdom, where they will become polygamous gods and goddesses to reign over another planet in some galaxy where this "Law of

Eternal Progression" will continue though the next cycle of this eternal system of god-making.

Those less righteous Mormons and those outside the church who were obedient to their faith or law will be sent to the Terrestrial Kingdom; and the most evil humans, murderers, liars, sorcerers, adulterers, anti-Mormons and so on will spend their eternity in the Telestial Kingdom.

What I have just shared is just the tip of a dark and dangerous iceberg, filled with death for its unsuspecting victims. Proverbs 14:12 says, *"There is a way that seemeth right unto a man, but the end thereof are the ways of death."* (KJV) Were the scriptures ever more direct in such a matter?

The Mormon people are like those of whom Paul spoke in Romans 10: *"Brethren, my heart's desire and prayer to God...is that they might be saved. For I bear them record that they have a zeal for God, but not according to knowledge. For they, being ignorant of God's righteousness, and going about to establish their own righteousness, have not submitted themselves unto the righteousness of God."*

There is a real zeal to serve God manifest in the lives and actions of the Mormon people. It is my prayer that the information I have gathered over the last fifty years presented herein will give you the opportunity to share that true joy of Christ's righteousness and love with your Mormon friends and loved ones! Let them know that there is only one God, and the job is taken; and He was not one born of man on some other planet in some outer galaxy.

There is one and only one savior, and He took all the laws and ordinances that were against us and moved them out of the way, nailing them to His Cross. (Colossians 2:13-15)

CHAPTER ONE

The Law of Eternal Progression

The LDS doctrine of where we came from, where we are going and what we must do to get there.

I am often asked, "Do the Mormons *really* believe those things, or have you dug up old material from some obscure past to make your points?" The question might also be, "Aren't you flogging a dead horse? The average Mormon family wouldn't know anything about that stuff! Why don't you make reference to something that someone below the rank of an apostle would have access to?"

It is my firm position that the very basic doctrines of Mormonism clearly separate it from Christian orthodoxy. No matter how many times the LDS church uses the name of Christ; they are, without a shadow of a doubt, completely outside Christianity.

If I have been told once, I have been told a thousand times by Mormons that they must surely be Christians because the church is named "The Church of Jesus Christ of Latter-day Saints." That just isn't good logic.

If you went into a restaurant with a big sign on the window stating it was "Tony's Pizza Parlor" and once inside, found out that they only served BBQ Chicken, you can chew on that chicken leg all day long, but it isn't going to turn into a slice of pizza. That actually happened to my family on a vacation years ago. We all piled out of our van and raced into the only pizza place in a small community; only to find out they were out of pizza dough and were only serving BBQ Chicken. We were not happy campers as we chewed on chicken.

The signs outside the LDS churches may use the words *Jesus Christ,* but the words do not reflect what is served inside the doors. The Mormons worship a different god; have a different Jesus, and a very different Holy Spirit. Mormons are polytheists in the highest sense. Not only do they teach that there are countless other gods, they teach that man may also attain godhood through "obedience to the (Mormon) laws and ordinances of the (Mormon) gospel."

The simplest expression of this is what the Church calls the Law of Eternal Progression:

"As man is, God once was; as God is, man may become."

Think about all that this holy axiom means. It means that God does not exist outside this creation called Earth, but is a sexually conceived being sent here from some other galaxy system, to begat the people of this planet and guide them to their own god-hoods. Let's take a deeper look at this core heresy, from which all the false doctrines of Mormonism hang.

In order to show that the support documentation for this doctrine is readily available to the average, active, LDS family, I have listed Mormonism's basic heresies in this regard and have documented them from books and materials that an LDS family would have in its home.

This doctrine of endless generations of created gods has birthed the entire theology of Mormonism. From the Temple rituals for the living to those for their dead, from the teaching that "Families are Forever" to the pressure on parents to send their youth to the mission fields across the world, the Mormon people are committed to a controlled program that maps out their entire lives as they seek their own exaltation and godhood.

Let's look at this mystery religion in simple terms. One of the most offensive (to Mormons) bits of work we have produced over the years is a 7-minute animation that accurately describes this LDS law. It was first used in the film, "The God Makers."

Today, you can go to the video website, **YouTube.com** and type the word *Mormon* in the search box, and you will find "Cartoon banned by the Mormon church" listed as the number-one video on the subject of Mormonism. In fact, on the day that I wrote this, I clicked through the videos posted on **YouTube** regarding this animation, found eight postings of it **with almost a half million viewings**. The many comments of unbelief tell the tale. The animation says that:

> *Mormonism teaches that trillions of planets scattered throughout the cosmos are ruled by countless gods who once were human like us.*
>
> *They say that long ago, on one of these planets, to an unidentified god and one of his goddess wives, a spirit child named Elohim was conceived. This spirit child was later born to human parents who gave him a physical body.*
>
> *Through obedience to Mormon teaching, death and resurrection, he proved himself worthy and was elevated to godhood as his father god before him.*
>
> *Mormons believe that Elohim is their Heavenly Father and that he lives with his many wives on a planet near a mysterious star called Kolob. Here the god of Mormonism and his wives, through endless celestial sex, produced billions of spirit children. We spirit children come to earth through human birth to gain physical bodies so we may have the bodies we need to become gods.*

By maintaining a rigid code of financial and moral requirements, and through performing secret temple rituals for themselves and the dead, the Latter-day Saints hope to prove their worthiness and thus become gods. The Mormons teach that everyone must stand at the final judgment before Joseph Smith, the Mormon Jesus, and Elohim.

Those Mormons who are sealed in the eternal marriage ceremony in LDS temples expect to become polygamous gods or their goddess wives in the Celestial Kingdom, rule over other planets and spawn new families throughout eternity. The Mormons thank God for Joseph Smith, who claimed that he had done more for us than any other man, including Jesus Christ. The Mormons claim that he died as a martyr, shed his blood for us, so that we, too, may become gods.

Shocking? Incomprehensible? Maybe to you and to me, but this is the core of Mormon theology, and it binds its believers away from the real Jesus, the real gospel and the real spirit of truth as surely as though they were locked away in chains of metal.

My Words or the Words of the LDS Leaders?

Over the many years of my ministry, I have been continually accused of using lies, misrepresentations, half-truths and misquotes to make a weak case seem strong. On many occasions, both public and private, I have asked the challenger(s) to give me the best shot, the worst lie, misrepresentation or misquote. I have offered to shut down my ministry if I could not document my statement from authorized LDS documents, with the understanding that the challenger would renounce Mormonism if I did prove the statement. In thirty years of ministry, I have documented every such challenged statement. As you may suspect, none of the challengers renounced the church when I gave them the data.

This goes to the core of the issue, biblically. Romans 1:18-25, in the New King James Version, states:

> *For the wrath of God is revealed from heaven against all ungodliness and unrighteousness of men, who suppress the truth in unrighteousness, because what may be known of God is manifest in them, for God has shown it to them. For since the creation of the world His invisible attributes are clearly seen, being understood by the things that are made, even His eternal power and Godhead, so that they are without excuse, because, although they knew God, they did not glorify Him as God, nor were thankful,*

but became futile in their thoughts, and their foolish hearts were darkened.

Professing to be wise, they became fools, and changed the glory of the incorruptible God into an image made like corruptible man—and birds and four-footed animals and creeping things. Therefore God also gave them up to uncleanness, in the lusts of their hearts, to dishonor their bodies among themselves, who exchanged the truth of God for the lie, and worshiped and served the creature rather than the Creator, who is blessed forever. Amen.

Here Are Some of Those LDS Proof Texts

Bruce R. McConkie: "That exaltation which the saints of all ages have so devoutly sought is godhood itself."[1]

Joseph Smith: "You have got to learn how to be gods yourselves...the same as all gods have done before you. My Father worked out His Kingdom with fear and trembling, and I must do the same; and when I get my kingdom, I shall present it to my Father, so that He may obtain Kingdom upon Kingdom, and it will exalt Him in glory. He will then take a higher exaltation, and I will take His place, and thereby become exalted myself."[2]

If God became God by obedience to all of the gospel law with the crowning point being the celestial law of marriage, then that's the only way I can become a god. [answer] Right![3]

(12-15) The endowment is the celestial course of instruction...being enabled to give them the key words, the signs and tokens, pertaining to the priesthood and gain your eternal exaltation in spite of earth and hell.[4]

Speaking of Baptism for the dead:

For therein are the keys of the holy priesthood ordained, that you may receive honor and glory.[5]

For their salvation is necessary and essential to our salvation, as Paul says concerning the fathers—that they without us cannot be made perfect—neither can we without our dead be made perfect.[6]

In the celestial glory there are three heavens or degrees; And in order to obtain the highest, a man must enter into this order of the priesthood [meaning the new and everlasting covenant of marriage]; And if he does not, he cannot obtain it.[7]

This is my [God's] work and my glory to bring to pass the immortality and eternal life of man.[8]

The Doctrine and Covenants Explains Godhood

The glory and reward of exalted beings in the celestial kingdom:

53 And who overcome by faith, and are sealed by the Holy Spirit of promise, which the Father sheds forth upon all those who are just and true. 54 They are they who are the church of the Firstborn. 55 They are they into whose hands the Father has given all things. 56 They are they who are priests and kings, who have received of his fulness, and of his glory;

57 And are priests of the Most High, after the order of Melchizedek, which was after the order of Enoch, which was after the order of the Only Begotten Son. 58 Wherefore, as it is written, they are gods, even the sons of God—70 These are they whose bodies are celestial, whose glory is that of the sun, even the glory of God, the highest of all, whose glory the sun of the firmament is written of as being typical.[9]

Celestial marriage and a continuation of the family unit enable men to become gods:

19 And again, verily I say unto you, if a man marry a wife by my word, which is my law, and by the new and everlasting covenant, and it is sealed unto them by the Holy Spirit of promise, by him who is anointed, unto whom I have appointed this power and the keys of this priesthood; and it shall be said unto them—Ye shall come forth in the first resurrection; and if it be after the first resurrection, in the next resurrection;

and shall inherit thrones, kingdoms, principalities, and powers, dominions, all heights and depths—then shall it be written in the Lamb's Book of Life, that he shall commit no murder whereby to shed innocent blood, and if ye abide in my covenant, and commit no murder whereby to shed innocent blood, it shall be done unto them in all things whatsoever my servant hath put upon them, in time, and through all eternity; and shall be of full force when they are out of the world; and they shall pass by the angels, and the gods, which are set there, to their exaltation and glory in all things, as hath been sealed upon their heads, which glory shall be a fulness and a continuation of the seeds forever and ever.

20 Then shall they be gods, because they have no end; therefore shall they be from everlasting to everlasting, because they continue; then shall they be above all, because all things are subject unto them. Then shall they be gods, because they have all power, and the angels are subject unto them.[10]

Did you read that? ***Then shall they be gods, because they have all power, and the angels are subject to them.*** **That is the goal of every believing Mormon Man – from the Mormon Missionary at your door to Mitt Romney, the Mormon Candidate – the man who would be god.**

And from the Temple Marriage Manual:

(1-12) The Lord commands marriage.

(1-13) Exaltation is based on celestial marriage.

(1-14) Then shall they be Gods, because they have no end.

(1-15) Only resurrected and glorified Beings may become Parents of Spirit Offspring.

(1-17) Celestial marriage prepares men to be Kings and Priests unto God.

(1-18) Celestial marriage makes women Queens and Priestesses to their husbands.

(1-19) Celestial marriage makes it possible for us to claim our moral children in eternity as well as to propagate ourselves throughout eternity.[11]

Men called to be polygamists now and a must for the next life.

It is still Mormon scripture today.

1 VERILY, thus saith the Lord unto you my servant Joseph, that inasmuch as you have inquired of my hand to know and understand wherein I, the Lord, justified my servants Abraham, Isaac, and Jacob, as also Moses, David and Solomon, my servants, as touching the principle and doctrine of their having many wives and concubines—

2 Behold, and lo, I am the Lord thy God, and will answer thee as touching this matter.

3 Therefore, prepare thy heart to receive and obey the instructions which I am about to give unto you; for all those who have this law revealed unto them must obey the same.

4 For behold, I reveal unto you a new and an everlasting covenant; and if ye abide not that covenant, then are ye damned; for no one can reject this covenant and be permitted to enter into my glory.

5 For all who will have a blessing at my hands shall abide the law which was appointed for that blessing, and the conditions thereof, as were instituted from before the foundation of the world.

6 And as pertaining to the new and everlasting covenant, it was instituted for the fulness of my glory; and he that receiveth a fulness thereof must and shall abide the law, or he shall be damned, saith the Lord God.

61 And again, as pertaining to the law of the priesthood—if any man espouse a virgin, and desire to espouse another, and the first give her consent, and if he espouse the second, and they are virgins, and have vowed to no other man, then is he justified; he cannot commit adultery for they are given unto him; for he cannot commit adultery with that that belongeth unto him and to no one else.

62 And if he have ten virgins given unto him by this law, he cannot commit adultery, for they belong to him, and they are given unto him; therefore is he justified.

63 But if one or either of the ten virgins, after she is espoused, shall be with another man, she has committed adultery, and shall be destroyed; for they are given unto him to multiply and replenish the earth, according to my commandment, and to fulfil the promise which was given by my Father before the foundation of the world, and for their exaltation in the eternal worlds, that they may bear the souls of men; for herein is the work of my Father continued, that he may be glorified.

64 And again, verily, verily, I say unto you, if any man have a wife, who holds the keys of this power, and he teaches unto her the law of my priesthood, as pertaining to these things, then shall she believe and administer unto him, or she shall be destroyed, saith the Lord your God; for I will destroy her; for I will magnify my name upon all those who receive and abide in my law.[12]

Celestial marriage is the new and everlasting covenant of marriage.[13]

The fact that Mormonism teaches that we come from heavenly parents who sexually birthed us as spirit beings in the pre-existence is evidenced by the Latter-day Saint hymn "O My Father," (#292). This hymn clearly speaks of a heavenly mother:

In the heavens are parents single?
No, the thought makes reason stare.
Truth is reason: truth eternal
tells me I've a mother there.

In actuality, there are uncounted numbers of Elohim's celestial wives, mothers to the billions of spirits who have come to earth to gain bodies. Some feminist Mormons have adopted the practice of praying to the Heavenly Mother. However, LDS Church President Gordon B. Hinckley has opposed this practice, saying that Mormons should not pray to the Heavenly Mother. A feminist professor was fired from Brigham Young University for teaching prayer to Heavenly Mother in her class.[14]

CHAPTER TWO

A New Face for an Old Scam

How and why the Mormon Church keeps changing as it seeks to be included in the Christian Orthodoxy it privately mocks and rejects.

A lot can happen in a hundred years. At the beginning of the 20th century, the possibility of having a Mormon senator from the recently and reluctantly admitted state of Utah was more than the country could handle. Sending Reed Smoot off to the United States Senate all but brought the Federal troops back into Utah. That's a bit of an exaggeration, but it may have appeared that way to the Mormons who had to live through what probably seemed to them like the Spanish Inquisition.

Reed Smoot's story is important to our understanding of the changing face of Mormonism. It was from that incident that the LDS church caught a glimpse of the future struggle it would face in changing its direction from one of isolationism toward a path that would link it with the rest of humanity. The highly publicized Smoot Hearings of 1903-1907 had an impact on the Church with repercussions continuing to the present time.

The *Mormon Encyclopedia* gives us penetrating insight into the issues involved from the LDS perspective:

> The 1890's had seen the church pass through some of its most challenging times, including the tumultuous political fight for Utah statehood following the Manifesto of 1890 (officially curtailing new plural marriages) [in the U.S.] and Presidential amnesty for Church Officers who had practiced Polygamy, *initiating the process of accommodation and acculturation to mainstream America* [My emphasis added.]. Euphoria, however, was short lived.
>
> The election to the U.S. Senate of Reed Smoot, a highly visible Church leader, unleashed intense anti-Mormon sentiment, which had subsided after statehood..., creating a furor that forced the Senate to examine the case. The prosecution focused on two issues: Smoot's alleged Polygamy and his expected allegiance to the Church and its ruling hierarchy, which it was claimed would make it impossible for him to execute his oath as a United States senator....it soon became apparent that it was the Church that was on trial.[1]

Church leaders were called and questioned about the power the church had over its members, especially over the General Authorities, of which Reed Smoot was a member. Again, from the Mormon perspective:

> Some of the testimony revealed situations and circumstances that put the Church in an unfavorable light. President Joseph F. Smith received especially harsh treatment in cross-examination....
>
> The victory for Elder-Senator Smoot was a victory for the church, providing the legitimacy it had been seeking since 1850.... Perhaps more than any other individual, Reed Smoot molded and shaped the positive national image the Church was to enjoy throughout the twentieth century.[2]

This victory held the answer to the deep dilemma in which the Church was mired. A few years earlier, they had come out of their hiding place in the desert and asked the government to grant them statehood, *just as they were* polygamy and all. It never happened. They had to first shake themselves loose from the stigma of polygamy and their unique brand of "Kingdom of God" theocracy. Only after the Manifesto of 1890 that was not a revelation from their living prophet, but a politically expedient declaration, were they marginally accepted into the brotherhood of States.

Then came the massive, unexpected blow-up over Reed Smoot. I can only *imagine* that first closed-door meeting with the Council of the Twelve Apostles on the return to Utah of "Prophet" Joseph F. Smith after he had just been raked over the coals on the witness stand regarding the strange quirks of his faith. It is my personal opinion that a policy of some sort was made at that time to accede to public pressure from time to time on serious doctrinal issues, which, if greatly publicized, could affect their assimilation into normal American society.

From that time until World War II, Utah and Mormonism quietly sat on the back burner, avoiding most controversy. Meanwhile, one other major change was secretly taking place behind the closed doors of the LDS Temple.

An Oath of Vengeance

During the LDS Temple ritual, certain oaths and covenants are made before God that are said to be both solemn and eternal. All participants are required to verbally take every oath. One such oath, which was part of the ritual until it was removed in early 1927, [3] was called *The Oath of Vengeance*. It was actually sworn against the United States of America in retribution for the deaths of Joseph and Hyrum Smith.

You and each of you do solemnly promise and vow that you will pray, and never cease to importune high heaven to avenge the blood of the prophets on this nation, and that you will teach this to your children and your children's children unto the third and fourth generations.[4]

You can imagine that following the humiliations of the Smoot hearings, The Brethren could only shudder at the thought of what the public disclosure of this oath would bring. (The very highest officials of the LDS Church are referred to by the faithful as The Brethren. This includes the Prophet, the First Presidency, and the Council of The Twelve Apostles.) There had been some chewing around the edges of this issue during the hearings, and The Brethren wanted no more of it. The oath was quietly removed from the ritual without ceremony or announcement.

While this oath was removed, and Mormonism moved further into general acceptance, the oath itself was an *eternally binding one,* given in the holiest of places, under the power of their eternal Melchizedek priesthood. Under those *eternal* circumstances, the vow once taken could not be undone. **Mitt Romney is among those of the third and fourth generations for whom this curse is still valid.**

Every LDS President from Brigham Young, including Gordon B. Hinckley in 2007, has been of an age to have taken that oath when they *"took out their own endowments"* in the LDS temple, prior to 1927, and therefore, they and their fourth generations, are *still bound under those oaths.*

Has a single one of the LDS Brethren officially renounced this oath? Or are they still under its power? Has Gordon B. Hinckley, the "living prophet," renounced it? If he has *not* renounced it, how can he presume to lead over six million American citizens under Article 12 of the LDS Articles of Faith *(We believe in being subject to kings, presidents, rulers and magistrates, in obeying, honoring and sustaining the law)* and still be bound to call upon heaven to heap curses upon our nation?

If The Brethren have secretly renounced it, is it just arrogance that prevents them from clearing the matter up for the general church membership? If they have secretly renounced it, how do they justify having sworn such a bitter, eternal oath in their sacred temple before their god and then reneged on it? This surely places an untenable dilemma upon all the LDS people who have gone through the temple and sworn oaths of total obedience to these very same leaders. What of the Mormons who hold office in our government or serve in the Military? There is an obvious conflict of interest between their oaths of office and their higher loyalty to a group of men who are sworn to seek vengeance against this great nation.

Bruce R. McConkie states, "While the oaths of the saints have furthered righteous purposes, similar swearing by the wicked has led to great evil." [5]

What is this if it isn't evil? In the Bible, Jesus states:

Again, ye have heard that it hath been said by them of old time, Thou shalt not forswear thyself, but shalt perform unto the Lord thine oaths: But I say unto you, swear not at all; neither by heaven; for it is God's throne: Nor by the earth for it is His footstool. (Matthew 5:33-37)

That should be plain enough, yet in their oath taking, these unrighteous Mormon leaders have denied the strong admonition of Jesus Christ Himself and reverted back to exactly that which He has told us *not* to do!

The Biblical gospel has a different way of dealing with enemies. Christ said:

I say unto you, which hear, Love your enemies, do good to them which hate you. Bless them that curse you and pray for them which despitefully use you. (Luke 6:27-28)

Paul instructed the church to "bless them which persecute you: bless and curse not" (Romans 12:14).

I have no personal vendetta against a group of elderly men who swore ungodly oaths in their youth, but it is important to point out that the LDS church has been in the cleanup business for over 100 years. Having had their hands stung in the Reed Smoot fiasco, they spent the next 40 years in near isolation until their service in World War II drew them back into the heart of American life.

An Incredible Revelation: Canceling the Curse on the Blacks

When I joined the Mormon Church in 1957, the Church was experiencing a time of peaceful growth and enjoyed strong societal favor. In fact, I really can't recall a single time that we Mormons were the subjects of *any* public debate. Privately, people may have thought some of our outward habits were odd, but what was said about the Mormons was generally positive, dealing with the wholesome attributes the church tried to communicate. We were known as "the people who took care of their own." If there were any anti-Mormons out there, I never saw or heard of a single one of them. Only once did a Christian couple in my neighborhood attempt to sit down with me and try to discuss the Mormon faith from their viewpoint. They were horribly unequipped to do so.

Most of the Church's growth during that time came from white Anglo-Saxons just like me. According to Mormon teachings, the Blacks were still under the curse of Cain, and the gospel was not presented to them.

Once, in the mid-60s, a group of Blacks picketed the LDS Church building I attended during Sunday school. Several of the Mormons went out and invited them in so that they could see what they were objecting to firsthand. They left rather quickly, but the Mormon leaders saw the gathering storm clouds on the horizon.

On June 9, 1978, Mormon President Spencer W. Kimball announced to the Saints that he had received a *revelation* ending the Church's ban on Blacks in the priesthood. President Kimball said that he had received the revelation "after extended meditation and prayer in the Salt Lake Temple. That same revelation came to his counselors and to the Quorum of the Twelve Apostles in the Temple, and then it was presented to all of the other General Authorities who approved it unanimously." The Revelation declared that the "long promised day has come when every faithful, worthy man in the Church may receive the holy priesthood" [6]

Shock waves reverberated through the Church membership. An actual eternal doctrine of the church had been reversed. However, time and a good deal of public relations on the doctrine of progressive revelation (which says that new eternal revelations can supersede older eternal revelations) brought the clamoring to an end. Today, the revelation—actually now called a declaration, and apparently one-step below an actual revelation—is Mormon scripture (*Doctrines and Covenants*, Declaration 2).

It had earlier been believed that Blacks would never hold the priesthood in mortality because they bore the "mark of Cain," and had been born through his lineage as a punishment for their failures in the pre-existent life we lived on the planet near the star, Kolob.

According to Mormon scripture, when Cain rebelled and rose up to slay his brother, God cast him away from His face and cursed him to be a vagabond and a fugitive. A mark was placed upon him that would make him known to all who see it: "I the Lord set a mark upon Cain, lest any finding him should kill him" (*The Pearl of Great Price*, Moses 6:40).

Early prophets of the Church taught that this mark of Cain was a black skin. They also taught that the real curse was that all who bore the mark of Cain would be forbidden to hold the Mormon priesthood. In the LDS scriptures attributed to father Abraham, we are told that this curse of black skin was carried on across the flood through the black-skinned Egyptian wife of Ham, the son of Noah. The LDS Scripture further confirms this when it states, "Now, Pharaoh, being of that lineage by which he could not have the right of Priesthood..." (*The Pearl of Great Price*, Abraham 1:21-27).

Early Mormon Church leaders had many racist and bigoted things to say about the Blacks, under the guise of their special, revelatory spiritual knowledge. **Joseph Smith** especially felt that something needed to be done with the Blacks.

> Had I anything to do with the Negro, I would confine them by strict law to their own species, and put them on a national equalization.[7]

Brigham Young, second prophet of the Church, was quite vocal about his opinion of the Blacks:

You see some classes of the human family that are black, uncouth, uncomely, disagreeable and low in their habits, wild, and seemingly without the blessings of the intelligence that is generally bestowed upon mankind.... Cain slew his brother....and the Lord put a mark on him, which is the flat nose and black skin.[8]

Shall I tell you the law of God in regard to the African race? If the white man who belongs to the chosen seed mixes his blood with the seed of Cain, the penalty, under the law of God, is death on the spot. This will always be so.[9]

John Taylor, third prophet of the Mormon Church, explained how and why the Blacks survived the flood:

...after the flood we are told that the curse that had been pronounced upon Cain was continued through Ham's wife, as he had married a wife of that seed. And why did it pass through the flood? Because it was necessary that the devil should have a representation upon the earth as well as God....[10]

Joseph Fielding Smith, tenth Prophet of the Mormon Church, put it in full perspective for us when he wrote:

Not only was Cain called upon to suffer, but because of his wickedness, he became the father of an inferior race. A curse was placed upon him and that curse has been continued through his lineage and must do so while time endures. Millions of souls have come into this world cursed with a black skin and have been denied the privilege of priesthood and the fulness of the blessings of the gospel. These are the descendants of Cain. Moreover, they have been made to feel their inferiority and have been separated from the rest of mankind from the beginning.... We will also hope that blessings may eventually be given our Negro Brethren, for they are our Brethren—children of God—not withstanding their black covering emblematical of eternal darkness.[11]

President Joseph Fielding Smith was a little kinder when speaking about this doctrine publicly. He told one national magazine reporter:

I would not want you to believe that we bear any animosity toward the Negro. Darkies are wonderful people and they have their place in our church.[12]

LDS Apostle and Theologian **Bruce R. McConkie** gave a solid description of the godly reasons for the Black's curse.

Those who were less valiant in the pre-existence and who thereby had certain spiritual restrictions imposed upon them during mortality are known to us as the *negroes.* Such spirits are sent to earth through the lineage of Cain, the mark put upon him for his rebellion against God and his murder of Abel being a black skin.... Noah's son Ham married Egyptus, a descendant of Cain, thus preserving the negro lineage through the flood.... The negroes are not equal with other races when the receipt of certain spiritual blessings are concerned, particularly the priesthood and the temple blessings that flow there-from, **but** this inequality is not of man's origin. It is the Lord's doing, based on His eternal laws of justice, and grows out of the lack of spiritual valiance of those concerned in their first estate.[13]

"Racial degeneration, resulting in differences in appearance and spiritual aptitude, has arisen since the fall. We know the circumstances under which the posterity of Cain (and later of Ham) **were** *cursed* **with what we call** *negroid racial characteristics."* [14]

"Though he was a rebel and an associate of Lucifer in the preexistence, and though he was a liar from the beginning whose name was *Perdition, Cain* managed to attain the privilege of mortal birth.... **As a result of his rebellion, Cain was** *cursed with a dark skin;* **he became the father of the**

negroes, and those spirits who are not worthy to receive the priesthood are born through his lineage. He became the first mortal to be **cursed** as a son of perdition." [15]

"Through Ham (a name meaning *black*) 'the blood of the Canaanites was preserved' through the flood, he having married Egypt, a descendant of Cain.... Negroes are thus descendants of Ham, who himself also was cursed apparently for marrying into the forbidden lineage" [16]

"...in a broad general sense, **caste systems have their root and origin in the gospel itself,** and when they operate according to the divine decree, the resultant restrictions and *segregation* are right and proper **and have the approval of the Lord.** To illustrate: **Cain, Ham, and the whole negro race have been** *cursed with a black skin,* **the mark of Cain**, so they can be identified as a caste apart, a people with whom the other descendants of Adam should not intermarry" [17]

Revelation or Public Relations: Putting a Spin on the Black Curse

Mormons had been always taught that Negroes were doomed to the curse until after the return of Christ for His millennial, thousand-year reign. It was all part of that battle in their so-called pre-existent world when that great Council of God's chose Jesus' plan for the earth instead of Lucifer's. One third of their spirit brothers and sisters chose to fight the decision and therefore, in this second estate, here on earth, they could not enter the Mormon Temple or receive the priesthood, and therefore could never become gods and goddesses.

Eventually, civil rights legislation brought the LDS Church once again into conflict with American standards. LDS leaders were forced to reconsider Smith's racist pronouncements against the Blacks. In the mid-seventies they hired one of America's largest general management and consulting firms—Cresup, McCormick and Paget (CMP) of New York—which subsequently recommended "a careful review" of certain potentially embarrassing "doctrinal policies" such as the Negro issue and "a serious reconsideration" of such policies in light of past public relations problems.

The report strongly urged that Church leaders re-assess the race issue and its "relevancy" for the future. Following these suggestions, Prophet Spencer W. Kimball conveniently received "a divine revelation" and once again a clumsy Mormon policy was rescinded.[18]

This change of heart over admitting Blacks to the Mormon priesthood brought the desired response. *Time* and *Newsweek* magazines stopped their presses to include the "revelation" and the President of the United States, Jimmy Carter, commended President Kimball for his "compassionate and courageous" decision.[19]

In reviewing these last few decades of turmoil, *US News and World Report* stated:

The doctrines with the greatest potential for divisiveness concern Blacks and women. For most of its history, the Mormon Church relegated Blacks to a position of inferiority and divine disfavor. Only in 1978 when Spencer W. Kimball, then the church's president, received divine revelation did the church declare Blacks eligible for the priesthood—a title bestowed upon all faithful males.[20]

The High Road to Change and Here Come the Ex-Mormons

By the mid 1970s, a great many ex-Mormons who had become orthodox Christians began to surface and suddenly represented a very vocal threat to their former church. While the movement was dismissed as a rag-tail army of rejects, it soon became apparent that it would not go away and it would not be quiet. For the most part, these former Mormons had a real zeal to bring the true gospel of grace to their former brethren.

By the end of the seventies, the many single groups of former Mormons had loosely joined into a nationwide network that was gaining the ear of the general public. In 1979, several dozen leaders in this movement met to strategize a campaign of deliverance for those still lost in Mormonism. By the mid-eighties, the **Annual Capstone Conference,** sponsored by **Saints Alive,** was drawing hundreds of group leaders from around the world.

It was the first time in the history of the Mormon faith that an organized movement of former Mormons, people who knew the innermost secrets of the Church, had begun to grow. These crusaders knew the Church's weaknesses and dared to challenge the LDS Church publicly on its many areas of unorthodox, anti-Christian doctrine. During the next decade the Mormon Church would make more changes of greater scope than in all its preceding 150 years. I am strongly convinced that because of the LDS Church's desire to slip in quietly among mainline Christian groups, it could not publicly defend itself against the severity of the ex-Mormon charges. It was easier to quietly change the aberrant doctrine and put their efforts into creating friendship ties with ecumenical organizations and churches.

Their plan has been working. Many of these ecumenical groups already consider the Mormons as Christian brethren and the bolder, more evangelistic ex-Mormons as a radical fringe group that should be shunned and rebuked.

The changes in Mormonism are far from over. Quite probably one of the next "eternal" practices to go will be the daily wearing of the LDS Temple garment, a holdover from the days of long johns. I fully expect that while this book is still in active circulation, a new decree will be issued mandating that the garment be worn only during temple rituals with the other special clothing used only inside the Temple.

Mitt Romney wears secret undergarments marked with sacred talismanic symbols that he believes will keep him protected as he works his way to godhood. *These are the very same markings that Lucifer claims in the LDS Temple ritual are the emblems of his power and priesthood.* **In fact, the Mormons' perverted belief that humans can ascend to godhood mimics Satan's tempting of Eve in the Garden of Eden.**

Romney is truly a presidential candidate with an actual, definable god complex, and an "other world" spiritual power that should *never* be seated in the Oval Office.

While I am on this delicate subject of the holy Mormon temple underwear, it too has had a long history of surreptitious change. It started out as an ankle-to-wrist length longjohn-type garment, with string ties and with secret markings on the breast, navel and knee. It has worked its way down to a mid-calved, short-sleeved, buttoned outfit, available in several styles, including a modernized two-piece model. So much for another God-given, unchangeable mandate about man's holiest piece of sacred clothing.

The Changing Role of Mormon Women

For women in the church, changes have come more slowly. A small but growing feminist movement in the church is making little headway against the patriarchal power structure. Feeling disenfranchised, some Mormon feminists made it known they were praying, not to God the Father, as is tradition, but to God's wife, their "heavenly mother," of whom Mormon Scriptures say next to nothing. When officials denounced the practice, the women agreed to stop but said they would ask god to reveal more about his wife.[21]

Not withstanding The Brethren's pronouncement of near apostasy for women praying to their heavenly Mother, the Church hymnals have contained the proof of her presence there. The following hymn was published in 1882 by Joel H. Johnson:

To Kolob now my thoughts repair,
Where God, my Father reigns above
Where Heav'nly Mother, too, is there,
and many kindred whom I love.
Oh, let me, then, return again
To see my parents, whom I love.
And with my children live and reign,
In worlds where I once lived above.

And

"O My Father"
I had learned to call thee Father,
Through thy Spirit from on high,
But until the key of knowledge
Was restored, I knew not why.
In the heavens are parents single?
No, the thought makes reason stare!

> Truth is reason, truth eternal
> Tells me I've a mother there.

In 1990, the church again revised the temple marriage ritual, substituting a woman's pledge to obey her husband with a pledge to obey God. Many women had stayed away from the temple because they felt "discomfort and alienation," said Lavina Fielding Anderson, then editor-elect of the *Journal of Mormon History*. While women's rights advocates applauded the reforms, they say the church has a long way to go. Women are still barred from the priesthood and from top leadership posts and are excluded from participating in child-blessing ceremonies.[22]

Priesthood Power?

D. Michael Quinn wrote some startling things in a 44-page essay in a work called *Women and Authority: Re-emerging Mormon Feminism*. The volume, edited by Maxine Hanks and published by Signature Books, had sixteen other contributors. However, not one has stirred the corporate Beehive like Quinn has:

> There is compelling documentary evidence that Joseph Smith gave women priesthood power in the temple "endowment" ritual, in which women are anointed to become queens and priestesses. "It is

an explosive issue," Quinn said, "...particularly at a time when church leaders face growing pressure from Mormon feminists for a more active role in a faith dominated by its male priesthood." Mormons define priesthood as the literal power of God and as the authority to act in God's name. They believe the "keys" to the priesthood came to Smith through heavenly intermediaries from Jesus Christ and have been passed on to the church's 12 successive presidents. Quinn explained that there is no evidence a woman was ordained to specific priesthood offices (elder, high priest, bishop, apostle). But in the early church there was clear distinction between priesthood power—available to women in the temple endowment—and priesthood office. Still, for nearly 100 years after Smith's death in 1844, Mormon women were authorized to perform the priesthood function of healing other women by anointing and blessing.[23]

Quinn reported that "two weeks before Smith organized the Female Relief Society of Nauvoo, Illinois, in 1842," he told the women that "the Society should move according to the ancient Priesthood" and he was "going to make *this society* a kingdom of priests as in Enoch's day—as in Paul's day."

"Much later," Quinn reported, "in printing the official minutes of Smith's remarks, the official "History of the

Church" omitted Smith's first use of the word "Society" and changed the second "Society to "Church." Those two alterations changed the entire meaning of his statement," said Quinn.

In the 1920s, Church apostles maintained women merely "enjoy the blessing of the priesthood through their husbands." Since the 1950s, Church leaders stressed that even though they are not ordained to the priesthood, Mormon women are the equals of men through a divinely mandated partnership of motherhood and priesthood. In 1988, Apostle Boyd K. Packer wrote that the well-being of all humanity depends on protecting motherhood. "The addition of such duties as would attend ordination to the priesthood would constitute an interruption to, perhaps an avoidance of, that crucial contribution which only a mother can provide."[24]

Church officials were not happy about this kind of talk to come at a time when the problem with women in the church was becoming a tender subject. In one careful response to the above article, Elder Boyd K. Packer, of the Council of the Twelve Apostles, gave the following insight:

> It should not disturb either men or women that some responsibilities are bestowed upon one and not the other, duties of the priesthood are delegated to men and are patriarchal which means "of the Father." From the very beginning this has been so. The scriptures plainly state that they were "confirmed

to be handed down from father to son." ...there are differences among men and women but there is no inequity.... "Intelligence and talent favor both of them, but, in the woman's part, she is not just equal to man, she is superior. She can do that which he can never do, not in all eternity can he do it. There are complementing rewards which are hers and hers alone.[25]

A Woman's Place

Back in the old days, the average family could get by with one paycheck, and most men were secure in their work place. Mormon women stayed at home and lived the life of the happy homemaker—baking, sewing and waiting at the door with a warm welcome for the breadwinner.

The goal of every young Mormon girl was to be there waiting for her missionary to return home to his family and rush with her to the temple to be married for time and all eternity. Even if the young lady went to college, it was to advance her performance as a wife and mother. Careers for women were not greeted with smiles by The Brethren.

However, in today's world, where two paychecks are barely enough to keep food on the table and job security is a rarity, even the most faithful Mormon women are being pulled into the work force, and it is tearing apart a vital cord within the very structure of the faith.

The late LDS President, Ezra Taft Benson, spoke to this issue in a special television address that was broadcast to more than 1,000 Mormon Church meetinghouses throughout the United States and Canada. President Benson urged young wives to stay in their homes and not seek a job in the workplace. "There is no more noble work than that of a good and God-fearing mother," he said. "The counsel of the church has always been for mothers to spend their full time in the home in rearing and caring for their children." He said that young Mormon wives should not delay in having their children nor limit the size of their families to obtain household luxury items.[26]

However, most LDS mothers were already working to help put food on the table and to pay the LDS tithes and other offerings that often add up to 20 percent or more of their gross income. Most couldn't even think in terms of luxury items. A week later, President Ezra Taft Benson said that a mother's role (at home) was vital to her exaltation and to the salvation and exaltation of her family.[27]

Splinter Group Ordains Women

While the Utah church had drawn a line with regard to giving Mormon women the priesthood, one early Mormon splinter group, **The Reorganized Church of Jesus Christ of Latter-day Saints**, *[now called "the Community of Christ]* threw in the towel on the matter:

Female elder – Emily Fern "Bunny" Spillman, in 1985, was ordained as one of the first female elders of the Reorganized Church of JCLDS, one of 85 women nationwide to be ordained in the RLDS... the culmination of a lifetime of work in the church. "I just want to be a worthy servant." The Missouri-based RLDS church split off from the main Mormon Church in the 1840's over who should lead the church: Brigham Young or the descendants of Joseph Smith, the founding prophet of Mormonism. In 1984, church president Wallace B. Smith, the great grandson of Joseph Smith, decreed that women should be ordained into leadership roles.[28]

CHAPTER THREE

The Birth of Heresy

Going back to the beginning days of Mormonism and looking at the root heresies.

Before I continue this probe of the secrets and intrigue of the modern-day Mormon Church, I need to take some time out to answer the question. Where did it all really begin? How did this major religion ever get such a foothold into the center of the American mind? To find out, we have to go back to almost 200 years ago.

The early nineteenth century was a time of great religious excitement in the Northeastern United States. New York State was rocked with spiritual renewal from every direction. While mighty men of God such as Charles Finney, sparked by the power of the Holy Spirit, led so many thousands of people to the cross of Calvary, there also arose those who captivated the few with the fruits of their own vanity and drew them away into the doctrines of a different gospel.

One such man was Joseph Smith, born into a struggling rural farm family in 1805. The Smith family was given to dabbling in the mysteries of divination. His father, Joseph Sr., had a special gift of visions, through powers from the unseen world.

Joseph Smith Jr. was to set his own mark in the world through a series of bold and visionary declarations. He was to claim that in the spring of 1820, he retired to a grove of trees near his home in Manchester, New York. There he sought the Word of the Lord concerning which church he should join of all those experiencing revival. He later testified that both God the Father and Jesus Christ appeared physically before him, hovering above him in a pillar of light, above the brightness of the sun.

He said that they instructed him that he was to join none of the churches, for they were all wrong; all their creeds were an abomination in God's sight, and those who professed these creeds were corrupt. According to Joseph's declarations, the true gospel of Jesus Christ was lost to the world. The power and authority of God was taken from the earth in the First Century AD, and only now was it about restored.[1]

In the evening of September 23, 1823 [Joseph reported later], while in his bedroom and in an act of prayer and supplication, seeking divine direction regarding the next step in God's plan for his life, God moved again. Another extraterrestrial being, which identified itself as the Angel Moroni, descended in a brilliant pillar of light and repeatedly instructed Joseph in the next steps of the restoration of the true gospel through Joseph's holy calling to that purpose.

Moroni told him of a stone chest he had buried in the nearby "Hill Cumorah" in the beginning of the fifth century. It held a book of scripture written upon gold plates, containing the "fullness of the everlasting gospel" as delivered by the Savior to the ancient inhabitants of the American continent, who were actually the descendants of Jewish settlers led there from Jerusalem by God 600 years before Christ. The chest also contained the Urim, Thummim, and Breastplate of Jewish antiquity for the purpose of translation.

Led to the site by Moroni, Joseph was instructed not to remove the items until given permission. He visited the location annually for four years, until told the time was ready for these scriptures to be translated. And so *The Book of Mormon* came forth, which Joseph Smith translated from the "Reformed" Egyptian characters inscribed on the gold plates.[2]

Joseph later described the return of John the Baptist, who descended in a cloud of light on May 15, 1829, and ordained Joseph and his scribe, Oliver Cowdery, to the Levitical Priesthood of Aaron, and gave them the authority to baptize. A short time later, Peter, James and John were to descend and confer the Holy Melchizedek Priesthood, which would hold the keys to all the spiritual power of Christ. Other visitors, such as Moses, Elisha and Elijah would later appear with their special messages and keys of "Restoration."

With revelation and prophecy abounding, Joseph began the building of his church. Moving often, and seeking Zion, the true gathering place of the Lamb, the era of Joseph Smith was at its peak in Nauvoo, Illinois.

With over 20,000 members, the Church had become a force to be reckoned with! It had political power and influence, as well as its own small army of 2,500 armed men under the charge of General Smith, who now often wore the uniform of that position.

Always fearful of attack from without, the final chapter of Joseph's life came from within and through "the conspiracy of traitors and wicked men." On the 27th of June, 1844, Joseph Smith died a martyr at the hands of a mob in the jail at Carthage, Illinois, thus sealing his testimony of *The Book of Mormon* with his own blood, as church history relates.[3]

While the church split in several directions at his death, the main body of the resolute believers trekked to a Rocky Mountain retreat—the New Zion—and named it Deseret. It is now known as Utah. Through hard work and a special brand of zeal, they carved an empire out of the desert under the powerful direction of Brigham Young.

Over the years, Mormonism has been one of the fastest growing religions in the United States and many countries. If Mormonism were truly a Christian work, drawing people to the Cross of Calvary, we could only cheer at the sidelines! *But the doctrines of Mormonism are not the doctrines of the Christian faith.* Let's examine this brief history of Mormonism in the light of Christian Scripture. In 2 Corinthians 13:1, we are warned that from the mouth of two or three witnesses shall every word be established; therefore, we will put Mormonism to that test!

The Plumb Line of Mormon Heresy

In 2 Corinthians 11:3 and 13, Paul warns us that "if people come and preach another gospel, another Jesus, another spirit...such are false apostles—deceitful workers, having the appearance of ministers of righteousness, whose end shall be according to their works." (Not Christ's mercy). We are warned in verse 14 of the same chapter that Satan himself is transformed into an Angel of Light.

If Joseph Smith really did see what he claimed, two personages appeared to him in a pillar of light. They claimed to be God the Father and Jesus, His son.

The very first clue that something was wrong was that a physical man appeared in the role of God the Father. We are told that *"God is not a man that he should lie; neither the Son of Man that he should repent"* (Numbers 23:19). John 4:24 says that *"God is spirit, and they that worship him must worship him in spirit and in truth."* Jesus specifically taught that a spirit does not have flesh and bones (Luke 24:39). In Matthew 16:17, Jesus declares that His father in heaven is not of "flesh and blood." John 1:18 states that no man has seen God at ***any*** time. It seems to be pretty clear.

Well-known Christian speaker, the late Dr. David Breese stated: *"Someone who says, 'I saw the Father' is dealing presumptuously, short-circuiting good Christian theology. It is the Son Who alone reveals the Father"* (John 1:18; Colossians 1:15).

This is no small matter, and it is the very plumb line of Mormon heresy. Mormons believe that God is an actual, physical, resurrected man, and that we can become just like Him. Dr. Breese's response to this blasphemy is:

> *A God cannot be made. God cannot be created. The definition of the eternal God is that He is eternal, immortal, invisible (1 Timothy 1:17; 6:16; Revelation 1:18; 2 Peter 3:8). That is Who the God of the universe is, and there is none other. A man is a created being and as a created being, it will always be the case with him, that in God he lives, and moves, and has his being. He is dependent upon the Fountainhead of life, God Himself He cannot move by his own volition, or anybody else's, to the level of Godhood—although that (concept) is very appealing to certain individuals.*
>
> *There is a question before the house in Christianity in our time that really is, Can a man become God? That question is answered in the affirmative by many*

of the cults, like the Mormons, like the New Age Movement. I assure you, it is totally presumptuous.[4]

This concept of godhood does not appeal to Mormonism alone. It is an ancient philosophy underlying much of pagan thought which proliferates through the New Age Movement today.

Did Jesus Fail?

Even if the appearance of God the Father as a man did not alert Joseph Smith to the deception, the first words out of the mouth of Joseph's Jesus should have brought loud clanging warning bells. He declared that the creeds of all the churches were an abomination to him, that all those who professed those creeds were corrupt. The Christian pastors were deceivers, agents of Satan. There was no authority of God left on earth!

What was the Christian confession in that day? The same as it was at the time of Christ! The same as it is today! Let's just look at two of the most common Creeds of Christendom and see what Joseph Smith's Jesus found that was filthy in his eyes:

THE APOSTLES CREED, AD 340

I believe in God the Father Almighty, Maker of heaven and earth, and in Jesus Christ, His only Son, our Lord; who was conceived by the Holy Ghost, born of the Virgin Mary; suffered under Pontius Pilate, was crucified, dead and buried; He descended into hell; the third day he rose again from the dead; He ascended into heaven and sitteth on the right hand of God, the Father Almighty; From thence He shall come to judge the quick and the dead.

I believe in the Holy Ghost; the Holy Christian Church; the communion of saints; the forgiveness of sins; the resurrection of the body; and the life everlasting. Amen.

THE NICENE CREED, AD 381

I believe in one God, the Father Almighty, Maker of heaven and earth and of all things visible and invisible.

And in one Lord Jesus Christ, the only-begotten Son of God, begotten of His Father before all worlds, God of God, Light of Light, Very God of Very God, Begotten, not made, being of one substance with the Father, By whom all things were made;

Who for us men and our salvation came down from heaven and was incarnate by the Holy Ghost of the Virgin Mary and was made man; and was crucified also for us under Pontius Pilate. He suffered and was buried; and the third day He rose again according to the Scriptures; and ascended into heaven, and sitteth on the right hand of the Father; And He shall come again with glory to judge both the quick and the dead; whose kingdom shall have no end.

And I believe in the Holy Ghost, the Lord and Giver of Life, Who proceedeth from the Father and the Son, who with the Father and the Son together is worshipped and glorified, who spake by the prophets. And I believe one holy Christian and Apostolic Church. I acknowledge one Baptism unto the remission of sins, And I look for the resurrection of the dead, and the life of the world to come. Amen.

Can we believe that the power of God, as it was established by Christ and carried forth by his Apostles and followers, was lost to mankind? Did the world become void of the authority of God? Did Jesus fail? Don't you believe it!

Isaiah 9:7 claims that there will be no end to the increase of Christ's government and peace. His Kingdom shall be established from henceforth even forever! Why? Because the zeal of the Lord of Hosts will perform it! We are promised that Christ will reign forever, and there shall be no end of His Kingdom (Luke 1:33). Jesus, being the Petra—the bedrock itself—proclaimed that upon that rock (Petra) He would build His church, and the gates of hell will not prevail against it (Matthew 16:18)!

One need only skim through *Foxe's Book of the Martyrs* and read some of the many testimonies of the Christian martyrs throughout the centuries to know without a doubt that the zeal of the Lord of Hosts has never stopped performing the establishing of His Kingdom!

And what about the Holy Spirit? Was He so less a power of God that He could not fulfill His divine function? The Holy Spirit came with awesome power in that upper room and did not and will not leave us. Jesus said He would abide with us forever, to dwell with us and in us (John 14:16-17)! He promised that the Holy Spirit would teach us, being a testimony of Christ, bringing all things of Jesus into our remembrance (John 14:26). To receive the message of Joseph Smith's first vision would be to call God a liar, Jesus a failure, the Holy Spirit without function and the Bible of no merit or truth!

Gold Plates and Angels

The next episode in the Mormon Restoration centers around the Angel Moroni, who prepared Joseph Smith to succeed where Jesus failed. Moroni, appearing as an angel of light, brings Joseph word of the gold plates and *The Book of Mormon*, which were to contain the fullness of the everlasting gospel.

Paul gave clear warning about anyone, even an angel from heaven, preaching any other gospel. He said that they should be accursed (Galatians 1:8). He repeated himself to be sure the message was clear.

> ***But even if we, or an angel from heaven, preach any other gospel to you than what we have preached to you, let him be accursed. As we have said before, so now I say again, if anyone preaches any other gospel to you than what you have received, let him be accursed.** (Galatians 1:8-9)*

Here again, the warning flag waves frantically!

The Book of Mormon

The Book of Mormon claims to contain the sacred writings of the Jewish people who relocated from Jerusalem to the western shores of the Americas in 600 BC. The first warning sign that something is terribly amiss is that this passage was written in Egyptian, a cursed language to the Jews. There has never been a verse of Hebrew Scripture written by Jews for Jews in Egyptian. It would be blasphemous! Nehemiah made that clear. He cursed those who had traffic with Egypt, smote them and yanked out the hair of the offenders (Nehemiah 13:23-27).

Secondly, *The Book of Mormon* speaks of a great civilization, with 38 major cities and Temples as great as Solomon's—built from 600 BC to AD 400. Yet there is not so much as a stone tablet, or a stick that the Mormon archaeologists can identify as *Book of Mormon* archaeology. This is in spite of thousands of discoveries of other cultures in the supposed *Book of Mormon* "locations."

The Hill Cumorah, where Joseph unearthed the gold plates, was said to have been host to a great battle in AD 385, where approximately a half million people died with all manner of weapons of war. The site would have to hold a mountain of archaeological evidence, yet not a single piece of evidence has been produced in proof of the greatest battle in this hemisphere in the history of all mankind.

The Redefined Holy Priesthood

Joseph's later claim that John the Baptist descended and restored the Levitical priesthood of Aaron can only lead one to believe that he had little or no knowledge of the Bible or Jewish tradition at the time.

John the Baptist never held the Levitical priesthood, and could not restore something he never had, even in Mormon theology. John wore the skins of an animal and ate food that was considered unclean to the Levitical priesthood. He functioned in the streets and by-ways, proclaiming Jesus Christ, calling people to repent and be baptized. The priesthood functioned within the temple at the altar. It doesn't match up.

If he were a member of the priesthood of his day, its leaders knew nothing of it. When challenged by Christ regarding this very subject, they were ignorant of John's authority (Matthew 21:23-27). Further, the Mormon priesthood that Joseph Smith claimed was a restoration does not deal with the key functions of the early Aaronic priesthood, the offering of gifts according to the law (Hebrews 8:4).

Jesus has given us a better Covenant, established upon better promises and has made the old to vanish away (Hebrews 8:6,-7, 13). Why would Jesus want to restore what He had come to put an end to?

Joseph Smith claimed that Peter, James and John came and restored the Melchizedek priesthood. This declaration, like each before it, cannot meet the test of Scripture, or logic.

In Mormonism, no man can hold the Melchizedek priesthood without first holding the Aaronic priesthood. Those great Apostles of the Lord most obviously were not operating as Levitical priests. Everything they did within the record of the Word of God places them totally outside that dead priesthood.

The true Melchizedek priesthood was always a priesthood of only one! It existed *before* the law was given

(Genesis 14:18) and *after* the law was ended (Hebrews 7:11-17). It sprang forth with the first offering of bread and wine (Genesis 14:18). It reappeared only when the final offering of the broken body of Christ and His shed blood ended the penalty of the law as He became our sin offering by the sacrifice of Himself (Hebrews 9:12-14).

The final irony of Joseph Smith's life came in the story of his death. The Mormon Church pronounces him a martyr, sealing the testimony of *The Book of Mormon* with his blood. Yet truth, and Mormon history, tells another story.

By 1844, Joseph already claimed 27 "Celestial" wives, by Church count, and 48 by Historian Fawn Brodie's count.[5]

Always on the lookout for more, he finally provoked several leading men within the Church to take action. Austin Cowles, first Counselor to the Church at Nauvoo, and William Law, Smith's second Counselor, published charges (of heresy, adultery and fornication) against Joseph Smith in the Nauvoo Expositor.[6]

Joseph destroyed the press, and charges were filed against him in Carthage, Illinois, the nearest community having non-Mormon officials. At first, Joseph fled and hid, but was convinced to return at his wife's pleading, by Orrin Porter Rockwell, his bodyguard. Upon his return, Smith was arrested.

An Ignominious Death

Joseph was in the second floor of the jail, with visiting friends and an unlocked door. After members of his own militia retired to their homes for the night, a mob formed outside, shouting insults. As some of the mob came up the narrow stairwell, Joseph discharged his pistol into their midst, killing two men and wounding a third. He and his brother, Hyrum, were killed in the exchange of gunfire.[7]

Under no circumstance can Joseph Smith be described as a martyr, sealing his testimony of *The Book of Mormon* with blood. He died in a gunfight, in a tragic ending caused by his own carnal, sinful use of other men's wives. The biblical account of a martyr is seen in the death of Stephen. Stephen was stoned to death for his testimony of Christ as the Messiah. He knelt down as he was killed, crying "Father, lay not this sin to their charge!" (Acts 7:60)

Whom should we follow? Jesus Christ, the Alpha and Omega, who said "Before Abraham was, I AM" (John 8:58), or Joseph Smith, the man who said, "I have more to boast of than any man had—neither Paul, John, Peter nor Jesus ever did it. I boast that no man ever did such a work as I." [8]

By every test of a prophet, Joseph failed. By every test of man, he was a fully debauched heretic. Yet, today, over twelve million people follow his teachings in spiritual blindness, and the numbers are climbing.

The Day That Mormonism Began

Let's take another look at that day when Mormonism began. It was the day Joseph Smith said he went out into the woods to pray and ask God which of all the churches was the true one. I have already shared that the information he claimed came from Jesus in the presence of a physical God, the Father, was extremely unbiblical. But, there is something else here to reveal.

The Bible is very clear that there can be demonic interaction, seducing spirits bringing the doctrines of devils.

> *Now the Spirit speaketh expressly, that in the latter times some shall depart from the faith, giving heed to seducing spirits, and doctrines of devils; Speaking lies in hypocrisy; having their conscience seared with a hot iron...* (1 Timothy 4:1-2 KJV)

Listen as Joseph Smith describes his experience in the woods:

> *So, in accordance with this, my determination to ask of God, I retired to the woods to make the attempt. It was on the morning of a beautiful, clear day, early in the spring of eighteen hundred and twenty. It was the first time in my life that I had made such an attempt, for amidst all my anxi-*

eties I had never as yet made the attempt to pray vocally.

After I had retired to the place where I had previously designed to go, having looked around me, and finding myself alone, I kneeled down and began to offer up the desires of my heart to God. I had scarcely done so, when immediately I was seized upon by some power which entirely overcame me, and had such an astonishing influence over me as to bind my tongue so that I could not speak. Thick darkness gathered around me, and it seemed to me for a time as if I were doomed to sudden destruction.

But, exerting all my powers to call upon God to deliver me out of the power of this enemy which had seized upon me, and at the very moment when I was ready to sink into despair* and abandon myself to destruction—not to an imaginary ruin, but to the power of some actual being from the unseen world, who had such marvelous power as I had never before felt in any being—just at this moment of great alarm, I saw a pillar of light exactly over my head, above the brightness of the sun, which descended gradually until it fell upon me.

It no sooner appeared than I found myself delivered from the enemy which held me bound. When the light rested upon me I saw two Personages, whose brightness and glory defy all description, standing above me in the air. One of them spake unto me, calling me by name and said, pointing to the other— This is My Beloved Son. Hear Him!

My object in going to inquire of the Lord was to know which of all the sects was right, that I might know which to join. No sooner, therefore, did I get possession of myself, so as to be able to speak, than I asked the Personages who stood above me in the light, which of all the sects was right (for at this time it had never entered into my heart that all were wrong)—and which I should join.

I was answered that I must join none of them, for they were all wrong; and the Personage who addressed me said that all their creeds were an abomination in his sight; that those professors were all corrupt; that: "they draw near to me with their lips, but their hearts are far from me, they teach for doctrines the commandments of men, having a form of godliness, but they deny the power thereof."

He again forbade me to join with any of them; and many other things did he say unto me, which I cannot write at this time. When I came to myself again, I found myself lying on my back, looking up into heaven. When the light had departed, I had no strength; but soon recovering in some degree, I went home.[9]

Was this a visitation of God and Jesus with new truths or demons with their doctrines of darkness?

Let's look at these doctrines of Joseph.

1) God a Physical Man

The Father has a body of flesh and bones as tangible as man's... [10]

He has a body of Flesh and Bones

2) Jesus Renounces His Church

All creeds are filthy in His eyes
All professors (testifiers) are corrupt
Gates of hell prevailed against His church

3) Jesus gave him secret knowledge

"and many other things did he say unto me, which I cannot write at this time" [11]

Remember 2 Corinthians 11:13-15?

For such are false apostles, deceitful workers, transforming themselves into apostles of Christ And no wonder! For Satan himself transforms himself into an angel of light. Therefore it is no great thing if his ministers also transform themselves into ministers of righteousness, whose end will be according to their works.

Deceiving spirits with the doctrines of demons?

Let's put them to the test of God's Word. On that very first day...of Mormonism

Who was that marvelous power, this actual being from the unseen world?

Well, according to the doctrines of Jesus and the Apostles, it wasn't God, was it...and it wasn't Jesus, was it...or His angels, were they?

This was an angel of light...

What doctrines did this angel of light, this marvelous being bring?

A different God, a different Christ, a different gospel and a different spirit.

But I fear, lest somehow, as the serpent deceived Eve by his craftiness, so your minds may be corrupted from the simplicity that is in Christ. For if he who comes preaches another Jesus whom we have not preached, or if you receive a different spirit which you have not received, or a different gospel which

you have not accepted—you may well put up with it!
(2 Corinthians 11:3-4)

If we can believe Jesus and the Apostles

Now the Spirit expressly says that in latter times some will depart from the faith, giving heed to deceiving spirits and doctrines of demons, speaking lies in hypocrisy, having their own conscience seared with a hot iron. (1 Timothy 4:2)

Therefore I was angry with that generation, and said,

'They always go astray in their heart, and they have not known My ways.'

So I swore in My wrath, 'They shall not enter My rest.' (Hebrews 3:11)

So we see that they could not enter in because of unbelief. (Hebrews 3:19)

Therefore, since a promise remains of entering His rest, let us fear lest any of you seem to have come short of it. For indeed the gospel was preached to us as well as to them; but the word which they heard did not profit them, not being mixed with faith in those who heard it. (Hebrews 4:1-2)

Because of false teachers, the Mormons do not have faith in full, for God once delivered for all, His Holy Word.

Brethren, my heart's desire and prayer to God for Israel [and The Mormons] is that they may be saved. For I bear them witness that they have a zeal for God, but not according to knowledge. For they being ignorant of God's righteousness, and seeking to establish their own righteousness, have not submitted to the righteousness of God. For Christ is the end of the law for righteousness to everyone who believes. (**Romans 10:1-4**)

CHAPTER FOUR

Behind Closed Doors

Looking at the destructive forces of heresy and false faith in the lives of families.

Although Mormonism is highly regarded for it social concerns, statistics from the State of Utah, whose population is overwhelmingly Mormon, indicate that Mormonism cannot produce a lifestyle that is any freer from societal ills than the rest of the country. That "Happiness is Family Home Evening" image of Mormonism doesn't go over so well at home in Utah!

Their high profile goodwill programs may include soup kitchens, aid to the homeless, flood victims, earthquake survivors and hurricane casualties, yet their "own members" often suffer neglect due to poor management practices of the LDS welfare program. Even secular welfare systems in Utah have had the same problems: Some disabled people in Utah have had to sell everything just to survive while others have waited up to five years for payments of benefits. In early 1992, disabled Utahans claimed that the terrible management of the Utah Division of Determination Services caused delayed benefits to over 4,000 people.[1]

John Heinerman, an active Mormon at the time, is the co-author (with Anson Shupe) of *The Mormon Corporate Empire* and was the Director of The Anthropological Research Center in Salt Lake City, Utah. John fully affirmed Utah's social problems in his own interview for the film "The God Makers II":

> The Mormon Church is caught up in the dilemma of having to, for the first time, face the reality that there are major problems within its organization, with its membership that are just not going to go away. One of these (problems) is homosexuality. In 1981, homosexuality was in another category called "other moral offenses." In '82 it was taken out, and put into a category by itself.... Homosexuality has increased by 50%, 100%, 200%, and it has just gone upward.
>
> Also adultery. The number one reason that the church excommunicates is for adultery, and its numbers are staggering and increasing every year. Another area of concern is the rising amount of child abuse within the LDS church...it is a growing problem.[2]

Among Heinerman's other concerns was the amount of prescription drug abuse and other types of crimes growing at Brigham Young University, in Provo, Utah, which is the showcase of Mormonism:

> Here [at BYU] you have runaway abuse of prescription drugs. I quoted (in a talk I gave last night in La Mirada, California) from an FBI report that now Brigham Young University is not as safe as the University of Utah in Salt Lake City. Brigham Young University has more aggravated crimes, and assaults...they smoke, and drink, and have gay clubs and lesbian clubs.

Heinerman concludes: *"So what it shows is, that all is not well in Zion, and that there are major problems confronting our religion."*[3]

Homosexuality at BYU

Heinerman's comments about homosexuality at BYU were not surprising. As early as 1982, students at BYU published a two-part series on LDS homosexuality and the gay lifestyle and the ways BYU and the LDS Church had chosen to deal with the phenomenon.

The report was published in an off-campus student paper called the *Seventh East Press*. Staff writer Dean Huffaker presented an extremely balanced look at the collision course between homosexuality and Mormonism. Centering on the problems gays have at BYU, he interviewed "gays and homosexuals on and near campus—including a former BYU instructor, a former BYU professor, and former and current BYU students." He reported on the weekend exodus of gay BYU students to one of the most popular gay bars in Salt Lake and their regular visits to a gay bath in Salt Lake. The danger was always that BYU Security, along with its undercover agents, were always trying to ferret out the gays who would be targeted for immediate disciplinary action.[4]

Huffaker reported that one homosexual, a former BYU professor named Steve, said that he struggled with the obvious inner turmoil for ten years while teaching at BYU. "While Steve was teaching at BYU, he was receiving help from the counseling center. His therapist told him that he was seeing three hundred students with the same problem."[5]

Readers of the articles were left with no doubt that the LDS Missionary program was a cradle of homosexuality. The *Seventh East Press* reported that in one group of 15 homosexuals alone, 13 were returned Missionaries.

The Church was stunned by the *Seventh East Press'* blatant disregard for the propriety or protocol one should use in dealing with church "problems." Those responsible for the indiscretion were called in and warned. In a follow-up issue, an article dealing with *Book of Mormon* discrepancies pushed church leaders past their level of tolerance. Key people within the *Seventh East Press* staff were transferred out of BYU and the Press died a quick and ignominious death. But, the secret was out: Mormonism was and still is a hot bed of homosexuality.

The church's program of taking young men (and women) out of their natural environments, isolating them from all family and friends at a time when their hormones are raging at their highest levels, bunking them in extremely close quarters with one other lonely and frustrated youngster, is a classic formula for trouble.

In the spring of 1990, *Evergreen,* an organization of Mormons, ex-gays and friends, held a private, by invitation only, meeting in Salt Lake City, touting cures for homosexuality. The conference, "LDS Men Overcoming Homosexuality," attracted about 150 participants, [6] including Mormon Bishops and gay men. Obviously, there is more than just a small problem there in Utah, when gays, ex-gays and the LDS church leaders are meeting to come up with *some answers* to the homosexual dilemma in which they now find themselves.

Today, LDS homosexuality is out of the closet and out on the web. Gay and Lesbian Mormons have found an open forum at such web sites as www.affirmation.org and www.gaymormon.com.

- Mormon attitude towards homosexuality softens (August 20, 2007) Tony Grew

- A new instruction pamphlet issued by the Mormon Church advises parents not to reject gay children, in what is being seen as a softening of attitudes towards homosexuality.
- *God Loveth His Children* is aimed at church members who are "troubled with same-gender attraction" and was released at the end of July.
- It states that gay people do not "choose" their orientation and counsels that homosexuals should remain celibate.
- Previously the Mormons, more correctly known as The Church of Jesus and the Latter Day Saints, had encouraged gay men and women to enter into heterosexual marriages.
- "Notwithstanding your present same-gender attractions, you can be happy during this life, lead a morally clean life, perform meaningful service in the Church, enjoy full fellowship with your fellow Saints, and ultimately receive all the blessings of eternal life," the sixteen-page pamphlet reads.
- "God does indeed love all His children. Many questions, however, including some related to same-gender attractions, must await a future answer, even in the next life."

The work appears on the LDS website, but its authors remain anonymous.

It reiterates that Heaven is a place for families only, but predicts that gay and lesbian people will become heterosexual in the afterlife if they remain celibate.[7]

Alarming Statistics

In a State monopolized by a religious group that advertises marital harmony, Utah's marriage and divorce statistics are alarming. In the years reported, Utah's divorce rate was higher than the national average.[8] Fifty five thousand women were being abused annually by their partners.[9] Child abuse and neglect had increased 212 percent in the last decade, with over ten thousand new cases in one year alone.[10] Rape and sexual assault for adults had increased 93 percent during the same period.[11]

In child labor law violations, Utah ranked number one in a six state region.[12] The Utah Department of Health admits pregnancies of unwed teenagers is a growing problem. In 1988, 48% of all teen births were out of wedlock.[13] In addition, Utah's prison system was ranked fourth for the rate of inmate population growth in 1989, with a 21 percent increase in the prison population.[14]

There has also been a staggering 379% increase in child sexual abuse to children under.[15] Much of the abuse is incestuous, and sadly, the perpetrators are given lenient sentences because of an oddity in Utah law that accommodates sexual abuse by a Mormon relative.[16] While State law provides stiff penalties for people who abuse children to whom they are not related, if a father sexually abuses his *own* children, the judge has the option of waiving any sentence and letting the Church step in and deal with him through their ecclesiastical system.[17]

The Mormon god in the Courtroom

A case in point was the appeal of Allen Hadfield in 1989. Hadfield had been convicted of sexual abuse of his 12-year-old son and 10-year-old daughter and was appealing to the State Supreme Court. *The Salt Lake Tribune* reported that Hadfield's attorney claimed that his client's children were influenced to lie about him by a therapist. Hadfield, who is an LDS, was convicted on four counts of sodomy and three counts of child abuse in a ritual satanic form.

In spite of the heinous nature of the crimes, Hadfield served only served six months on a work-release program. Usual mandatory sentencing for such crimes is 10 years. But Hadfield was under *church* counseling. As we said above, Utah law allows judges like staunch Mormon Cullen Y. Christensen of Provo's 4th District Court to invoke an incest exception. Christensen found Hadfield qualified for probation under this exception, since he was being counseled for his deviant behavior by the church.[18]

In looking at the particular section of the referenced Utah Code, it is obvious that the Mormons manipulate even the *intent* of the exception. The actual wording states:

> ...the defendant has been accepted for mental health treatment in a recognized family sexual abuse treatment center which specializes in dealing with the kind of child sexual abuse occurring in this case.[19]

Nevertheless, when a defendant walks into a Utah court with his Bishop and letters of affirmation by other leaders in the Mormon hierarchy, and the Bishop advises the Mormon Judge that the church will handle the counseling, the deal is as good as done. The Mormon god and his priesthood authority have entered a plea on behalf of the defendant. What LDS judge would dare risk his own exaltation to godhood or his re-election by disagreeing?

Another example of the power of the Mormon religion to control decisions in Utah courtrooms was reported in an article "Did God Influence Jury? Court Asked to Decide."

> The Utah Court of Appeals has been asked to determine if God's influence in a jury room is an improper interference of jury deliberations during a criminal trial. Two people charged with conspiracy to hide evidence of an office-building burning were found guilty after a male in the jury "asserted his spir-

itual authority in the said religion" [Mormonism] and thereby "influenced his fellow adherents to submit the question of guilt to *the will of God* by joining him in group prayer" claimed the defense attorney, Loni Deland. "Immediately following the prayer, the said juror expressed the "answer" to the prayer—that [the defendants] were guilty." After that, Mr. Deland said, all prayer participants changed their opinions to *adhere to the will of God,* and a 6-2 vote in favor of acquittal became a 6-2 vote in favor of conviction without further evidentiary considerations.

In his brief he said, "It is an undeniable fact of life in the state of Utah that one religion dominates virtually all aspects of life. The State Legislature openly acknowledges that the approval of the Mormon Church's hierarchy is a prerequisite to successful passages of proposed laws touching on that religion's tenets. It is also common knowledge that church adheres to a male-only priesthood which governs on the premise that the church president is a prophet and rules with divine inspiration and authority which flows from him to the faithful via the priesthood." Mr. Deland said that "all prayer participants changed their opinions to adhere to "the will of God," without further "evidentiary considerations" when they learned that the male juror after calling for prayer "indicated he had divine guidance that the defendants were guilty." Deland said, "The juror who asserted his spiritual authority" manipulated his client's verdict.[20]

I have been an expert witness in a number of LDS-related sexual child abuse legal cases. In every case, the church and its own system had protected the perpetrator from legal action that would have helped the victims and stopped the abuse. In one case, the perpetrator had been moved from one Ward where he had sexually abused children and to another, where he was made a Home Teacher (authorizing his authority to visit church member homes in the name of the church) for several Single Mother homes where he immediately began the abuse cycle all over again.

I have just taken you through a minefield of social problems that are out of control in Utah, problems that the LDS church pretends do not exist. *The fruit doesn't fall far from the tree.* If it really were the only true church, operating with divine, holy revelation on a daily basis, then the LDS church, its prophet of god, and its social, welfare and religious systems would have turned Utah into a virtual Garden of Eden. But it hasn't. Far from it. It is a living hell for thousands.

Worse, because when the LDS church would rather the sins of its common people not be there, *they aren't.* The good LDS people live in a perpetual state of denial, and when sin *does* push its ugly head through the roof of the house so all can see, it's then blamed on the failure of the individual to live up to the standards of the Church. The Church is *always* right, *always* pure, *always* without spot or wrinkle. What the LDS people end up as are either robots or as broken people unable to see a way out of this paradox. Where do they go with their sin?

Years ago, in the early days of Saints Alive, I was doing a daily radio program that was broadcast into most of Utah. While the program generated a lot of correspondence in most areas, there were certain rural pockets from which not a single letter came. Saints Alive had no idea if anyone even listened to the show in those areas. When time and scheduling problems made it impossible to maintain the daily program, it was eventually closed down.

Not long after they went off the air, I received an unsigned letter with no return address. The postmark on the envelope was from one of those "silent" towns. The writer told of how she was a physically abused Mormon wife and mother who was a virtual prisoner in her own house. She shared how she had tried to get help and counseling from the local Bishop. He told her husband that she was complaining about him and that only brought on more beatings. Her own parents told her that she was not working hard enough at being a good Mormon wife. She thought about suicide often.

One day, alone at home, she turned on the radio and tuned in to the Saints Alive program, "Dialogue." She listened as my co-host Jim Witham and I talked about the love and grace and joy of knowing Christ. She gave her life to Jesus a few days later while listening to us call the lost to Calvary. The program became her one hope, her only contact with reality. She organized her schedule around those 15 minutes each day and her life became a new one, centered in Jesus, filled with peace. In spite of all the turmoil in her life, she had found joy and a solid anchor in a raging storm. She wanted me to know how much good that program had done for just one Mormon woman. She wanted me to know that Jim and I had been carrying the bulk of her heavy burden in the love and caring we had shown each day on the air.

That's the way I feel about my own role in helping to create *The God Makers* and *The God Makers II* books and films. That's how I feel about the publication of this book. Someone has to speak for these silent victims; someone must be their voice. Someone needs to stand up to this giant "Big Brother" masquerading as a benevolent family-centered church that preaches Christ.

On The Road with "The God Makers II"

The reader needs to understand that when the original "God Makers" movie was released over twenty-five ago, relatively little was known about Mormonism in mainstream Christianity. The film hit like a bombshell and was being shown in as many as a thousand churches per month. Scores of ministries to the cults across the country were showing the

16 mm version of the film almost non-stop for several years. Even today, more than twenty five years later, the video and DVD versions of the film have been Jeremiah Films' all-time bestsellers. It is a rare church library that doesn't have a video or DVD copies of these films on its shelf, along with the film, *The Mormon Dilemma*.

Today, Mormonism is no longer a quiet, quaint, little Quaker-type sect tucked away in the mountains of Utah. It is a major business conglomerate/religion with its tens of thousands of missionaries wielding the power of American wealth and success around the globe.

Mormon leaders may have been asleep when the first film hit, but they were ready and waiting for the new one! The first copies of "The God Makers II" video went out of the mailrooms at Jeremiah Films and Saints Alive without covers or jackets. Too many people couldn't wait to see this new look at the Mormonism of the nineties. The initial response was tremendously positive. In early December 1992, I brought the new video into Utah for three premier showings, scheduled for Salt Lake City, Brigham City and Ogden.

Even before I arrived in Utah to premier the film, its detractors pulled out all the stops. The day before I arrived, an organization called *The National Conference of Christians and Jews (NCCJ)* had issued a widely distributed news release attacking the yet-to-be-seen film that went out across the country over AP wires. It was as follows:

A STATEMENT FROM THE NATIONAL CONFERENCE AND THE UTAH CHAPTER: FOR RELEASE DECEMBER 10 AT 10:00 AM: A statement by Gillian Martin Sorensen, President of the National Conference, about "The God Makers II": [Contact Chris Bugbee (1-212-206-0006)]

Like its predecessor, God Makers II presents an intemperate polemic against the Mormon faith disguised as an objective documentary. Using a carefully selected mix of sensational and unsubstantiated first-person accounts, lurid allegations, and a highly subjective interpretation of Mormon teachings, God Makers II draws upon the incendiary arsenal of religious bigotry.

Frank discussion of the truth claims of different faiths is a legitimate avenue of inter-religious dialogue," Sorensen acknowledged. "But, base appeals to fear and hatred have no place in such efforts, and must be condemned wherever they are encountered."

"With its depiction of the Mormon Church as an evil empire founded upon sexual exploitation, predatory greed and Satanism," Sorensen said, God Makers II carries the odious scent of unreasoning prejudice. Let the public beware.

President Sorensen's statement reflects the feelings and has the endorsement of the Utah Chapter of the National Conference of Christians and Jews," said presiding Co-Chair Ted Speros. "A statement of our mission is to promote understanding and respect among all races, religions and cultures through advocacy, conflict resolutions and education. God Makers II is an affront to religious understanding.[21]

What the AP report did not say was that the NCCJ was the same group that claimed the very same things about the first movie, way back in 1984. At that time, they claimed to have spent a major effort in researching the movie before they concluded it was "religious pornography." Yet, the NCCJ failed then and failed again to contact Jeremiah Films, Saints Alive, or any single participant for a single document to support a single statement. I would guess that their only input in a blatant attempt to discredit this film was the Public Relations office at the Mormon Church.

The NCCJ failed to identify over a dozen Mormons in their first study group, failed to mention that there wasn't a single orthodox Jew or conservative Christian on the team, either time. They also failed to state who the Mormon members of their Board presently were, or how they had managed to get this Statement ready for release in Utah on December 10th, the day before I arrived there. It had taken them nearly a year to release their report on the first "God Makers" film. This one was out within a month of the first videos being shipped out from Jeremiah Films. The Mormons could sit back and smile while this unorthodox group, led by Mormons within it, did their cleanup work. The NCCJ news release and its authors were without merit! Who gave them the authority to judge what specific lines of doctrine separate any group from Christian orthodoxy when they themselves weren't even part of it?

The one sad part of the matter is that several other "ministries" to Mormons joined in with the NCCJ to take some shots at the film and at us. These groups felt we should be strictly intellectual in our statements. A lady from one such group in Utah was interviewed both in the press and on television and stated that "the things [they] object to [in Mormonism] can be laid out and documented. I can present logical reasons not to believe in Mormon claims. The Decker film appeals more to emotion in a supermarket tabloid style."[22]

The fact is, the movie clearly stood on its own merit and is more than well documented. I wanted to face these accusations in Utah. If something was out of order, it was far better to face it openly and honestly right at the start. I read the NCCJ report in full and the negative public statement by the fellow Christian ministry above, after each showing, and took a vote on who was telling things straight. By a show of hands the film easily won by a ratio of well over 50 to 1.

The people in Utah already know Christian fact from Mormon fiction. They have to live with this dark side of Mormonism every day. The film was a welcome bit of reality. The other ministry continued on, so tied to the intellectual approach of dealing quietly with Mormonism, that they missed the move of the Holy Spirit that brought hundreds of Mormons to the altars and Christ at every one of our showings. I'm with Paul, the real apostle, who saw revivals or riots wherever he went to preach.

I wish you could have been with me in Utah as the movie was shown. The audience participation times were so alive and positive. There was a great, enthusiastic response in the center of the area where the film would obvious meet its severest criticism, virtually at the front door of Mormonism.

In one of the meetings, a man in the audience stood and said he had a statement to make. He said that he had been a Mormon for many years and he had just one thing to say about the movie. I fully expected to be called to repentance by the man, but was in for a surprise. The man stated that he had watched the film with great intent and *"every single thing in that film is...absolutely true!"* He said that he had been gathering notes on the Church over the years and had over 1,200 pages of documentation that supported the exact same things the film pointed out. He was amazed that we had not made the film from his own notes.

Someone in the audience asked him why he was still a Mormon if he believed the things the film had revealed were true. He was silent for a moment and then responded. He said that his wife was bedridden, an invalid for whom he did everything from clothing and cleaning to feeding. But, his wife was a Mormon and had told him that if he released his data, she would leave him even if she had to crawl out of the house. He told me later that he could never get anyone from the church to come to help him, even for a few hours. Yet, even though she relied on him for everything, the church had a spiritual death grip on her that was stronger than anything he could offer her.

Yes, the film was hard hitting and *yes,* the Mormons were less than thrilled. But this was not a witnessing tool for wooing Mormons. It was a film to warn the Christian church! To warn an apathetic church, a church that has gone back to sleep and a church that is ignoring the wolves ravaging its own flocks! It is time to wake up that slumbering church once more to the shouts of danger!

Purging the Radicals

In the fall of 1992, Mormon-watchers began to pick up rumblings of an uncharacteristic *purifying* within its ranks of members who would be an embarrassment to the new ecumenical face of Mormonism. The reverberations broke through the wall of silence toward the end of November, when local, regional, and national wire services carried the story of another one of the secret plans of The Brethren gone wrong. *The Salt Lake Tribune* released an article that was a balanced presentation of the outcry.

The Church of Jesus Christ of Latter-day Saints is purging hundreds of Mormon dissidents who church officials say are preoccupied unduly with Armageddon. This massive housecleaning may be one of the church's largest since the 1850s, when thousands were excommunicated for everything from poor hygiene and low church attendance to disobeying the Ten Commandments. In recent months, Mormons from Utah, Nevada, Arizona and Idaho have been expelled and many others have been threatened.

Those interviewed by *The Salt Lake Tribune* say they had faced church discipline for a range of transgressions—from having too much emergency food storage to adhering to the doomsday predictions of then popular Mormon presidential candidate Bo Gritz, who received more than 28,000 Utah votes in the November [1992] election.

Targeted were those obsessed with the early speeches of LDS Church President Ezra Taft Benson and who believed the ailing 93-year-old leader has been silenced because his opinions no longer are politically popular.

LDS Church leaders from central and southern Utah complained of such "troublesome ideologies" during a Nov. 13-14 meeting at the Edgemont Stake Center in Provo. Elder Jeppson outlined a profile of dissidents. Stake presidents have used that profile [later to be defined as an unofficial list] to compile a list of warning signs.

The profile [list] apparently was used to finger Elaine and Jim Harmston. "Our stake president said, 'You cannot discuss the gospel in your own home with anyone outside your own family or you will be excommunicated,'" says Elaine Harmston. *"That was something we couldn't go along with."*[23]

Apparently, the Harmstons were running a study group in their home that included a form of prayer that was prohibited outside the temple. Conducting any home study, especially one where some form of temple type of prayer would be used, is virtually unthinkable within orthodox Mormonism. When the Bishop issued a warning from the pulpit that attending the Harmstons' study group would bring the risk of discipline, the study group immediately *increased* in size. The *Salt Lake Tribune* article said that, as the group swelled, area church leaders began surveillance on the Harmstons' house, taking down visitors' license plate numbers. The visitors were then called in for disciplinary action.

Can you even imagine such a thing taking place in a normal Christian church? If a Christian minister behaved in this way, either the pastor would be looking for other work or the outlawed study group would break their ties. The group would probably become the nucleus of a new church, where the people would be concerned with being taught the meat of the real gospel, instead of bowing before the strong arm tactics of their pastor.

What was extremely rare in this case was that Mormons actually disobeyed the direct instruction of their bishop. What the Harmstons saw was that the people who came in spite of the threats were hungry for truth and "tired of the pabulum they're getting from the church." While I don't necessarily agree with what the study group was teaching, I certainly have to admire their spunk in standing up to such church pressure.

A key point is that the LDS Church operates with such dictatorial control that the members of any particular local LDS church cannot escape it. They are forced to deal with the judgment and the discipline of *that* local bishop. It didn't matter why they attended the study group. If the bishop said it was wrong to do it, they were wrong to go and in spiritual rebellion to do so. These people put their Mormon Church membership, their Temple recommends and their actual salvation on the line by going.

Further, members who were in conflict with leadership could not avert their problems by going to some other Mormon Church in town. Mormons *must* go to the local ward (church) where they are assigned. Many Mormons have friends living a block or two away (and in some extreme cases, even across the street) with whom they would dearly love to attend church and share the many fellowship programs associated with church attendance. But, the LDS Church *assigns* members to wards they must attend, based upon geographic boundaries established in a clerk's office somewhere in the system.

Censured Mormons must either conform quickly and quietly or face swift expulsion from what most of them consider to be the only true church. What was so strange about this purge was that the very things that Mormons were encouraged to do just a few years ago, like food storage and home schooling, were now putting the same people in danger of Mormon Church discipline.

Checklist for Apostasy

Sometimes it pays dividends to have a friend in Utah who is also an active Mormon, privy to certain things not readily available to the average non-Mormon. My friend sent me two sheets of data that were significant to this story. The first sheet appeared to have come from the General Handbook of Instruction, in use at the ward level. It had the heading, Dealing with Apostate and Splinter Groups, and under the subheading below, listed 14 things Mormon leaders should watch for:

Inappropriate and Questionable Activities

1. Teaching false doctrines.
2. Teaching against the direction of local or general leaders.
3. Being in sympathy with apostate individuals or groups, including studying with them.
4. Teaching sacred doctrines and ordinances of the temple in one's home or elsewhere.
5. Practicing, teaching, studying or sympathizing with polygamists or others who have been excommunicated from the Church.
6. Conducting temple-like prayer circles or other unauthorized rituals outside the temple.
7. Following and teaching the words of dead prophets as being more authoritative than those of the living prophets.
8. Inappropriate interpretation or teaching of the scriptures or statements of The Brethren.
9. Claiming to have special divine authority or callings outside of established priesthood channels.
10. Refusing to follow priesthood leaders' specific counsel and instruction in Church-related matters.
11. Divorces among splinter group members which may result in plural marriages with other group members.

12. "Proselytizing" members into special groups who teach questionable doctrine and practices.
13. Receiving so-called "inspiration" or direction for others.
14. Teaching that individuals receive inspiration or have a higher knowledge or level of spirituality which gives them greater insights or abilities than ordained Church leaders.

When The Brethren began the purging of radical members who might be an embarrassment, some standards were set for what constituted LDS radicalism. Elder Jeppson, who outlined a profile of dissidents, presented these standards at the Edgemont Stake Center in Provo on November 13-14, 1992. This profile was used to implicate Elaine and Jim Harmston, the couple who started the home study group discussed earlier. The undated document as is follows:

Profile of the Splinter Group Members or others with Troublesome Ideologies.

- They follow the practice of home school.
- There is a preoccupation with the end of the world and the events preceding the coming of the Savior.
- Many have John Birch membership or leanings.
- Many do not work and have no jobs.

- They study the mysteries, feeling that what is provided in our meetings today is superficial.
- They meet in study groups.
- They listen to tapes such as the "Bo Gritz" tapes and others about such topics as Armageddon.
- They are inordinately preoccupied with food storage.
- They feel and teach that there is a great conspiracy, that the government is corrupt and that you can trust few people.
- They feel many of the members and Church leaders have gone astray.
- They feel that President [Benson's] counselors have muzzled the prophet so that he cannot tell us the things he would like to tell us, especially about the last days.
- They staunchly profess that they sustain the prophet and local leaders, but when asked to stop doing certain things, like meeting in groups to study the mysteries, they tell you straight out they will have to take the matter to the Lord to see what He tells them before they will agree.
- Some have met or are meeting with leaders of the Church of the Firstborn.
- They believe we must be super spiritual to know the will of God or even our leaders may lead us astray.
- They read the books of Avraham Gileadi and other materials which are unapproved by the Church.

- Many of these folk are on state welfare and others try to obtain Church welfare.
- We observe that many of these people reportedly have visions and dreams which they share with group members but not priesthood leaders.
- The element of plural marriage, though seldom spoken of outside this group, continues to surface as a part of the belief structure of many.
- Some have held prayer circles in full temple clothing outside the temple.
- While this practice has now been stopped, some of these folks would linger in the celestial room of the Manti Temple for hours to teach one another.

True Gritz

Seen as one of the key agitators, who had stirred the pot, was Bo Gritz, a highly decorated former green beret. He was the ultraconservative Mormon who made an unsuccessful third party bid for president in the 1992 elections, but actually made a strong showing in high Mormon population areas.

The press reported that Gritz was warned by Mormon Church leaders to be careful of what he taught. He was told that some of his views were out of line with the Church. Gritz was the first member of his family to convert to the church, in 1984 and was still active at the time. Still, the report said, Gritz quickly acknowledged that he doesn't agree with everything the Church teaches. "I don't personally believe we will be gods," said Gritz. "I don't think God was ever like we are, very frankly. I don't know whether Joseph Smith was a prophet a little bit, a long time or always or never. It doesn't make any difference to me."[24]

In a related story, Gritz added, "A lot of folks, they would die if their bishop were to criticize them or if their membership were threatened. To me, it's more important what my personal relationship is with the savior."[25]

In 1993, Gritz changed his emphasis again and began offering a course called SPIKE (Specially Prepared Individuals for Key Events), which taught paramilitary and survivalist skills. He also established a community in Idaho called Almost Heaven. Both of these proved to be even more controversial than his past activities, attracting charges from anti-racist watchdog groups that he was trying to build a community of Christian Patriot believers and train them in paramilitary skills for a showdown with the government.

The Church of Jesus Christ of Latter-day Saints responded to his newfound activities by disfellowshipping Gritz, revoking his temple recommend, to which Bo responded by resigning his membership in the LDS Church. He eventually cut his ties to the Almost Heaven community and returned to Nevada.[26]

Reversing the LDS Pro-Life Stand

When I was in Utah premiering the new film, "The God Makers II," one of the TV stations did a news report on the Church disciplinary action being taken against some people who were pro-lifers. In a literally *unbelievable* turn of events, the LDS church had *reversed its almost militant pro-life position* and LDS bishops were counseling young women to have abortions. 20 years earlier, such counseling would have caused a bishop to be immediately excommunicated from the Church! Here is the actual transcript of the report:

Anchor:
The LDS Church says it has consistently opposed elective abortions, but some Mormons claim they are being disciplined for preaching the Pro-Life message. Paul Murphy has this exclusive report.

Murphy:
They say they are faithful Latter-Day Saints, but claim they are being disciplined for their anti-abortion views.

Sharp:
It is murder—the shedding of innocent blood, for which there is no forgiveness.

Murphy:

Sharp says he was excommunicated in July only over abortion. His Stake President says it was only one of four issues leading to the discipline. John Abney was a ward clerk until he expressed his views against abortion. Now he and his wife are scheduled for a church disciplinary court.

Abney:

We do not want to have the blood and the sins of this generation to come upon our garments, either in or out of the church.

Murphy:

Roxanne Abney said she couldn't believe the conversation she recently had with her stake president.

Mrs. Abney:

One of the lord's representatives, discussing abortion, me being against it, him being for it, and I'm on the wrong side of the fence.

Murphy:

The LDS General Handbook now says that abortion is not murder, and is permissible in cases of rape, incest or when the life or health of the woman is in danger, or the fetus is not likely to survive birth. But, as recently as 1975, the LDS President said abortion is wrong, even in cases of rape. And Utah's Right-to-Life Director says she has received a lot of calls from girls who say their Bishops counsel them to have abortions.

Director Goodnight:
So it wasn't for rape and it wasn't for incest and it wasn't for fetal deformity...

Murphy:
And the Bishop still counseled these girls to have an abortion?

Director Goodnight:
The Bishop is still advising them to have an abortion.

Murphy:
These are confusing times for Sharp and the Abneys. They thought they were in line with Mormon doctrine. Now they find themselves on the way out.

Paul Murphy, KTVX 4 News.

Anchor:
Tomorrow night, a group of Pro-Life Mormons will be meeting at the Copper View Community Center in Midvale to discuss their future in the LDS church.

Reporter: Paul Murphy

Anchor: Randall Carlyle

1st LDS: William Sharp

LDS Couple: John and Roxanne Abney

Director of Utah Pro-Life group: Rosa Goodnight

Prophet quoted is Spencer W. Kimball, 1975
    Video showed page of Bishop's handbook to show new rules[27]

Freedom of Thought at BYU

In a subtler way, other members of the Church of Jesus Christ of Latter-day Saints are also feeling the heat. LDS historian, D. Michael Quinn, once a highly esteemed educator, published some things about the history of Mormonism that did not bring joy to The Brethren.

First, there was his research about Church-sanctioned polygamy after 1890, when the church had publicly ended the practice. Quinn said several apostles secretly tried to have him disciplined for that in 1985. Then there was the book about the occult beginnings of the Church, *Early Mormonism and the Magic World View,* which caused quite a stir. Then came his contributions about women in the Church, and finally an article entitled "150 Years of Truth and Consequences about Mormon History," in which Mr. Quinn described the punitive actions taken against those who write about controversial aspects of Mormon history."[28]

The *Salt Lake Tribune* reported that Quinn, at the time *still an active, believing Mormon,* was under investigation for Apostasy!

> Mormon historian D. Michael Quinn has been on the lam for five years. Ever since three apostles encouraged his stake president to start excommunication proceedings against him when he was teaching at Brigham Young University, Mr. Quinn has managed to stay one-step ahead of the Church of Jesus Christ of Latter-Day Saints ecclesiastical process servers. Until last weekend.
>
> Mr. Quinn's first encounter with his local LDS leaders since moving back to Salt Lake last summer was a request to defend himself in an apostasy investigation. "No welcome visit, no home teachers, no

invitations to attend ward meetings, just a summons to defend myself," says Mr. Quinn.

Quinn isn't playing the game, however. "I vowed I would never again participate in a process which was designed to punish me for being the messenger of unwanted historical evidence," he wrote in a letter of response.... In his letter, Mr. Quinn reiterated his belief in the core doctrines of Mormon theology.[29]

It was obvious that the Church had a loose cannon on its hands when a Mormon historian was caught between reporting on actual Church history or rewriting Church history in a manner that fit the image The Brethren wanted to project. Michael Quinn was obviously no longer associated with BYU, but he was a highly esteemed, visible scholar and his excommunication would bring a literal wave of negative response from the large body of more liberal-minded intellectuals within the church. The Brethren were between a rock and a hard place of their own making.

Some of the lowly students at BYU weren't quite as visible or lucky as D. Michael Quinn. In what I consider to be a major step back from the LDS race to ecumenicalism, BYU officials ordered the immediate expulsion of students who quit the LDS church. Associated Press writer Vern Anderson reported on this strong action against students who leave the faith while attending BYU.

Policy Says Re-baptism is Only Route to Gaining Reinstatement. Mormon students at Brigham Young University who leave the faith or affiliate with another religion will be barred permanently from the school under a new written policy governing such cases. Only rebaptism in the Church of Jesus Christ of Latter-day Saints will allow a student to return to the Mormon Church-owned school, according to the policy approved by BYU's Board of Trustees.

> To attend BYU, a student must complete an annual Continuing Ecclesiastical Endorsement form, promising to adhere to the school's strict honor code. It must be signed by an ecclesiastical leader after an interview to determine if the student is "worthy" to continue. Mormon students must be interviewed by their ward bishops, while the 1.5% to 2% of non-Mormons among the student body of 27,000 can see their own clergy. As part of the written policy, BYU officials expanded a section of the endorsement to include a question asking if a student has been excommunicated or disfellowshipped, requested that their name be removed from church rolls or "formally joined another church."[30]

Cookie-Cutter Saints

The many purges and continuing clampdown on individual freedom of thought should concern all Mormons greatly:

> Salt Lake attorney (Paul Toscano) presiding over the Mormon Alliance, a group formed last summer to investigate cases of Mormons who believe they've been unjustly disciplined...says, "It is very much in the interest of world-sphere Mormonism or visitor-center Mormonism to eliminate anybody who thinks." Brigham Young called it the "iron bed of conformity." Disciplining of conservative Mormons and stepped-up pressure on liberal and intellectual Mormons portrays a leadership concerned that all members be cut from the same moderate mold. Worldwide Mormons need to be like Utah Mormons and Utah Mormons need to be more cookie-cutter.[31]

The Mormon Church may want cookie-cutter Saints, but it just isn't going to happen that easily. The Church will have to enlarge its court system before it is able to censure all thinking members, even if they are victims of LDS control games. The gigantic break-though with computer and web technologies in the years following these secret purgings opened hundreds, if not thousands, of "Unhappy Mormon" websites and blogs. Just go to YouTube or MySpace and search under *Mormon* or *LDS*, and see the hundreds of posts by today's computer-wise radicals. I just "Googled" *radical Mormons* and found over 1,000,000 hits! Typing in *Leaving Mormonism* gave another million-plus hits. *LDS Error* gave up 824,000 hits and *False Prophet Joseph Smith* brought up only 686,000. *Mormon Erotica* gave up 816.000 hits. *Gay Mormon Missionaries* produced 487000 references.

The Cookie-Cutter Saints are getting out of the box! [32]

CHAPTER FIVE

Cleaning up the Unchangeable Temple Rituals

The unchangeable Temple Ritual that keeps changing with the times.

If you work on the premise that the Mormon Church is true, *or even possibly* true, the LDS temple ritual has to be at the center of your faith. It is only through the sacred temple that you would have *any* hope of personal exaltation or godhood. The path to Mormon godhood will be explained in detail later. For now, it is important to know that without the ritual and the keys the temple provides, there can be no entrance into Mormon godhood. To an active Mormon, the temple is like the doorway to heaven. It is so holy that Mormons, even those who have carpooled to the temple, remain absolutely silent on *anything* regarding the rituals in which they have just participated once they step outside the temple doors.

Prelude to Change

When the film "The God Makers" was released in 1982, it had a monumental impact that went far beyond the film itself or any expectations of its makers. For the first time ever on film, the heresies of Mormonism were revealed, and the world was exposed to the darkest secrets and doctrines of the Latter-day Saints.

While the film was difficult enough for Mormons to deal with in its entirety, the parts that showed LDS temple ordinances struck so deeply that many felt a deep violation of their deepest privacy.

Suddenly, rituals performed in solemn sanctity within the Mormon Temples under the most consecrated conditions were being shown on movie screens in as many as a thousand Christian churches each month. The secret ceremonies became the subject of numerous radio and television shows, bringing the things Temple Mormons had done in secret into the glaring light of day. In the movie, the reenactments of the rituals were displayed in full, authorized Temple costume, and were performed and supervised by former, longtime Temple workers Chuck Sackett and his wife, Dolly.

The movie not only displayed the Mormons' deepest secrets to the world but also gave sound evidence that they were occult in every respect, with large portions of their ceremony taken from Blue Lodge Freemasonry. In fact, one "secret" about the film itself was that the LDS temple scenes were filmed in an actual Masonic lodge room that was rented for the purpose because of its similar ambiance.

No one dared challenge the accuracy of the Temple ritual reenactment. First, Mormons were bound by Temple oath to never speak of them outside the Temple. Second, the word from the LDS pulpits was that Mormons who wanted to stay in good standing in the church had better stay away from any showings of "The God Makers." Third, the people reenacting the ceremonies in the film were working from a script containing the actual, *verbatim* rituals.

Going Public

While still officiating in the Los Angeles Temple, Chuck Sackett covertly took a small tape recorder into the Temple with him and recorded the secret rituals. The next business day, Chuck notified the Temple president of what he had done and said that he intended to publish the ritual. He let the president know that he was making himself available for both Church and legal action. He was willing to risk everything to let the world see the real LDS temple ritual. When Chuck made the material available to other ministries to Mormons, the LDS response to was to deny that this was anything more than a few dissidents playing at what they *thought* they knew.

When another tape recording appeared with excerpts of the ceremonies from *two other Temples,* that validated Chuck Sackett's tape, we made the decision to create a film that would center on this critical element of the Latter-day heresy. "The Temple of the God Makers" was born. Its swift and wide distribution was credited to the great success of the first film and the tremendous interest the public had in seeing the inner darkness of Mormonism revealed. The film showed in detail that what really went on behind closed Temple doors was not bringing Mormons into a closer walk with God, but actually driving them away from God into a bizarre, occult ritual of self-glorification.

At this time, Chuck and Dolly Sackett published the full rituals,[1] and thousands of copies of their book spread across the United States and many foreign countries. *The Mormon Temple secrets were secret no longer.* They were also hardly sacred. Their cultic, anti-Christian mockery stood open and indefensible.

At that time, I was broadcasting daily radio programming in much of Utah, Idaho, and Arizona. One week I ran a series of programs detailing the heresies within the Temple, showing significant parallels with Freemasonry, the occult, and Luciferianism. The programs compared the rituals to the Biblical warnings against such practices. The station broadcasting the programs to the Salt Lake City area was darkly warned to take it off the air. After the second segment played, the station's broadcast tower facility was burned to the ground, and the station was unable to operate for nearly six months. We realized that these were no idle threats.

Meanwhile, the Sacketts took their presentation on the road, dressed in all their temple regalia teaching and calling Mormons to repentance in hundreds of communities. They appeared on radio and television programs nationwide, boldly proclaiming the truth about Mormonism to potential audiences of millions.

Looking at Mormonism from a different angle was Idaho pastor Jim Spencer, a former Mormon and author of several books on Mormonism that showed the parallels between Mormonism, Witchcraft, and Freemasonry. His book, *Mormonism's Temple of Doom*, was publicly endorsed by the great Christian apologist, Dr. Walter Martin. He issued this statement in a letter to James Spencer, January 6, 1989.

> When I first read *Mormonism's Temple of Doom* in July of 1987, I recognized it as an important work helping to document the connections between Mormonism and the occult.
>
> Controversy has arisen over the book in that some people have understood the authors to be saying that Mormonism is a lineal descendant of specific occult organizations (i.e. Freemasonry). I can understand how that conclusion can be reached. The authors,

however, have—on many occasions—stated that their position is "remarkable and undeniable similarities exist between Mormonism and other occult organizations." They contend, in *Mormonism's Temple of Doom*, that disciplines such as Mormonism, Freemasonry, and Wicca are streams of the same Satanic river. This can be substantiated as fact.

I do not agree with every line of this book. However, I believe the authors' hearts are squarely centered on the side of winning Mormons to the Kingdom of God. I therefore commend the authors for their bold witness, and this book to God's service.

Its volatile charges caused an explosive reaction within Mormonism and a great deal of controversy among the less confrontational ministries to Mormons, such that the wedge between the more intellectual ministries and the more evangelical ones widened further. Even Walter Martin's ministry, following Martin's death, pulled away from endorsing the book. Yet the book is still a powerful tool in understanding the deep occult bedrock of Mormonism, the Mormon Temple.[2]

In the fall and winter of 1989, a revived flurry of radio programs seemed to reopen the bleeding wounds of the Mormons about their Temple. Perhaps the straw that broke the camel's back was a two-day presentation of the rituals on the late Dr. Walter Martin's Christian Research Institute's nationwide radio program, *The Bible Answer Man*.

Broadcasting live across the country on hundreds of stations, Chuck and Dolly Sackett laid the ceremonies out once again, playing segments of the actual rituals from Chuck's original tape recording and answering callers' questions from all parts of the country.

While all of this intense activity was going on, faithful Mormons were becoming extremely unhappy over the Church's silence against the charges of heresy and occultism.

To make matters even more cumbersome was that many of the women in the church were getting tired of being treated like chattel in the Temple ritual and were starting to become vocal about their feelings of their subordinate stature in the eternal complexities of Mormonism.

A Remarkable Event

We have no way of knowing what caused The Brethren to act. We suspect it was the culmination of the many attacks, not only from the army of former Mormons but increasingly from within the Mormon Church. What we do know is that several months later, the LDS Church closed its U.S. Temples for what everyone believed were normal renovations and repairs. On April 10, 1990, immediately after the General Conference (the Church's largest ecclesiastical gathering of the year), the doors were opened again to those Mormons with Temple recommends, except this time something besides the carpeting had changed. Major revisions had been made *to the rituals themselves*. As Chuck Sackett remarked in his detailed report of the changes:

> No announcement was made of a new revelation, nor was a sustaining vote taken, as church rules require. Mormons have been taught that the Temple rituals were a direct revelation from God to Joseph Smith, Jr., the founder of Mormonism. Such drastic changes should only be made through another revelation to Ezra Taft Benson, the current Mormon Prophet. Mormons have been taught that such revelations must be reported at General Conference [in early April] and a sustaining vote taken to give the revelation official approval and sanction of the membership.[3]

It was apparent that the church chose to wait until immediately after the semi-annual General Conference to effect the changes and sidestep embarrassing member concern over it at the leadership meetings. Mormons, as we noted earlier, are under solemn oath not to discuss things of the Temple outside its doors. To do so would bring swift and grim judgment. By the time of the next General Conference in October, The Brethren had things under control and the drastic changes never became an issue.

What is most fascinating about the changes is that the Church had literally ripped out almost everything in the temple ceremony that the many ministries to Mormons had been exposing since Chuck Sackett walked out of the LA temple with that tape recording in his pocket. **The deleted parts were the *very* things being declared as grievous to God across the nation on radio and television, and in newsletters and books.** The sections that were expunged were primarily those that Chuck and Dolly Sackett reenacted in both "The God Makers" and "The Temple of The God Makers!"

Mormon leaders took the only road out of the swamp. They radically changed a ritual that had supposedly been *restored to its original form* when it was given to Joseph Smith *from the very mouth of* God. I will deal with the new Mormon doctrine of progressive revelation more fully in another chapter, but as briefly noted earlier, it is the quasi-doctrine of concession that states that the revelations of any living prophet can supersede the revelations of any former prophet. What an open door to heresies within heresies!

The Details

When news of the Temple changes came, the specifics of the reformation were sketchy. The very first week, a number of calls came from far and wide about the changes. The exact details surfaced when a friend of a friend passed the details of the changes to a Mormon ministry in Salt Lake City.[4]

This material clearly confirmed the changes Chuck Sackett reported in his April 1990 report, which received wide circulation when it was duplicated in full in the September 1990 edition of *The Evangel*, a monthly newspaper produced by the ministry of John L. Smith, in Marlow, Oklahoma.

The Sackett report detailed a number of significant changes, and with his permission, we will quote from his description of the changes at length:

1. The execution of the penalties has been removed from the Priesthood Signs. No longer will every initiate be required to perform the three morbid gestures associated with having their lives taken if they reveal any of the temple secrets. These gestures were:

    A. Running the right thumb across the throat from left ear to right ear, signifying having one's throat slit from ear to ear.
    B. Drawing the right hand across the chest from left breast to right breast, signifying having one's chest ripped open and one's heart torn out.
    C. Running the right thumb across the abdomen, signifying having one's body cut asunder and one's vitals and bowels gush out.

What a relief this will be to thousands of civilized and sensitive Mormons who have been offended by this barbaric atrocity with each temple visit, also to those who decline to attend the temple because of this highly offensive aspect.

2. The most awesome spectacle of the entire series of temple rituals is gone! *The Sign of the Second Token of the Melchizedek Priesthood, the Patriarchal Grip, or Sure Sign of the Nail* has been eliminated. No longer will temple initiates be required to chant in unison the infamous *"Pay Lay Ale, Pay Lay Ale, Pay Lay Ale"* as they raise and lower their arms three times in the universal gesture of obeisance. No longer will thinking Mormons travel home wondering, as we did so often, what does *"Pay Lay Ale"* really mean?

3. The Masonically inspired *Five Points of Fellowship* through the temple veil has been eliminated. No longer will temple initiates be required to embrace "the Lord" through the veil in this mystical, highly occult configuration while they whisper in his ear the *Name of the Second Token of the Melchizedek Priesthood, the Patriarchal Grip, or Sure Sign of the Nail.*

The embrace is out, but it is likely that the incantation associated with it is still in. Apparently initiates will still be required to repeat back to "the Lord" through the veil: *"Health in the navel, marrow in the bones, strength in the loins and in the sinews. Power in the Priesthood be upon me and upon all my posterity, through all generations of time and throughout all eternity."*

4. Lucifer's hireling lackey, the Christian Minister, is out. No longer will initiates watch the devil hire a Christian pastor (representing all Christian clergymen) to teach his Satanic doctrines to Adam. No longer will they watch him mock and ridicule the most basic doctrines of Christianity. No longer will they watch as this Christian hireling abandons his faith and teachings and changes altars to join Adam and Eve in the Mormon Priesthood program of works and rituals.

    The liturgical significance of this change is profound. It is through the initiate's personal identification with Adam or Eve, as they renounce and deny the basic tenants of Christianity, that the purging of all remnants of Christian commitment in the initiates is accomplished. This crucial act in the Mormon conversion process would seem to have been eliminated! What will be substituted to accomplish this vital function spiritually bonding the initiates to LDS Priesthood power?

5. Women will no longer be required to veil their faces during the prayer in the Endowment prayer circle.

However, they will still wear the veil as their regular head covering. This was a vital symbol of the subservience of women in the Priesthood and the dominance of the man in all aspects of Mormonism. The veil is to be lifted only by her worthy resurrected husband in his process of resurrecting her.

6. Women (single and married) will no longer be required to swear an oath and covenant of obedience to their husband. This change may have the most radical effect on Mormonism of all! The Mormon god in the temple will no longer officially impose the oppressive stigma of female singleness. Single women will be somewhat relieved of the extreme pressure to marry. The wife will no longer be reminded with each temple visit that her only channel to her god is through her husband and that his faithfulness determines her eternity. Each Mormon husband can no longer rely on his wife (or wives) to constantly prod and motivate him to do his duty to the church based upon her total dependence upon him for her eternal exaltation. What will become of the church as a result of the change? How many worthy Priesthood leaders will become indifferent or lazy due to this major doctrinal change? We will have to watch and discern the inevitable decline in vigor taking place."[5]

One of the more interesting asides to this story of the temple ritual change was the removal of the words of the chant, *"Pay Lay Ale, Pay Lay Ale, Pay Lay Ale."* A number of years ago, the Sacketts showed that the words were a quick step-to-the-side from words in Hebrew that mimic, in their harshest translation, *"O Marvelous Lucifer."* In a far more conservative translation, the words read, *"O marvelous god"* with the god being defined as that one to whom the words were spoken. Using that approach, one can see in the ritual that the words had to refer to Lucifer, who was the one who responded when Adam cried out these words in the Lone and Dreary World.[6] Their report on *"Pay Lay Ale"* became an issue of debate even within a few of the ministries to Mormons. Surely, ex-Mormon theorists could argue the points until the end of time. But in the Temple, when Adam called out those words, Lucifer was the *only god* who answered. Most importantly, the Church responded to that charge by pulling the entire sequence containing the *"Pay Lay Ale"* chant from the ritual. There is no way of proving that the chant was removed because of the Sacketts' observations, but why else would such a critical portion of the original ritual be dropped?

One of the news reporters who interviewed me in Salt Lake City, during the premier showings of the film, "The God Makers II," wanted to know why we had portrayed examples of the old temple ritual in it. I told him that we did it because we didn't want the Mormon hierarchy to get away with secretly removing key portions of what they claimed was a sacred ritual restored to the purity of its first century order by the holy power of God. The theology of godly restorationism *cannot* allow you to change something that has already been restored to its original perfection.

The alterations in the Temple ceremony made headline news across the county. One report in the *Arizona Republic* particularly caught the flavor of the many facets of change involved.

> Revolutionary changes in temple ceremony...are seen as a move to bring the secret ceremony closer to mainstream Christianity.... The changes are the most drastic revisions of the century, rivaled only by the church's removal at the turn of the century of an oath to avenge the killers of church founder Joe Smith, according to Mormon insiders. The (asking to remain anonymous) member said, "They are substantive, I would say, in the cosmetics of the thing rather than in substance." A former member said...the climax has been eliminated. Removal of that part of the ritual is the equivalent of taking the Eucharist out of the Roman Catholic mass.
>
> Not all Mormons are happy with the ceremony changes. "I have Mormon friends who will see it as a step toward apostasy and an accommodation to the world," said one practicing Mormon in Utah.[7]

Most Mormon Church members quoted in news stories about revisions in the Church's confidential temple ceremony were quickly summoned for interviews by church officials.... The sacred confidentiality of the temples was reemphasized by the public communications office of the Church. John Dart, a religion editor, noted this in a *Los Angeles Times* news story:

> When the [Mormons] leave the house of the Lord, they are under obligation to be true to a sacred trust not to speak of that which is holy and sanctified; therefore, it is appropriate that church leaders visit with members when comments about the temple or other sacred matters are made public and are attributed to them in the news media...." Ron Priddis [one-time editor of the *Seventh East Press*] said he was reprimanded during his interview with a church authority (for talking to the press) and called the revisions "the most significant change in the church since Blacks received the priesthood in 1978.... In a church that is so patriarchal, that's quite a step."[8]

Bringing members in for "personal interviews" with Church leaders is one way the Mormon Church controls its members. As you will see, not every member who disagrees with The Brethren gets off so easily.

One of the most awkward and often demeaning portions of the LDS Temple Ritual takes place during the Washing and Anointing procedure where temple workers wash and anoint with oil certain parts of the human anatomy. Many former Mormons, most of them women, have talked about the strange feelings they had during this portion of the ritual.

It is especially unnerving to the first-time "patron" who also receives his/her "new name" and the sacred Garment of the Priesthood following their washing and anointing. This procedure was first revealed to the world in the Saints Alive/ Jeremiah film "The Temple of the God Makers." Literally, thousands of Mormons responded to the exposure of this cultic practice by leaving the church.

Again, the Eternal, Divinely Restored LDS Temple Rituals Change

One would think that, having a direct line to God through a holy prophet, the above corrections to the eternal temple ritual would have been complete for this generation, but in the spring of 2005, The Brethren felt the need to (very) quietly make further corrections to their earlier corrections.

Now, once again, The Brethren have cleaned up their occult act and removed the more graphic of the ritual from the Temple ceremonies they used to claim were divinely restored to their perfection, for time and all eternity. *Have*

I said that before? The ritual was changed quietly without any announcements or discussions with temple patrons. An active Mormon Temple worker wrote me this email:

> ***Dear Ed...*** *I am also an ordinance worker in the XXXXX temple. I have noticed a change in the initiatory ordinance. It used to be that one went in naked except for the shield that was worn. They entered a booth, where a worker washed them, and then washed certain parts of the body (eyes, ears, bowels, loins, legs, arms etc.) They then proceeded to the anointing portion where one was anointed with olive oil (with all this why go to a day spa) and the same thing was repeated. Finally they stepped out of the anointing booth to a booth wherein they were clothed in the garment. This has changed within the last two weeks. I am wondering if this is a Church-wide change. (I am assuming it is, as a friend of mine just went through Logan to get his own endowments and said it was different than his parents had told him.)*
>
> *We have been asked not to discuss these changes outside the temple, and we have not been given ANY information regarding this change. I feel bad for the old people who spend so much time trying to memorize this stuff. At least for me I can quickly learn the stuff. But I wanted to let you know of the changes. They no longer wash and anoint specific parts of the*

body. One is washed on the forehead, and the same words are used, but those body parts are not washed. They then go to the anointing booth, where they are anointed as if given a blessing. All the same words are used, but no specific [body parts] anointing. They then go and are clothed in the garment, but oddly enough they wear their one piece garment throughout the entire ceremony now. The temple gets stranger and stranger. Maybe someday we will also do away with the green little apron.

It seems to me that every bizarre and heathen practice in the temple is being slowly removed to make the temple seem less occult and strange. Try what they may, The Brethren will never correct what is evil without full repentance and renunciation. The bondage it brings as these people wallow in the necromantic bowels of pagan temple rituals leads to the burning fires of Hades unless the Mormon people flee from it for their very lives.

CHAPTER SIX

Mormonism, the American Islam

There is nothing new under the sun. The astonishing parallels of Mormonism and Islam.

A Second Mohammed

A few years back, I returned to the college (now a university) where I went to school in Logan, Utah. The Utah State Special Collections Library there has all the records of my ministry that I have gathered over the last 30-plus years and have cataloged it in the Ed Decker Manuscript Collection (MSS 210). Utah State is where I discovered Mormonism and a fitting place for my archives.

However, this time I was there to lecture on "Mormonism, the American Islam," and there was an overflow audience at the meeting. In fact, I had forgotten what a large Muslim population there was on campus. While I expected that the Mormons would be quite upset at the comparison, the Muslims were almost climbing up onto the stage to stop me from defiling Allah, Mohammed and the Koran, by making any comparisons with the LDS Church that they considered to be a pagan, multi-god and ancestor-worship cult. I felt that if I had not arranged for very tight and visible security, the meeting would have ended in violence.

I drew a strong comparison between the amazingly similar claims of Mohammed and Joseph Smith: visitations of an angel of light, the claim as God's last and greatest prophet, the Koran and *The Book of Mormon*.

I compared their similar doctrines of the nature of God, personal salvation and the afterlife with those of orthodox Christianity. The auditorium became too small for the large gathering, and we filled the large commons area of the Student Union beyond capacity and overflowed throughout the large student center and entrance.

Utah State University had certainly grown from that small agricultural college I attended in the early 1950s. Because it has been a long-time Land Grant school, many Muslims live and study there. The meeting was packed with Muslims and Islamic clerics, extremely offended at any reference to any comparison as Mormonism.

During the presentation of my evidence, there was much murmuring and shouting. When I opened the floor for the Question and Answer time, I faced a number of very agitated and verbally abusive Muslims. In fact, the Muslim interaction totally overshadowed any dialogue on Mormonism. Had there not been security guards all around, I am sure there would have been serious difficulties. The next day, I met with two local Muslim leaders and began a series of contacts that forced me to take a deep look at its history, its tenets of belief and its comparisons to orthodox Christianity.

As I was researching the religion of Islam and its similarities to Mormonism, I came across the following facts on the Internet. There were no references to ownership, so along with my own thoughts, I publish them here, in part.

In the heat of the Missouri "Mormon War" of 1838, Joseph Smith made the following claim:

"I will be to this generation a second Mohammed, whose motto in treating for peace was 'the Alcoran [Koran] or the Sword.' So shall it eventually be with us – 'Joseph Smith or the Sword!'"[1]

It is most interesting that a self-proclaimed Christian prophet would liken himself to Mohammed, the founder of Islam. His own comparison invites us to take a closer look as well. And when we do, we find some striking—and troubling—parallels. Consider the following.

Mohammed and Joseph Smith both had humble beginnings. Neither had formal religious connections or upbringing, and both were relatively uneducated. Both founded new religions by creating their own scriptures. In fact, followers of both prophets claim these scriptures are miracles since their authors were the most simple and uneducated of men.[2]

Both prophets claim of having angelic visitations and of receiving divine revelation to restore pure religion to the earth again. Mohammed was told that both Jews and Christians had long since corrupted their scriptures and religion. In like manner, Joseph Smith was told that all of Christianity had become corrupt, and that consequently the Bible itself was no longer reliable. In both cases, this corruption required a complete restoration of both scripture and religion. Nothing which preceded either prophet could be relied upon any longer. Both prophets claim they were used of God to restore eternal truths which once existed on earth, but had been lost due to human corruption.

Both prophets created new scripture which borrowed heavily from the Bible, but with a substantially new "spin." In his Koran, Mohammed appropriates a number of Biblical themes and characters—but he changes the complete sense of many passages, claiming to "correct" the Bible. In so doing he changes many doctrines, introducing his own in their place.

In like manner, Joseph Smith created *The Book of Mormon*, much of which is plagiarized directly from the King James Bible. Interestingly, he claims that this same Bible has been substantially corrupted and is therefore unreliable. In addition, Joseph Smith went so far as to actually create his own version of the Bible itself, the "Inspired Version," in which he both adds and deletes significant portions of text, claiming he is "correcting" it. In so doing he also changes many doctrines, introducing his own in their place.

As a part of their new scriptural "spin," both prophets saw themselves as prophesied in scripture, and both saw themselves as a continuation of a long line of Biblical prophets. Mohammed saw himself as a continuation of the ministry of Moses and Jesus. Joseph Smith saw himself as a successor to Enoch, Melchizedek, Joseph and Moses. Joseph Smith actually wrote himself into his own version of the Bible—by name.

Both prophets held up their own scripture as superior to the Bible. Mohammed claimed that the Koran was a perfect copy of the original which was in heaven. The Koran is therefore held to be absolutely perfect, far superior to the Bible—and superseding it. In like manner, Joseph Smith also made the following claim: "I told the Brethren that *The Book of Mormon* was the most correct of any book on earth, and the keystone of our religion, and a man would get nearer to God by abiding its precepts, than by any other book."[3]

Despite their claim that the Bible was corrupt, both prophets admonished their followers to adhere to its teachings. An obvious contradiction, this led to selective acceptance of some portions and wholesale rejection of others. As a result, the Bible is accepted by both groups of followers only to the extent that it agrees with their prophet's own superior revelation.

Both Mohammed and Joseph Smith taught that true salvation was to be found only in their respective religions. Those who would not accept their message were considered "infidels," pagans or Gentiles. In so doing, both prophets became the enemy of genuine Christianity, and have led many people away from the Christ of the Bible.

Both prophets encountered fierce opposition to their new religions and had to flee from town to town because of threats on their lives. Both retaliated to this opposition by forming their own militias. Both ultimately set up their own towns as model societies.

Both of these prophets were polygamists who had many wives. Polygamy became the reward for the faithful men who followed them without question and would be the sub-leaders under these men-prophets.

Both the Islam and Mormonism have splinter groups that follow the "original doctrine" of the founding leaders; and like these founding leaders, they are violent, polygamists, and have revelations justifying their actions. The Islamist fundamentalists have no problem in slaying the weaker Muslims who have given in to the "traditions of men," and the LDS fundamentalists still believe in the doctrine of "blood atonement" or the offering up of spilt blood of the unworthy as a sweet aroma to god.

Both Mohammed and Joseph Smith left unclear instructions about their successors. The majority of Mohammed's followers, Sunni Muslims, believe they were to elect their new leader; whereas the minority, Shiite Muslims, believe Mohammed's son was to be their next leader.

Similarly, the majority of Joseph Smith's followers (Mormons) believed their next prophet should have been the existing leader of their quorum of twelve apostles, whereas the minority, The Re-organized Church or the RLDS (now called "The Community of Christ," to further distance itself from the Utah Mormons) believed Joseph Smith's own son should have been their next prophet. Differences on this issue, and many others, have created substantial tension between these rival groups of each prophet.

Mohammed taught that Jesus was just another of a long line of human prophets, of which he was the last. He taught that he was superior to Christ, and when Jesus talked about another to come (The Holy Spirit), Mohammed said that Jesus was foretelling of his rise to prophet-hood. In comparison, Joseph Smith made this following claim.

"I have more to boast of than ever any man had. I am the only man that has ever been able to keep a whole church together since the days of Adam. A large majority of the whole have stood by me. Neither Paul, John, Peter, nor Jesus ever did it. I boast that no man ever did such a work as I. The followers of Jesus ran away from Him, but the Latter-day Saints never ran away from me yet."[4]

In light of these parallels, perhaps Joseph Smith's claim to be a second Mohammed unwittingly became his most genuine prophecy of all.

It is ironic that back in 1899, Sir Winston Churchill, in defining the darkness of Islam also defined Mormonism in its kinship to the Ishmaelites:

How dreadful are the curses which Mohammedanism lays on its votaries! Besides the fanatical frenzy, which is as dangerous in a man as hydrophobia in a dog, there is this fearful fatalistic apathy. The effects are apparent in many countries. Improvident habits, slovenly systems of agriculture, sluggish methods of commerce, and insecurity of property exist wherever the followers of the Prophet rule or live. A degraded sensualism deprives this life of its grace and refinement; the next of its dignity and sanctity. The fact that in Mohammedan law every woman must belong to some man as his absolute property either as a child, a wife, or a concubine, must delay the final extinction of slavery until the faith of Islam has ceased to be a great power among men.

Individual Moslems may show splendid qualities, but the influence of the religion paralyses the social development of those who follow it. No stronger retrograde force exists in the world. Far from being moribund, Mohammedanism is a militant and proselytizing faith. It has already spread throughout Central Africa, raising fearless warriors at every step; and were it not that Christianity is sheltered in the strong arms of science, the science against which it had vainly struggled, the civilization of modern Europe might fall, as fell the civilization of ancient

Rome." (Sir Winston Churchill, *The River War*, first edition, Vol. II, pp.248-50)

CHAPTER SEVEN

Let's Be Christians about this...

The reasons behind the Mormon zeal to convert the world.

Every Member a Missionary

One of the voices you hear as "The God Makers II" film opens is the frustrated voice of a young ex-Mormon named Lisa, as she says, *"The biggest danger was that they took me in, and I was thinking it was a Christian church, and it wasn't a Christian church; it was a cult."* Lisa had bought the lie. She fell victim to that seductive spirit of Mormonism, and it wasn't until she had been in the system for a while that her strong Christian background sent out enough danger signals that Lisa paid attention and left the Mormon Church.

Lisa isn't alone. She is in a fellowship that spans the globe. The word "cult" conjures up images of Charles Manson or saffron-robed Hare Krishnas with shaven heads bobbing up and down in mindless repetitions. We can all vividly remember when the whole world watched as FBI and ATF agents waited outside a heavily armed compound near Waco, Texas, while polygamist cult leader David Koresh waited for the divine word from God to torch the place and turn it into another Jonestown.

My solution would have been to put a security fence around the perimeter of the property and put them under safe and secure house arrest until Koresh came out and surrendered. Or, perhaps they could have just picked him up in town any Monday night while he watched Monday Night Football at a local tavern.

There are thousands of cults world wide, and in light of such divergent cult forms, let me define what I mean by the word *cult*.

Defining a Cult

Billy Graham characterized cults this way:

> In general, I would say a cult is a group that follows religious ideas (usually taught by a strong leader) which are not in accordance with the Bible. Sometimes cults will have certain writings for which

they claim supernatural authority in addition to the Bible. Often the leader of the cult will demand total, blind obedience to his word and may even separate children from parents.

While cults differ greatly with each other, they have in common one thing: they reject Jesus Christ and the Bible as their authorities and therefore reject faith in Jesus Christ as God's way of salvation. Often, they attempt to disguise this by talking a great deal about Jesus. But frequently, the test of a cult is found in their answer to this question: How can I be saved? If the answer is anything other than trusting Jesus Christ, then the group may be a cult. This is particularly true if they say they alone have the truth and salvation is found by joining their group.[1]

Mormonism surely fits that definition, having added to the Word of God, with *The Book of Mormon*, *The Doctrine and Covenants* and *The Pearl of Great Price*. They have detracted from the Bible's authority with their holy scriptures, the final authority of their holy priesthood and the doctrine that God must have a holy prophet in place directing His church. Full salvation can only be found in Mormonism. Surely, one must beware of such wolves in sheep's clothing who come amongst the flock to steal and destroy!

While Mormons may wish to gloss over any objective criteria for distinguishing religions from "cults," here we use the term cult to designate "a religious group which claims authorization by Christ and the Bible but neglects or distorts the gospel, the central message of the Savior and the Scriptures."[2]

No matter how nice a group can appear, *nice* is not on the list of criteria for determining orthodoxy. That standard *Mormon* test for truth, the warm "burning in the bosom," *isn't* on the list either. In spite of that, the Latter-day Saints are still trying to sell the burning bosom softness of modern Mormonism to the world as evidence of orthodoxy. The frightening thing is that it appears to be working. It has been stated that 60%-80% of all converts to Mormonism come from evangelical Christian backgrounds. These are the people whose doors the Mormon Missionaries knock on.[3]

It's certainly a lot easier for someone to move from one Christian church to another than it is to move from an orthodox Christian church to Mormonism. First, one doesn't have to renounce one's profession of faith to walk across the street to that "other" neighborhood church, but leaping over into Mormonism is a jump over a high wall. The Mormon Church of today is putting all its efforts into motivating people to get over that wall.

In a series of meetings the summer of 2007, in Utah, I discovered that many of the evangelical churches of Utah have stopped what they call "apologetics evangelism."

Instead, they have lowered the wall of theological division, entered into friend-shipping relationships with their local Mormon leaders and find that Mormons can easily step over the two-inch wall of division and casually go back and forth without ever having their faith tested.

One minister in a town just south of Salt Lake City was happy to state that he has 25 to 30 Mormons at his services every week. When I asked how many have left the LDS Church and become born again, he said that I was still working off an old evangelism stratagem that would never work in Utah. I doubt that one church in twenty is preaching the real Jesus in Utah today. A Jesus who gives a Mormon the warm burning in the bosom is not the Jesus of the Bible.

In fact, many shepherds who are supposed to be protecting the flock are inviting the wolves in to play with the sheep. What the pastors are not talking about are the members of their churches who are crossing the almost non-existent line of *division and not coming back. The Mormons are leaving with the sheep.* It is in their blood, their DNA.

In a sense, you can't blame the Mormons any more than you can blame the wolves. They are both doing exactly what they are bred to do. With marauding wolves, the problem lies more with the shepherd and the flock. A shepherd who isn't keeping an alert, protective eye on the flock is going to lose sheep, and the sheep who will not keep an eye on the shepherd, but instead wander near the edge of the flock, are prime candidates for the wolf's supper.

Remember what the Lord said in this regard: *"Verily, verily, I say unto you, he that entereth not by the door into the sheepfold, but climbeth up some other way, the same is a thief and a robber"* (John 10:1, KJV).

In the *Latter-Day Sentinel*, a now defunct Mormon Newspaper, the Mormons boasted that:

> A recent study by the Southern Baptists revealed that an average of 282 members of their church join the LDS church each week. Coincidentally, the average Southern Baptist congregation has 283 members.... The Baptists lose 52 congregations each year to the Mormons.[4]

When you read this kind of report, it's hard to understand how any Christian minister can comfortably sit down for a casual good-buddies lunch with the Mormon bishop down the street and not be a little bit nervous; yet in the politically correct ecumenicalism of today, it would seem rude for him not to fellowship with the Mormon bishop.

In the mid 80s, I accepted an invitation to visit a local Baptist minister at his church office and answer his many questions regarding Mormonism. We had a long talk. His name was Walford Erickson, and he wrote a religion column every now and then for the *Journal American* (now called *The Eastside Journal*), a local daily paper in Bellevue, Washington. He has since passed away. I could say without fear of contradiction those articles were ecumenical, written to the "everyman" reader.

One day, Erickson put out a column that gave me some insight to the losses his denomination had been having to the Mormons. In an article entitled, "Mormon Tries to Reach Out to Other Faiths," he reported about a Mormon businessman/local missionary who had visited one of his minister friends. This Mormon, Darl Anderson, only wanted to make friends with the pastor. Erickson was smitten with the idea that this Mormon not only wanted to reach out and engage friendly dialogue with non-Mormon clergy, but had the backing of the LDS church to encourage and train up the area bishops to do the same.

While Wally Erickson was a fine man, it would seem he lacked discernment in this area, since he wrote that he and a few of his pastor friends around Bellevue took delight in drawing Darl into their inner circle.[5]

In a local letter to the Editor, I responded that Darl Anderson's attention to Walford and his friends was "no accidental experience, but part of an LDS program to neutralize ministers and civic leaders to the covert, predatory program of the Mormon Church. Darl and his missionary buddies steal sheep for their church! That's their job...."[6]

Darl Anderson conducted an in-house LDS lecture series he called "Win a Minister and Influence a Thousand" and was the Mormon author of *Soft Answers to Hard Questions* that illustrated the strategy LDS leadership had adopted to gain acceptance among the American Christian community. He said that the purpose of public communications was to "promote public goodwill and positive attitudes [towards Mormonism] so that people will be more receptive to the blessings of the glorious Restoration." In other words, he wanted local Mormon leaders to conduct themselves among Christians in a way which would make it possible to proselytize people who already are members of Christian churches. He wanted the fences lowered in the pastures.

Anderson devoted the book to ways of dialoguing with Christian ministers in an attempt to get them to perceive Mormons as something other than a threat. He related that at first, when he began to develop this approach, local ministers were openly hostile to him, but after a while they warmed to his gentle fellowshipping. He told how he eventually persuaded them to let him join the local ministerial association.[7]

The fact was that Darl Anderson had been "called and set apart," with the official backing of the Mormon Church "to lower barriers between Mormons and people of other churches." The purpose of the discussions of "friend shipping" was to "draw attention to those points that pastors and Mormons can 'agree on'."

The design of such strategy ultimately sways the naive Christians into the path of the Mormon agenda. Darl Anderson had already brought disruption to the evangelical Christian community in Mesa, Arizona, where one pastor, Roger Keller, invited the Mormons to come in fellowship.

Keller also spoke to LDS missionary groups about the things they held in common. He was the perfect example of what Anderson felt could be accomplished through his program. Keller ended up as a Mormon and his Presbyterian Church congregation was shaken to the core. Today, Keller is on staff at BYU and is a part of this new fellowshipping approach to opening the doors of the local Christian churches. In my opinion, the denomination leaders of such Christian churches in Utah who have bought into this inter-church fellowshipping program should remove every single pastor who has bought into it.

Anderson was then sent to Palmyra, New York, and was quoted in a church-related article: "If you can change that minister's attitude, you can change the attitude of hundreds.... Now if the minister is saying unkind things, it's turning people against the (Mormon) church. I look to the day when whole congregations will come into the church through their own leadership. We see quite a few ministers come into the church. There isn't any reason a minister couldn't lead them in the truths we teach...."[8]

Christian ministers aren't always treated so kindly, especially if they take a stand against the LDS doctrines. Michael Warneke who had been pastoring the Bible Baptist Church in Salt Lake City since 1979 wrote a letter to John L. Smith of Utah Ministries (a ministry to Mormons). In it, Warneke told of some of the frustration that came after a bit of a confrontation with the Mormons.

...the next Sunday, the LDS church sent many car loads of missionaries to our church. They went in and out of the services, to disturb us. Four or five would come in for five minutes and then get up and leave, slamming the doors as they went out. They kept this up through Sunday School and the morning worship service.

This was not unexpected, the pastor explains:

Upon moving to our neighborhood and buying our current home, upon finding out I was a Baptist teacher, the Mormons pulled out the trees in our yard and egged our house with rotten eggs. Since we built our church we have been robbed eight times in eight years. The windows have been knocked out of our bus three times, and we've been vandalized many times. Our boys play baseball.... It is nothing to see a Mormon kid with a 200 batting average picked to play over a non-Mormon with a 600 batting average.[9]

Dear Pastor

Once the Mormon Church openly and clearly positioned itself outside the realm of mainstream Christianity. Today it is very conciliatory. Efforts to make loving contact with local area pastors take the position that Mormonism and "other streams of Christianity" have more in common than not. Throughout the country, Mormon leaders are soliciting the friendship of Christian clergy and in some cases even applying for membership in the local ministerial associations. Books such as *We Are Christians Too!* and *Are Mormons Christian?* are arguing that Mormons and Christians are brothers in the Christian faith.

A recent addition to these publications is the Robert L. Millet book, *A Different Jesus?* It was published in 2005 by Eerdmans, a Christian publisher. To make matters more difficult, it has a Foreword and Afterword by Richard J. Mouw, president of Fuller seminary. It is very obvious that Mouw has little understanding of Mormon doctrine and little concern for Christian Orthodoxy as he travels around sharing the spotlight with his Mormon friends.

In the Mormon Tabernacle in Salt Lake City on Nov. 14, 2004 Mouw apologized from the pulpit there to the Mormons for the many lies evangelicals like me have told about Mormons not being true Christians. Mouw may get the applause from the deceivers and the deceived, but he will have to answer to God for his ungodly behavior as a supposed Christian leader.

And the Mormons aren't waiting for Christian pastors to walk into LDS bookstores to find such books. Not only are the many directors of Clergy Relations dropping off gift copies, but even the authors are getting the books out in direct force. Don and Brennan Kingsland, authors of *Are*

Mormons Christian? (one of the books mentioned above), sent a direct mail piece out to thousands of Christian pastors telling them that:

> The Christian community has enough problems today fighting Satan—without weakening itself by divisions within, from attacking each other. Unfortunately, many persons today are more interested in fighting over "who is right" and "who is wrong" than they are in promoting unity in the Body of Christ and spreading the Good News to those waiting to hear it....
>
> Don't be misled by attackers of the Church of Jesus Christ of Latter-day Saints. These individuals, incidentally, have developed affluent ministries and made lucrative businesses out of creating divisions in the Body of Christ.
>
> We are firmly convinced that Satan is behind the "divide and conquer" strategy we see being used so effectively by anti-Mormon leaders. To enable you to ascertain the TRUTH about our church, we are offering "MORMONS ARE CHRISTIANS, TOO!" at a special price to pastors....[10]

Even more recently, in a dialogue on BeliefNet.com, Mormon writer and activist Orson Scott Card posted an article on June 28, 2007, called "Who Gets to Define

Christian?" Card's article took the wall of theological separation between Mormonism and Orthodox Christianity and smoothed it down to "Christianity without a definitive edge."[11]

On July 5, 2007, Dr. R. Albert Mohler, president of the Southern Baptist Theological seminary, gave as good a response as I have ever read. He said, in part:

> Mormonism uses the language of Christian theology and makes many references to Christ. Mr. Card wants to define Christianity in a most minimal way, theologically speaking. If I were arguing the other side of this question, I would attempt the same. But Christianity has never been defined in terms of merely thinking well of Jesus. Mormonism claims to affirm the New Testament teachings about Jesus, but actually presents a very different Jesus from the onset. A reading of Mormonism's authoritative documents makes this clear.
>
> All these things point back to the reason the question is so important in our contemporary context. Mormons want their religion to be seen as another form of Christianity. In other words, they want to identify with what from their inception they sought to deny. There are advantages to Mormonism on this score, but this surely places them in an awkward position.

"The Church of Jesus Christ of Latter-Day Saints," as Mormonism is officially known, claims to be the only true church. As stated in the Doctrine and Covenants [1:30], Mormonism is "the only true and living church upon the face of the whole earth." According to Mormon teaching, the church was corrupted after the death of the apostles and became the "Church of the Devil." Mormonism then claims that the true church was restored through the Prophet Joseph Smith in the 1820s. This restored church was, Mormon theology claims, given the keys to the kingdom and the authority of the only true priesthood.

Why would Mormonism now want to be identified as a form of Christianity, when its central historical claim is that the churches commonly understood to be Christian are part of the Church of the Devil?

There is simply no way around the Mormon claim that the other churches hold to a corrupted theology and have no true priesthood — and are not true churches. Mr. Card may complain that traditional Christianity defines the faith in a way that rejects Mormonism. Fair enough. But Mormonism rejects historic Christianity as it makes it own central claim — to be the only true church, restored on earth in the latter days.[12]

Interfaith Relations

In an Associated Press Release that came out of Salt Lake City, the writer reported on how the Mormon Church was trying to smooth its relations with other denominations.

The issue of interfaith relations with the Mormon Church was brought to the forefront by the Presbyterian Church (USA), which held its General Assembly in early June in a land where Mormons outnumber Presbyterians more than 200-to-1. In response, Mormon leaders issued an appeal to set up informal meetings with Presbyterian officials, and the denomination's Theology and Worship Ministry Unit and Utah Presbytery both submitted reports on Mormon-Presbyterian relations.

Even as the Mormon Church seeks improved relations with other religious groups, many gentiles in the Mormon heartland say they face economic, political and social sanctions—or simply feel shunned.

Signs of change exist: a recently revised [temple] ritual no longer portrays non-Mormon clergy as agents of Satan, for example. But some ecumenical officials and church observers say the Church of Jesus Christ of Latter-day Saints has not entered the mainstream of American religious life.

"Mormons' exclusivist claim toward truth and being God's church is as strong as it's ever been," said the head of a liberal Mormon group who spoke on condition of anonymity. "That's probably the major stumbling block toward improving relations with other churches."

Jan Shipps, a professor of religious studies at Indiana University, said the recent elimination of the part of the church's endowment ceremony where Satan hired a non-Mormon preacher to spread false teachings "is a very important signifier the LDS church is moving away from its position that all other churches are false."

Shipps said though *no official policy* encourages ecumenical relations, there has been "a kind of relaxing" of rules allowing some local Mormon Churches to get involved with councils of ministries.[13]

The pattern is there in every corner of the Christian community. LDS leadership has reversed its elitist nature in areas that the Mormon faithful would have considered unbelievable 30 years ago.

For example, one Easter, a mailer went out from the pastor of one of the downtown churches in Bellevue, Washington, inviting local pastors and their congregations and choirs to participate in an interdenominational Easter morning procession of walking the Stations of the Cross, which would take place in various downtown locations.

Our home church sat on the edge of that area, and they were therefore invited to participate. I was shocked to see the Mormon Church listed as having already been assigned one Station where *they* would have the responsibility of leading the prayers and singing. I knew that they would have full freedom to lead the participants in Mormon prayer and singing. I had been present at a number of LDS Manti summer Pageants in Manti, Utah, where the cross of Jesus is mocked in each performance, and this was just unacceptable.

I was provoked by such anti-Biblical compromise to directly challenge the organizing pastor, saying in part, "It is with utter dismay that I have heard of your plans to have a joint celebration of Good Friday and Easter with the Mormon Church. I wonder if you *really* understand that while the LDS Church may certainly have a Christian ethic and use Christian terminology, they do *not* have an orthodox Christian theology."[14]

After few tense conversations, the Mormons pulled out. It was certainly an example of what an educated, motivated Christian could do to stop the Mormon infiltration into orthodoxy.

In another development, Mormon leaders in eastern Idaho asked to be part of the National Day of Prayer gathering. Not only were they invited, but one evangelical pastor, speaking not for men, but for God, asked for forgiveness, not for doctrine, but for "not responding to the LDS people in Christian character."

Dr. Rulon Robison, LDS Regional Representative for the area, welcomed the call for fence mending, saying, "We have long desired to break down these walls and build bridges of friendship and understanding and love."[15]

To the general public, these episodes might slip by as some sort of an *"oh, well, how could it hurt to have them praying with a crowd of Christians?"* However, it is highly significant to ex-Mormons who have spent years in the LDS church listening to speakers lifting up the Church as God's only true voice among the other churches in town, the "whores of all the earth."[16]

One writer, trying to explain the deep quagmire into which this kind logic has placed the Mormon Church, stated:

> Mormons believe Christian churches are apostate, but the LDS church is Christian, therefore the LDS [church] is apostate.... Mormons say Christian churches are apostate, [and] the LDS church is not apostate, therefore the LDS church is not Christian. Mormonism assumes that the LDS church is Christian, while at the same time assuming that Christianity is apostate; the only way out of this dilemma is for Mormonism to either discard the untenable theory of a total apostasy, or cease to claim to be Christian.[17]

Mormons have already shown their hand at political and religious integration on many fronts. One Associated Press article explained their approach:

> In 1986, Mormons became part of the Religious Alliance Against Pornography, a wide ecumenical cross-section. In 1984, they affiliated with Religion in American Life, involving most major US denominations in seeking to stimulate weekly worship. Also, in the mid-80's Mormons entered into inter-religious relief work, including aid to the homeless. They contributed about $5 million to relief efforts in famine-ravaged central Africa, much of it through Catholic Relief Services and the American Red Cross.[18]

We know that these are very worthwhile social efforts and should be applauded as such, but it is important to recognize that this is all part of a conditioning process that the Mormons have implemented in their efforts to become an acceptable part of the ecumenical body of general Christianity. In this same article, some other points were clearly laid out:

> Mormons, who generally have kept aloof from other Christian communities, are gradually – and in expanding ways – moving into working association with them.... "Some Mormons don't want it," said

former pastor Roger Keller, now of Brigham Young University in Provo, Utah. "Some of the others are suspicious of Mormons. But we've begun to break through the shell of isolation."

As misconceptions and scurrilous notions about each other are diminished, "more interchange becomes possible," he said. "I hope we are standing at the crossroads of genuine dialogue."

Let me break in here to say again that Roger Keller, who was just quoted, is the Presbyterian minister we told you about earlier in this chapter, who was seduced away from his church congregation in Mesa, Arizona, through the efforts of Darl Anderson.

Such dialogue has flourished for years among Protestant, Roman Catholic, Anglican, Eastern Orthodox and Jewish groups, reducing old prejudices and distortions. Nevertheless, Mormons who were denounced, persecuted and driven westward in their early years, generally have stayed apart from that inter-religious companionship and teamwork until recently. Dallin Oaks, a member of the Church's ruling Council of 12, said, "I think the outlook for our being involved with others is good.... And I think other groups need us, and we need other groups."[19]

We would all rejoice to see every Mormon come to Christ; however, Christians don't need the ungodly beliefs and practices of Mormonism. But Mormonism does need the credibility and blessing of Christianity. It is very frustrating to see Mormons work so hard to appear to be what they are not. It doesn't matter what they do. They can start a friendship with every Christian pastor in the world, but it will not make their doctrines Christian. If only they could see the futility of their errors and repent corporately. *In one day,* they could shed these doctrines of error and be set free in Christ. What a day of rejoicing that would be to see these people who are trying so hard at looking like Christians actually become *the real thing!*

More recently, in my home town, in the State of Washington, just a few miles down the road, the local LDS church announced, with paid advertising in most of the area daily papers, that they were hosting an open dialogue meeting to discuss "Are Mormons Christian?" They invited the public to come and hear what the Mormons *"really believe."*

Mormon Open House

On May 15, 2005, I went to the meeting that promised a presentation on the subject, to be followed by an open Q&A time as well as refreshments. I arrived, as did a number of other former Mormons, to a very upbeat and crowded Ward building filled with about 300 people. It came as no surprise that, except for a few others who were not ex-Mormons, the place was filled with the faithful, who laughed and chuckled at every Mormon inside joke from the podium.

The interesting thing we immediately noted was the Mormons were not dressed in the fashion they would dress in church. For example, most of the men were not wearing jackets, something I had never seen in an LDS church meeting before. It was apparent they were told to "dress down." And that was fine. It was a considerate thing, knowing that their neighbors would be a little uneasy sitting there in Levis and slacks.

The speaker did a fine job of sharing his passion for the gospel, for Jesus, for the church. He stayed totally within those areas of practice and theology where the Mormons are compatible with orthodoxy. Except, the same words he used had different meanings to the true Mormon and the true Christian, so we ex-Mormons were frustrated that there was no opportunity to set any ground rules before he gave his excellent speech.

He never discussed the things that made the world wonder if they really were Christians. No talk about becoming gods and goddesses, nothing about the rest of the world being the "whore of Babylon" or the LDS church having the only true authority to baptize and so on....

When he finished it was opened up to questions with the speaker, the Stake President and the Stake Relief Society President, acting as a panel. But when a few ex-Mormons asked key questions, they quickly danced away back to the warm and fuzzies. I stood during the Q&A and introduced myself to the meeting. Amid the loud rumbling sounds of discovery, the great anti-Mormon—the son of perdition, himself—was in their midst.

I thanked them for the effort but commented that the meeting could never cover the vast areas of difference and it would be good to meet more times and in private with the true seekers. In one case, the Stake President was asked directly about the priesthood authority and the only true authority to act for God on earth, and he sat there, refusing to give an honest answer.

At the end, they asked people to contact them for further dialogue, and I followed up with an email to Bishop Mike Murray, who seemed a wonderful, warm and caring person. I wrote them an email, asking for a private meeting to discuss areas of reconciliation whereby the Mormon Church *could* step into fellowship with Christianity. In it, I wrote, in part:

In my heart there is an urgency for reconciliation of the Church and Christian orthodoxy and Ed Decker. I would like to quietly and privately dialogue that potential with you and perhaps my Ward Bishop in my neck of the woods. Even some private time with Dr. Hilton [the speaker] would be wonderful.

I am not out trying to write another book. Just a broken heart for reconciliation. I am willing to lay down everything in that goal. I have no agenda, other than to sit and talk and pray for each other and perhaps come to a place of trust where we can talk about things that the Lord would have us discuss. (Edecker@nwlink.com to M. Murray June 6, 2005)

Bishop Murray replied on June 27, 2005, and in a very warm and sincere response, stated, in part:

Dear Ed, Thank you for this good email and for your attendance at the LDS Forum in Redmond. I'm glad you came up after the event and introduced yourself to me. I enjoyed our short visit.

I have reviewed your email carefully and appreciate the spirit in which it is written.

I do not have the authority to speak on the topic of reconciliation between the LDS Church and, using your term, Christian orthodoxy. Such dialogue will have to be pursued directly by you with the First Presidency of the Church.

Reconciliation, by definition, most often requires compromise as parties seek the lowest common denominator of agreement. In my mind such an outcome is neither spiritually nor intellectually satisfying as one is forced to tamper with his definition of truth. On the other hand, if what you are seeking is "letting bygones be bygones," then I would suggest that you get together with your local bishop.

I feel in my heart that the average Mormons are trying to sincerely find that path that will draw them into the mainstream of true Christianity. But, Bishop Murray said it best: *In my mind such an outcome is neither spiritually nor intellectually satisfying as one is forced to tamper with his **definition** of truth.*

Therein is the rub. One former president of the United States said something like this: "It all depends on what your definition of the word, IS is."

The Mormon leadership will not tamper with the definitions that have separated them from Orthodoxy for over 170 years. They *will* spend their time trying to look as Christian as possible so that they can draw in the converts needed to keep the great caravan rolling, however crooked its path.

The Only True Jews

The Mormons aren't just interested in stepping into mainstream Christianity; they have their other eye on Israel. It is the Mormons' secret claim to be the "true Israel." Even now the Mormon Church is reaching out for what it believes is its inheritance in Israel.

Chuck Sackett is the former Mormon who authored the book, *What's Going On in There?*, which details the actual LDS Temple ritual. Chuck was visiting in Jerusalem at the same time Jeremiah Films was there and agreed to an interview at the site of the extremely controversial BYU Extension on Mount Scopus.

I had been invited to Israel during the Extension's construction to explain the LDS doctrines to leaders at the Knesset. These secular leaders were shocked to find out that the god of Mormonism was an exalted man. It was equally shocking to the religious leaders of Israel. But political expediency overcame the very vocal objections of the conservative minority, and the Mormons were able to complete the project.

Former Mormon Chuck Sackett, standing in front of the LDS building, in actual Mormon Temple clothes for the filming, described the situation for us:

I'm standing here in beautiful Jerusalem. This impressive structure is built on the sacred site of Mount Scopus by the Church of Jesus Christ of Latter-day Saints, as an extension to Brigham Young University. I believe that it's very important for the Jewish people to know about the deception and misrepresentation that was employed in building this Mormon edifice. Mormons used political intrigue and great sums of money in order to cover up their true intent to proselytize Jews and convert them to Mormonism. Most of the religious Jews of Jerusalem consider this Mormon structure an abomination and sacrilege of holy ground and are outraged by its presence.

These clothes that I am wearing are the authentic Mormon Temple attire, which Mormons believe are copied from the actual attire that the priesthood wore in the temple of Solomon that stood on this site behind me. Mormons believe that there has been an apostasy in Judaism, and they hold the only true authority to administer in the rituals of the Temple that will be performed here in Jerusalem.[20]

As Chuck explained, Mormons believe that they are the only true Jews on earth today. They also believe they come from the tribes of Ephraim and Manasseh, and that they have the true blood of Israel. Mormon males are ordained into what they believe are both the Leviticus and the Melchizedek priesthoods. They believe that when they are baptized, their blood actually changes from Gentile blood into the blood of Israel.

Mormons believe that they will build the new Jerusalem near Independence, Missouri, and it will be the primary capital of the kingdom of God on the earth. And in Jerusalem will be the secondary capital, which will be administered by Jews.

The Church of Jesus Christ of Latter-day Saints came here to Jerusalem under the banner of Christianity to establish this edifice and to establish their presence here when they are no more true Christians than they are true Jews.[21]

When I was given my Patriarchal Blessing as a Mormon, I was quite surprised when told by the church patriarch that I was of the House of Ephraim. I was shocked because I am the son of a Jewish mother of the Levitical lineage. I wrote it off as strange and special mystery. It meant that God removed my Levitical blood (and DNA) from my body and replaced it with the blood line of Ephraim and a different DNA. Remarkable!

My bishop at the time told me to avoid the mysteries and focus on the joys of now having the bloodline of Ephraim flowing though my body. However, when I became a Christian and actually read the Bible, I discovered that the sons of Ephraim were a puffed-up, prideful bunch of cowards who ran from battle and refused to walk in the ways of the Lord (Psalm 78). God said He will cast them away because they did not hearken unto Him (Hosea 9:16-17). Not a great tribe in which to claim membership. Hey, give me back my Levitical blood!

The doctrine of blood physically changing into Jewish blood during a baptism ritual is rarely shared with those about to step into the waters of the baptismal pool. This information is withheld until the member becomes worthy enough and indoctrinated enough to be trusted with this higher level of knowledge. The member discovers this glorious mystery when he or she is worthy enough to have the "patriarchal blessing."

CHAPTER EIGHT

Testing the Prophet Joseph Smith

The core testimony of every Mormon is that Joseph Smith was a holy prophet. But was he a true prophet or a false prophet?

The very existence of Mormonism hinges on its central tenet that it was founded by Joseph Smith, who claimed that he was called of God to re-establish Christ's true Church on the earth. In the last chapter you saw that this could not possibly be true. However, Mormons revere Joseph Smith as a true prophet of God and the holy man upon whom God himself laid the authority to oversee God's people and usher in the last dispensation of time. If Smith's claims of having seen God and Christ and to have received his prophet-hood and authority from them really were true, two very important things would follow.

First, the Christian world would have to recognize that the "New Testament" era was over and a new era had begun. To understand this concept one needs to understand the place of the "office" of prophet. The calling of the Old Testament prophet was "one to whom and through whom God spoke. Their messages were very largely the proclamation of the Divine purposes of salvation and glory to be accomplished in the future."[1] The prophets and their messages were the pointers to Jesus!

In Luke 16:16 (KJV), the Lord clearly stated, *"The Law and the Prophets were until John: Since that time the Kingdom of God is preached, and every man presseth into it."* The time for declaring the forthcoming of the Kingdom was over; the kingdom itself was now to be declared by the Son himself!

Hebrews 1:1-2 (KJV) makes it even clearer. *"God, who at sundry times and in divers manners spake unto the fathers by the prophets, hath in these last days spoken unto us by His Son, whom He hath appointed heir of all things, by whom also He made the worlds."*

This was said after Christ had risen and the church was in operation. No prophet was appointed to be the head of the church and spokesman for God. Christ had fulfilled that empty office in His own right when he said, "It is finished." Yet as we read in 1 Corinthians, the *gift of prophecy* was active in the body of the Church, not something found only in the headship of the church (see 1 Corinthians 14).

So, if Joseph Smith was the spokesman through whom God would now issue His orders, then the established order of New Testament government would have to be ended, and the church would step into a new covenant that was not foretold by Christ, by whom God was to speak to us in New Testament times.

Second, if Smith's claims of having restored Christ's true church on earth were true, then we could step back from the responsibility of having *"every man presseth into it"* and simply listen to the instruction and counsel of the Mormon prophet, trusting and obeying the words from his mouth as they came directly from God.

However, before we take that step of obedience, it would be wise for us to check the Biblical tests of a prophet, as given in the Bible, and put this new-era prophet to the same simple tests by which every Old Testament prophet was judged. We need to do that with Joseph Smith. After all, Christ fulfilled over 300 exact prophecies in His birth, life, death and resurrection. Some of these prophecies were foretold over 900 years before His birth. Prophets can be checked out for accuracy.

One would think that any member of a "restoration" church which bases its very existence on its own personal latter-day prophet would be able to give any willing listener a long litany of "true prophecies." At least the earnest seeker would expect to find dusty volumes of such prophecies abounding in church libraries throughout the new kingdom.

Yet in Mormonism, they don't exist in mind or matter. While some people who claim both scholarship and membership have written books on the subject, the church does not receive them in any official capacity, especially since much of the work is contrived.

If you doubt that the true Mormon avoids such discovery, just ask a Mormon to extemporaneously recite five or six of his or her favorite Joseph Smith prophecies. You will rarely get past one or two of the most commonly used "faith promoting" stories that are hardly kingdom shaking.

One such story that really did come true (if Joseph actually gave it) was a "word" given to Orrin "Porter" Rockwell, Joseph Smith's bodyguard and church assassin for apostates of the early Mormon Church. Smith promised Rockwell a quiet death in bed if he never cut his hair. Porter Rockwell killed a lot of men through the years, never cut his hair and we are told he died in bed.

It is amazing that when the LDS missionaries share the joys of having a church led by a living prophet and are asked to produce a booklet or at least a list of the prophecies of their living prophet or any of their deceased prophets, including Joseph Smith, they cannot produce anything except a blank stare. You would expect that any reasonable, thinking person would flee from such foolishness. Yet millions of Mormons testify that they "know," by personal revelation, that Joseph Smith is a prophet of God.

In actuality, Joseph Smith meets the test of Scripture as one of the foretold false prophets who would come in the last days. A number of the prophecies of Joseph Smith, some of which were buried deep inside the LDS closet, certainly failed to come to pass. Judge them for yourself. Let me list a few:

The False Prophecies of Joseph Smith

Remember, as you read the following list, that according to Deuteronomy 18:20-22, it only takes one false prophecy to make a prophet false, just as it only takes one murder to make a person a murderer. As you read the many false prophecies of Joseph Smith, keep this Biblical teaching in mind.

The Abridgment of *D&C* 137

Although there are actually dozens of false prophecies I could begin with, I chose one which has come to newfound prominence in recent years. In 1976, Section 137 of *Doctrine & Covenants* was submitted to the General Conference of the Church of Jesus Christ of Latter-day Saints for a vote to be "sustained" as scripture. It is a narrative of a vision supposedly seen by Joseph Smith in Kirtland, Ohio, in 1836.

What the members who voted on this new addition to scripture were not told by "The Brethren" is that whole paragraphs (216 words) of the actual revelation as recorded in the History of the Church had been conveniently left out of the version to be included in the *D&C*. The reason for these omissions was that four obviously false prophecies were contained in the part of the revelation that was censored out. These were prophecies so blatantly false that even the average Mormon reader would pick up on them. Therefore they went down that ever widening and deepening "black hole" of Mormon history.

What exactly did these missing parts contain? If you go to the official History of the Church published by the church's own publishing company, you will easily be able to find the missing prophecies.[2] Here is what is *not* in the new *D&C* 137:

[Joseph Smith:] "...I saw *the Twelve Apostles of the Lamb, who are now upon the earth, who hold the keys of this last ministry*, in foreign lands, standing together in a circle, much fatigued, with their clothes tattered and their feet swollen, with their eyes cast downward, and Jesus standing in their midst, and they did not behold him. The Saviour looked upon them and wept."

I also beheld Elder M'Lellin in the south, standing upon a hill, surrounded by a vast multitude, preaching to them, and a lame man standing before him supported by his crutches; he threw them down at his word and leaped as a hart, by the mighty power of God."

Also, *I saw Elder Brigham Young standing in a strange land*, in the far south and west, in a desert place, upon a rock in the midst of about a dozen men of color, who appeared hostile. He was preaching to them in their own tongue, and the angel of God standing above his head with a drawn sword in his hand, protecting him, but he did not see it.

And I finally saw the Twelve in the celestial kingdom of God. I also beheld the redemption of Zion and many things which the tongue of man cannot describe in full...." [All emphasis added.]

Now, if this prophecy were true, it would have been a truly inspiring and wonderful declaration! Unfortunately, for the Mormon faithful, a short look at these missing parts reveals the false prophecies contained therein.

The most striking of these is that Smith claimed to see his original "Twelve apostles" all in the celestial kingdom.[3] This is difficult to imagine, since there was already division between Smith and the majority of the apostles, beginning with discord in Kirtland, Ohio. The first portion of the missing parts shows his less than subtle rebuke of their resistance to his will. *"...fatigued...tattered...eyes cast downward.... The Saviour looked upon them and wept."* Smith was calling them to get into line and submit themselves to his full authority. That's the carrot offered in the last portion,

"I finally saw the Twelve in the Celestial Kingdom of God." [All emphasis added.]

However, his "thus saith the Lord" must have had little effect on these men, because at least seven of the twelve were soon excommunicated or apostatized from the church: John F. Boynton and Luke S. Johnson (1837),[4] Lyman Johnson (1838),[5] William E. M'Lellin (c.1838),[6] Thomas B. Marsh and Orson Hyde (1838),[7] and William Smith (1845).[8]

How could they have ever attained the celestial kingdom under those conditions? They couldn't! They were not only accursed by their very acts of apostasy or excommunication, but fell victim to the LDS Church's own scriptural denunciation. *D&C* 84.40-41 clearly states:

> Therefore, all those who receive the priesthood, receive this oath and covenant of my father, which he cannot break, neither can it be moved. But whoso breaketh this covenant after he hath received it, and altogether turneth there-from, shall not have forgiveness of sins in this world nor in the world to come.

Although a few of these men later returned to the church, none of them were even close to the standards necessary for attainment of that highest degree of glory. The majority remained apart for life. Therefore, the prophetic utterance, "I finally saw the Twelve in the Celestial Kingdom of God" could not be true. It would have been false even if only one Apostle remained outside the fold.

In addition, the vision of M'Lellin preaching and working miracles in the south never came true because he apostatized from the church without ever doing it!

Brigham Young did bring the Mormons west and was a great colonizer and orator, but the vision of Brigham Young preaching to "men of color" in their own language, in some strange and faraway place in the southwest never took place either—or at least there is no trace of it in the very detailed records and diaries concerning his reign as prophet.

Finally, "Zion" (Independence, Missouri) was never redeemed, has never been redeemed in the 165+ years since the prophecy was made. Is it any wonder that The Brethren chose to remove whole chunks of this "inspired" revelation?

Was Emma Smith Destroyed?

One of the most significant sections of the *Doctrine and Covenants* is Section #132, which deals with the plural marriage (polygamy) revelation. However, it also contains many false prophecies!

> And as pertaining to the new and everlasting covenant [i.e.. polygamy or plural marriage], it was instituted for the fulness of my glory; and he that

receiveth a fulness there must and shall abide the law, *or he shall be damned, saith the Lord God...* (v. 6).

Let mine handmaid, Emma Smith [Joseph's first wife] receive all those [wives] that have been given unto my servant Joseph, and who are virtuous and pure before me; and those who are not pure and have said they were pure shall be destroyed, saith the Lord God.... And I give unto my servant Joseph that he shall be ruler over many things; for he hath been faithful over a few things, and from henceforth I will strengthen him. And I command my handmaid, Emma Smith to abide and cleave unto my servant Joseph, and to none else. *But if she will not abide this commandment [of plural marriage] she shall be destroyed, saith the Lord; for I am the Lord thy God, and will destroy her if she abide not in my law* (v. 52-54).

And if he have ten virgins given unto him by this law, he cannot commit adultery, for they belong to him, and they are given unto him; therefore he is justified (v. 62). [All emphasis added.]

Where do we begin? First of all, plural marriage was an "everlasting covenant" *that only lasted about 50 years.* It was officially done away with in 1890.[9] How can something that is ordained by God as "everlasting" ever stop? Second, according to verse 6, everyone who is not living in plural marriage in the LDS Church is damned. That means that *almost all Mormons* except for 40,000 or so Fundamentalists today, who still keep the original commandments of plural marriage, are damned!

Verse 53 says that Joseph Smith would be strengthened henceforth. Whether he was depends on one's definition of *"henceforth,"* as he was shot dead by his enemies *less than a year later!*

Verse 54 threatens Emma Smith with destruction if she doesn't let Joseph have all of his wives without complaint and acknowledge the divine origins of plural marriage. Emma *never* did these things. She fought against the plural marriage doctrine; and yet she lived to a ripe old age; and Joseph was shot just months later. Emma was so opposed to polygamy that she went off with Joseph's son Joseph Smith III and started the Reorganized Church of Jesus Christ of Latter-day Saints, which denies that Smith *ever* taught polygamy.

The Civil War Prophecy

This one is a little longer, but it should be looked at closely because the Mormons like to claim this prophecy as one of Joseph Smith's *true* prophecies. Yet it just doesn't bear up to close scrutiny. In *D&C* 87:1-8, we read:

> *Verily, thus saith the Lord* concerning the wars that will shortly come to pass, beginning at the rebel-

lion of South Carolina, which will eventually terminate in the death and misery of many souls; And the time will come that war will be poured out upon all nations, beginning at this place. For behold, the Southern States shall be divided against the Northern States, and the Southern States will call on other nations, even the nation of Great Britain…and they shall also call upon other nations, in order to defend themselves against other nations; *and then* war shall be poured out upon all nations.

And it shall come to pass, after many days, slaves shall rise up against their masters, who shall be marshaled and disciplined for war. And it shall come to pass also that the remnants who are left of the land will marshal themselves, and shall become exceedingly angry, and shall vex the Gentiles with a sore vexation.

And thus, with the sword and by bloodshed the inhabitants of the earth shall mourn; and with famine, and plague, and earthquake, and the thunder of heaven, and the fierce and vivid lightning also, shall the inhabitants of the earth be made to feel the wrath and indignation, and chastening hand of an Almighty God until the consumption decreed hath made a full end of all nations.

That the cry of the saints, and the blood of the saints, shall cease to come up into the ears of the

Lord of Sabaoth, from the earth, to be avenged of their enemies. Wherefore, stand ye in holy places, and be not moved, until the day of the Lord come; for behold it cometh quickly, saith the Lord. Amen.

This prophecy was given on Christmas Day, 1832, in appearance almost 30 years before the Civil War. Although the prophecy looks good on the surface, it must be realized that at the time this was brought forth, South Carolina was already involved in many rebellious acts, and this fact was available in the papers of the time.[10] Congress had passed a tariff in July of 1832 that South Carolina had declared unacceptable.

It was during that Christmas season when the nation's press expected and wrote about the impending outbreak of civil war, beginning with this rebellion in South Carolina. Even the U.S. Army was on alert. With these facts at hand, it didn't take much of a seer to predict the unfolding events. Even a paper published by the Mormons themselves contained such news![11]

However, the war did not come to pass. Added to the dating problems, the scope of the prophecy is not in balance. In just one item, the prophecy states that war would begin locally and pour out upon all nations and shall be the direct cause of an international global war. Even the great World

War I did not encompass all nations, and it was 50 years after the Civil War and had no possible relationship to it!

After having been given, the entire prophecy was shelved and never appeared again during Joseph Smith's lifetime. In fact, the first two editions of the *History of the Church* did not include it even though it was in the original manuscript. It reappeared in 1852 when the war again seemed imminent.

One former Mormon has pointed out that there are at least 20 elements in this prophecy, and for it to be a true prophecy, all of those elements would have to have come to pass.[12] In human terms, those odds are 1 in 1,048,576—a truly remarkable achievement, had Smith pulled it off. Obviously he did not.

In another example of failure in this prophecy, verses 4 through 6 state that the slaves shall rise up, the remnants left in the land shall rise up against the Gentiles (non-Mormons) and the bloodshed, famines, plagues (caused by this great war) shall bring with God's wrath, and "a full end of all nations." This did not happen. In fact, Smith only got two elements out of twenty right, and those were based on current events and common sense.

Pestilence and Earthquakes to Sweep Across the USA?

Here is an explicit false prophecy (given in 1833) from official Church history:[13]

And now I am prepared to say *by the authority of Jesus Christ*, that not many years shall pass away before the United States shall present such a scene of bloodshed as has not a parallel in the history of our nation; pestilence, hail, famine, and earthquake shall sweep the wicked of *this generation* from off the face of the land.... Flee to Zion before the overflowing scourge overtake you, *for there are those now living upon the earth whose eyes shall not be closed in death until they see all these things*, which I had spoken, fulfilled. [All emphasis added.]

Obviously, *none* of these dire predictions have come to pass, and it has been 170 years since they were given. No one is now left alive from that generation. The scope of the warning was centered on the *generation* in which the Mormons were still calling on their converts to leave their homes, cities and countries to "Come to Zion." They have long since stopped this mandatory migration to the center of Mormonism. That generation had passed by before the end of the nineteenth century.

Jesus' Return

Joseph Smith made this reference to the Second Coming of Jesus:

"Were I going to prophesy, I would say the end [of the world] would not come in 1844, 5 or 6, or in forty years. There are those of the rising generation *who shall not taste death* till Christ comes.

> I was once praying earnestly upon this subject, and a voice said unto me, "My son, if thou livest until thou art eighty-five years of age, thou shalt see the face of the Son of Man." I was left to draw my own conclusions concerning this, and I took the liberty to conclude that if I did live to that time, He would make His appearance. But I do not say whether He will make His appearance or I shall go where He is. *I prophesy in the name of the Lord God, and let it be written—the Son of Man will not come in the clouds of heaven till I am eighty-five years old. (48 years hence or about 1890)*[14] [All emphasis added.]

Interestingly enough, this passage is taken from Smith's diary; and modern LDS "historians" have removed the phrase "48 years hence or about 1890" because it so clearly demonstrated the falsity of the prophecy.

None of the "rising generation" ever saw Jesus' coming. Jesus certainly did not come in "about 1890." Over a century has passed since that date; and Smith's prophecy lies dead and buried along with him and that rising generation.

The Potsherd Prophecy

Although Mormons like to exhibit their patriotism, Joseph Smith was not overly fond of the US government. **This is one of Smith's prophecies that you will not hear Mitt Romney speak about**. In 1843, Smith declared:

> if the government, which received into its coffers the money of citizens for its public treasury, cannot protect such citizens in their lives and property, it is an old granny anyhow; and *I prophesy in the name of the Lord God of Israel,* unless the United States redress the wrongs committed upon the Saints in the state of Missouri and punish the crimes committed by her officers, that *in a few years the government will be utterly overthrown and wasted, and there will not be so much as a potsherd left...*[15] [All emphasis added.]

Congress failed to comply with Smith's demands. It did not protect the Mormons, and did not redress the wrongs done against them. In spite of this, the congress was never overthrown, and the U.S. government has never been destroyed, overthrown or wasted. After over 160 years, the United States is the most powerful country in the world!

Who *WAS* that guy, Oliver Granger?

Another personal prophecy of Smith's which fell to the ground was recorded as *Doctrine and Covenants* 117.12-15, which says in part:

> I say unto you, I remember my servant Oliver Granger; behold, verily I say unto him that his name shall be *had in sacred remembrance from generation to generation, forever and ever*, saith the Lord…. [All emphasis added.]

Ask 100 Mormons who Oliver Granger is, and 99 will give you a blank look. His name is supposed to be in everlasting remembrance from generation to generation, and millions of Mormons have never heard of him, nor if they do "remember" the name can give any reason why he should be held in sacred remembrance or who he even was.

Did Joseph Smith Triumph Over His Foes?

The section of *Doctrine and Covenants* where this prophecy is given, Section 121, is prefaced in the LDS Church introduction by being identified as "Prayers and Prophecies written by Joseph Smith the Prophet, while he was a prisoner in jail in Liberty…." Note what is said in verses 5-15:

...My son, peace be unto thy soul; thine adversity and thine afflictions shall be but a small moment; And then, if thou endure it well, God shall exalt thee on high; *thou shalt triumph over all thy foes*...And also that God hath set his hand and seal to *change the times and seasons, and to blind their minds*, that they might not understand his marvelous workings; and take them in their own craftiness...And not many years hence, *that they and their posterity shall be swept from under heaven, saith God*, that not one of them is left to stand by the wall.... [All emphasis added.]

This prophecy promises that Smith and his Church would triumph over all their foes. This never happened. They had just been driven out of their "Zion" in Independence, Missouri. Smith was to die by the hands of his foes, about five years later. The entire church was run out of the state about eight years later and had to flee to Utah! And Joseph Smith was dead in Carthage, Illinois. Can this be triumphing over your enemies?

Even in Utah, the power of the church was ultimately *broken* by the federal government, which forced the church leaders to submit to government authority and to do away with their cherished doctrine of plural marriage. More recently, the church was forced to succumb to outside pressure again and change its racist position on the blacks or else lose its tax-exempt status. Is this triumph?

We need to ask: When did God change the times and seasons on us? When did he blind the minds of Smith's enemies? When were every one of Smith's enemies "swept from under heaven"? In fact, most of them long outlived him!

Boastful Prophets

In the *Doctrine and Covenants* 3, verse 4 (given in 1828), we find this:

> For although a man may have many revelations, and have power to do many mighty works, *yet if he boasts in his own strength, and sets at naught the counsels of God,* and follows after the dictates of his own will and carnal desires, *he must fall and incur the vengeance of a just God upon him.* [All emphasis added.]

Bear this prophecy in mind, as we move ahead several years to 1844. In May of that year, Smith proclaimed this:

> *I have more to boast of than any man ever had.* I am the only man that has ever been able to keep a church together since the days of Adam.... Neither

Paul, John, Peter, nor Jesus ever did it. *I boast* that no man ever did such a work as I. The followers of Jesus ran away from him; but the Latter-day Saints never ran away from me yet.[16]

Just 30 days from making that boast, on June 27, 1844, Joseph Smith was murdered by a mob at the Carthage, Illinois, jail.[17] *It would seem that he fell, and incurred the vengeance of a just God upon himself.* This is not how Mormons see it; but at least this time, Joseph's prophetic word was true.

A Prophet without Prophecies and Revelations of Convenience?

Near the end of his life, Joseph Smith insisted, "There is no error in the revelations which I have taught."[18] Joseph Smith also said, "I am learned and know more than all the world put together."[19] Subsequent Mormon leaders have affirmed that once the prophet has spoken, the church has its marching orders. In one Ward Teachers' message [a monthly message sent by The Brethren to the homes of the members], they were told:

> He [Satan] wins a great victory when he can get members of the Church to speak against their leaders and do their own thinking.... *When our leaders speak, the thinking has been done.* When they propose a plan

– it is God's plan. When they point the way, there is no other which is safe. When they give direction, it should mark the end of controversy. God works in no other way. *To think otherwise, without immediate repentance, may cost one his faith, may destroy his testimony and leave him a stranger to the kingdom of God.*[20] [Emphasis added.]

Having made such a strong affirmation, one would think that the die had been cast and the words of Joseph Smith would live on in the hearts and minds of the Mormon people for eternity, but it isn't so. When the church changed the doctrine on African-Americans being allowed to hold the priesthood and go to the temple, these bedrock doctrines of Joseph Smith and Brigham Young were shattered and a new theology emerged.

The Brethren had already been at work, preparing the Saints for several decades of enormous change. At a BYU Stake fireside meeting on May 5, 1974, General Authority, S. Dilworth Young had already warned the students about modern revelation. "That is modern revelation," he said. "May I repeat? Modern revelation is what President Joseph Smith said, unless [then] President Spencer W. Kimball says differently."[21]

After the shock waves settled down following the African-Americans receiving the priesthood and being allowed in the temple, more revelation knowledge was given to the people. On February 26, 1980, a landmark speech was given before the student body of Brigham Young University by Ezra Taft Benson, who was at that time the President of the Council of Twelve, and soon to ascend to the presidency of the church upon the death of Spencer W. Kimball. His message, **"The 14 Fundamentals of Following the Prophet"** listed those things that set the LDS prophet apart from the rest of mankind. "Let us summarize this grand key, these 'Fourteen Fundamentals in Following the Prophet,' for our salvation hangs on them." Among the things he listed were:

First: The prophet is the only man who speaks for the Lord in everything.

Second: The living prophet is more vital to us than the standard works.

Third: The living prophet is more important to us than a dead prophet.

Fourth: The prophet will never lead the Church astray.

Fifth: The prophet is not required to have any particular earthly training or credentials to speak on any subject or act on any matter at any time.

Sixth: The prophet does not have to say "Thus saith the Lord" to give us scripture.

Seventh: The prophet tells us what we need to know, not always what we want to know.

Eighth: The prophet is not limited by men's reasoning.

Ninth: The prophet can receive revelation on any matter, temporal or spiritual.

Tenth: The prophet may be involved in civic matters.

Eleventh: The two groups who have the greatest difficulty in following the prophet are the proud who are learned and the proud who are rich.

Twelfth: The prophet will not necessarily be popular with the world or the worldly.

Thirteenth: The prophet and his counselors make up the First Presidency—the highest quorum in the Church.

Fourteenth: The prophet and the presidency—the living prophet and the First Presidency—follow them and be blessed; reject them and suffer.[22]

The door was now opened wide to begin the changes to the LDS doctrines that separated it from its understanding of mainstream Christianity. The trick was to be able to change just enough to slip in the back door of the ecumenical body of believers without giving up some of those *special* things that made their faith so much more to them. One of the reasons that changes could now be made to eternal doctrines is that the LDS people adore their prophet, seer and revelator. He is their door into the throne room of God and the instructor of their fate. How can they ever give him up or doubt his words? LDS General Authorities themselves can only acclaim the prophet with unmasked adulation:

We can all be blessed by the words of the prophets of the Lord—if we will only listen and follow their counsel. How fortunate we are that "the living God" has restored his "living Church" with "living prophets" and additional "living scriptures."

> Having a living prophet on the earth today is evidence that God loves us and is interested in us. When we speak of the prophet of the Church, we mean the President of the Church who is president of the High Priesthood. He is sustained by the membership of the Church as "prophet, seer, and revelator." He holds the "keys of the kingdom" (see *D&C* 107:91-92). The prophet and his counselors constitute the First Presidency of the Church. We sustain the First Presidency and the Council of the Twelve as prophets, seers, and revelators."[23]

As Elder Bruce R. McConkie explained, "Those called to preside over quorums, wards, stakes, or other organizations in the Church should be prophets to those over whom they preside." He pointed out that the First Presidency presides over all the presidencies in the Church and that they do so because of their apostolic authority, holding "both the fulness of the priesthood and all of the keys of the kingdom of God on earth. The President of the Church serves in that high and exalted position because he is the senior apostle of God on earth.... (He) is the presiding prophet on earth and as such is the one through whom revelation is sent forth to the world."[24]

The prophet is so vital to Mormonism that his writings and speeches are considered by the LDS Church as direct revelation from God. The only problem is that by the time a man works his way through the tangled hierarchy of the Mormon Church to the top spot, he is often too old to be more than a figurehead prophet. During much of his presidency, and in 1993 when the following report was published, Ezra Taft Benson had been so frail that he was nonfunctional.

"Ezra Taft Benson, the 93 year old president of the Church of Jesus Christ of Latter-Day Saints, broke ground on the gleaming, $24 Million San Diego Temple in 1988, but is too sick to attend its open house, which begins today." It is an irony that has not gone unnoticed by some Mormons who fear Benson is no longer able to receive divine inspiration to lead the 8.5 million member worldwide church.

Mormon historian D. Michael Quinn, who is under investigation by church leaders for apostasy, has described Benson as "mentally diminished." And Mario De Pillis, incoming president of the Mormon History Association, has gone so far as to say Benson is senile.[25]

During the time it took for Benson to pass away and a new prophet chosen, Gordon B. Hinckley, counselor to President Benson, continued to function as the acting president of the Mormon Church. Elder Hinckley also filled this same function for the then ailing Spencer W. Kimball, during the last years of his office.

It is interesting to note that the next in line to take the presidency and become the church's prophet upon the death of Benson was Howard W. Hunter, president of the Council of Twelve Apostles, who was already so frail that he must use a walker.[26]

Today, in 2007, Gordon B. Hinckley is the prophet and president of the Mormon Church, having outlived both Benson and Hunter. He, too, is limited now by age and frailty.

Revelations...of God or Man?

Hugh B. Brown, a high-ranking member of the Mormon hierarchy for 22 years up to his death in 1975, is recorded in his memoirs as saying that many church decisions called "revelations" were actually decisions first "thrashed out" thoroughly by the top authorities. Those decisions "are no less revelatory, but it is simplistic to think that it [revelation] comes as a bolt out of the blue," said the memoir's editor, Edwin B. Firmate, a grandson of Brown and a law professor at the University of Utah.

The decision-making procedure, Brown explained, generally worked like this:

> An idea is submitted to the First Presidency and Twelve, thrashed out, discussed and rediscussed until it seems right. Then, kneeling together in a circle in the temple, they seek divine guidance and the president says, "I feel to say this is the will of the Lord." That becomes a revelation. It is usually not thought necessary to publish or proclaim it as such, but this is the way it happens.[27]

CHAPTER NINE

A Massive Mess of Scripture

Mormons believe that the Bible is the weakest link in scriptures and place their full faith in three other books that contain their fullness of truth. But do they believe in vain?

Trying to sort out the massive complexities of the Mormon scriptures is somewhat akin to the frustration one might feel trying to rewind a pickup load of tangled fishing line. Every time you feel like you have made some headway, another mess pops up. It would be easier to just cut the line and clear up little sections at a time, but that's the basic problem!

Mormon scripture is comprised of four documents: the Bible, *The Book of Mormon*, the *Doctrine and Covenants* and *The Pearl of Great Price*. However, the Mormons have never really had to confront their scriptures as individual units within a full set of integrated documents that can be measured by simple "scriptural test" procedures. The average Mormon sees LDS scripture only in the inflexible context of classroom references within the rigid teaching structure imposed by the LDS instruction manuals. It is never looked at from a critical, Biblically based, scholarly perspective.

The Mormon is taught to unequivocally accept the LDS scriptures as the pure word of God, without error or inconsistency—except, ironically, the Bible, which is in fact the only real standard by which any doctrine can be tested. By discrediting the authority of the Bible, Mormons thereby cut the other three LDS scriptures loose from any Biblical accountability. The only acceptable measurement for LDS scripture is the LDS scripture itself and that has already been given the fullest approval of an "infallible latter-day prophet." There is no room for the application of generally accepted biblical scholarship.

The Eighth Article of the LDS "Articles of Faith," states, *"We believe the Bible to be the word of God as far as it is translated correctly; we also believe The Book of Mormon to be the word of God."*[1]

Mormonism teaches that there are several problems with the Bible. First, many of its books are missing, so it is only an incomplete compilation at best. Second, we are told that many plain and precious things were taken away from the Bible by that "great and abominable church," as recorded in

The Book of Mormon. The very document requiring Biblical testing discredits its only credible witness!

> 24 And the angel of the Lord said unto me: Thou hast beheld that the book proceeded forth from the mouth of a Jew; and when it proceeded forth from the mouth of a Jew it contained the fulness of the gospel of the Lord, of whom the twelve apostles bear record; and they bear record according to the truth which is in the Lamb of God.
>
> 25 Wherefore, these things go forth from the Jews in purity unto the Gentiles, according to the truth which is in God.
>
> 26 And after they go forth by the hand of the twelve apostles of the Lamb, from the Jews unto the Gentiles, thou seest the formation of that great and abominable church, which is most abominable above all other churches; for behold, they have taken away from the gospel of the Lamb many parts which are plain and most precious; and also many covenants of the Lord have they taken away.
>
> 27 And all this have they done that they might pervert the right ways of the Lord, that they might blind the eyes and harden the hearts of the children of men.
>
> 28 Wherefore, thou seest that after the book hath gone forth through the hands of the great and abomi-

nable church, that there are many plain and precious things taken away from the book, which is the book of the Lamb of God. (*The Book of Mormon*, I Nephi 13:24- 28)

The final severance from biblical accountability is the continued LDS teaching that what was left of the Scriptures has been so often and badly translated that our present Bible is of almost no "stand alone" value. Apostle Orson Pratt, an early Mormon theologian, summed up the LDS position when he stated:

> "...and who, in his right mind, could for one moment, suppose the Bible in its present form to be a perfect guide? Who knows that even one verse of the whole Bible has escaped pollution, so as to convey the same sense now that it did in the original?"[2]
>
> Joseph Smith taught, "I believe the Bible as it read when it came from the pen of the original writers. Ignorant translators, careless transcribers, or designing and corrupt priests have committed many errors."[3]

What they are saying is that the Bible, which, at best, represents only 25% of the LDS scriptures, is the weak link. Yet, Mormons are winning people to their biblically unfounded faith by carrying Bibles under their arms as though they read and believe it. It's just a ticket in the Christians' doors for the Mormons.

What the Mormons end up with is a set of spiritual laws that force them to judge their scripture as perfect, by their own measure of faith and not by any objective criteria. If there is an obvious contradiction with the LDS scripture and what the present prophet is teaching, the Mormons cannot judge or test the prophet by the scripture, history or fact. According to the late President and Prophet of the church, Ezra Taft Benson, the current LDS doctrine is that the living prophet is above scripture. There is absolutely no way out.

Burning in the Bosom

The finality of the Mormon theology is not based upon evaluation by scriptural evidence, but based entirely upon a "burning in the bosom." Again, LDS Scripture demands this final proof of itself and tells its members that this experience is what they must seek. Oliver Cowdery was the second elder to Joseph Smith in the founding of the church and in the translation of *The Book of Mormon*. In a word of admonition to him during the translation of *The Book of Mormon*, the Mormon god declared through Joseph Smith:

> "But behold, I say unto you that you must study it out in your own mind; then you must ask me if it is right, and if it is right I will cause that your bosom shall burn

within you; therefore you shall feel that it is right. But if it be not right you shall have no such feelings, but you shall have a stupor of thought that shall cause you to forget the thing which is wrong...."[4]

When the Mormon missionaries come into a home, they will talk about their first prophet, Joseph Smith and *The Book of Mormon* and will instruct the investigator to read *The Book of Mormon* and to pray about it. They will encourage the reader to seek that divine burning in the bosom which will prove that Joseph Smith is a prophet of God and *The Book of Mormon* is really scripture. Moroni 10:4 [*The Book of Mormon*] will be quoted:

"And when you have received these things, I would exhort you that ye would ask God, the eternal father, in the name of Christ, if these things are not true; and if ye ask with a sincere heart, with real intent, having faith in Christ, he will manifest the truth of it unto you by the power of the Holy Ghost."

The missionaries use this quote to put the burden of proof on the investigator's sincere heart, his real intent and his level of personal faith, rather than on fact.

Actually, the average investigator *will* feel good about it. It all becomes a subjective evaluation. The LDS scriptures and prophet are not to be tested. The LDS doctrines are not to be tested. In fact, none of the real heresies of Mormonism will have been shared with the investigator at this stage of conversion, so the investigator is praying about the taste of the icing on an unknown cake.

The Biblical knowledge and *The Book of Mormon* knowledge of the investigator are not to be tested. They are to just pray sincerely, and this divine burning in the bosom will be the proof that the missionaries are delivering divine truth directly from God.

My Own Personal Experience

I vividly recall my own experience with the burning in the bosom. I can clearly remember lying on my bed for the better part of a whole night, crying out to God for a burning in my bosom so that I would know the church was true. Hour after hour I lay there, with my breast lifted upward, as though it were on an altar of sacrifice, pleading for the evidence of this eternal truth. I knew that my heart was sincere, and yet the guilt of my not experiencing the manifestation was almost more than I could bear.

Finally, many hours into my vigil, that burning came. I felt an actual, physical burning sensation in my breast. I would later testify that it was as though I had a rise of 7 or 8 degrees in body heat. My chest was at a high fever temperature. I rejoiced in the certainty of my faith. I knew that the church was true, that Joseph Smith was a true prophet and that *The Book of Mormon* was the pure, true word of God. Yet, in retrospect, I never checked one single teaching of the missionaries against the Holy Bible to see if it matched up.

It is kind of interesting that when, as a born again believer, my wife, Carol, prayed that same prayer of Moroni 10:4 as she read *The Book of Mormon*, seeking to know of its truth, she would fall asleep and experience that stupor Oliver Cowdery was told would be the evidence of untruth. Perhaps she was praying to the wrong God. When I prayed it, not being born-again, I prayed as instructed by the missionaries. I received one answer, and she received a totally different one. Yet, we were both sincere. What was the difference? The difference was that Carol had become "born again" and had the real Holy Spirit to guide her.

An Inspired Version?

Mormons use only the King James Version of the Bible. It is also interesting to note that the LDS Church publishes its own edition of the King James Bible. An article, "Church Publishes First LDS Edition of The Bible," by Lavina F. Anderson, appeared in the October 1979 edition of the LDS *Ensign* magazine and described the enormous project and the intense commitment of the project workers to cross-reference this edition to the other standard works of the church.

Aside from the very obvious question of why the prophet did not take this opportunity to add back all the plain and precious missing parts and correct the translation errors the LDS Church claims have been plaguing the Bible all these years, one comment regarding the project almost flew off the page.

In the last paragraph of the article, the writer concluded, "Brother Rasmussen added, 'Sometimes Brother Patch and I would be discussing a matter of linguistics, and, as we concluded, one of us would remark, "That feels good." I suppose to some people this might seem like a slipshod way to be scholars, but we could tell when we were moving in the proper direction and we could certainly identify the stupor that came over us when we weren't.' He paused, then added quietly, 'In some ways, scholarship was the least important part of our work.'"[5]

As a by-product of referencing the new edition, one long-debated topic among the diverse sub-groupings within the various branches of Mormonism, including the numerous Josephite or Restorationist churches, was clarified. It dealt with the authenticity of a manuscript called *The Inspired Version of the Bible*, written by Joseph Smith shortly before his death. The copyrighted property of the Reorganized Church of Jesus Christ of Latter-day Saints, the Inspired Version, was never given full credentials by the Utah branch—until the release of the new *LDS Edition of the King James Bible*.

It was quite significant that this new edition firmly placed the Inspired Version in the position of a Standard Work or a fifth item of approved Mormon scripture, integrated into the fourth. The title page classifies the new edition as *"Authorized King James Version with Explanatory Notes and Cross References to the Standard Works of the Church of Jesus Christ of Latter-day Saints."* In the "Explanation Concerning Footnotes," on page VI, it identifies JST as the code for the Joseph Smith Translation. The Joseph Smith Translation (The Inspired Version) is referenced by footnotes throughout the new LDS Edition in clarification of some of the errors in the King James Edition.

The Problem with Inventing Scripture

During the question and answer time following an early showing of the film, "The God Makers," in Colorado Springs, Colorado, I made the point that all the extra-Biblical scripture was out of order with God's Word. Among the several references I gave was Revelations 22:18-19, which clearly stated that anyone who would add to the Word or subtract from it in any way was in deep trouble with God.

A Mormon woman in the group challenged me on this statement and emphatically declared that this was only in reference to the Book of Revelation in its single content and had no bearing upon any other book of Scripture, including any Latter-day Saint scripture. I asked her if these curses would be in effect if anyone had dared to alter just the Book of Revelation in any way. She replied that this was obviously so.

I then showed her that in the Joseph Smith Translation, Smith had added to, or subtracted from, the Book of Revelation over 85 times.[6] "Even in the smallest context of the warning, Joseph Smith stands condemned as a false prophet," I declared. She stared in shock. Later, a local LDS leader came up to me after the meeting and quietly whispered, "It doesn't matter; he was just adjusting the incorrect parts. I know that he is a true prophet!"

The Jesus of *The Book of Mormon*

Is *The Book of Mormon* "Another Testament of Jesus Christ," as the Mormons claim? Or is it a testament of another Jesus Christ? Let's check it with one simple test, comparing what happened when Jesus went to Calvary in the Bible and when he went in *The Book of Mormon*. If they are testifying of the same Jesus Christ, the testament should be the same!

The various New Testament writers in the Bible describe the events this way:

> *Jesus, when he had cried again with a loud voice, yielded up the ghost. And, behold, the veil of the temple was rent in twain from the top to the bottom; and the earth did quake, and the rocks rent; And the graves were opened; and many bodies of the saints which slept arose, And came out of the graves after his resurrection, and went into the holy city, and*

appeared unto many. Now when the centurion, and they that were with him, watching Jesus, saw the earthquake, and those things that were done, they feared greatly, saying, Truly this was the Son of God. (Matthew 27:50-54)

And Jesus cried with a loud voice, and gave up the ghost. And the veil of the temple was rent in twain from the top to the bottom. And when the centurion, which stood over against him, saw that he so cried out, and gave up the ghost, he said, Truly this man was the Son of God. (Mark 15:37-39)

And it was about the sixth hour, and there was a darkness over all the earth until the ninth hour. And the sun was darkened, and the veil of the temple was rent in the midst. And when Jesus had cried with a loud voice, he said, Father, into thy hands I commend my spirit: and having said thus, he gave up the ghost. Now when the centurion saw what was done, he glorified God, saying, Certainly this was a righteous man. (Luke 23:44-47)

When Jesus therefore had received the vinegar, he said, It is finished: and he bowed his head, and gave up the ghost. (John 19:30)

The word "earthquake" is used in the verses from Matthew 27 to state that the earth shook. It must not have been severe, since John doesn't even mention it. Luke indicates that people stood by as the earth shook and the sun went into eclipse for three hours. There is one clear thing. No one is mentioned as having died from the earthquake. At His resurrection on the third day, graves were opened and some saints were resurrected to walk into the city.

> *In the end of the Sabbath, as it began to dawn toward the first day of the week, came Mary Magdalene and the other Mary to see the sepulchre. And, behold, there was a great earthquake: for the angel of the Lord descended from heaven, and came and rolled back the stone from the door, and sat upon it. His countenance was like lightning, and his raiment white as snow: And for fear of him the keepers did shake, and became as dead men. And the angel answered and said unto the women, Fear not ye: for I know that ye seek Jesus, which was crucified. He is not here: for he is risen, as he said. Come, see the place where the Lord lay. (Matthew 28:1-6)*

Again, the word "earthquake" is not used in the destructive sense. The earth shook and the stone rolled away from the door. People were not killed.

It's Not Quite the Same in *The Book of Mormon*

The Book of Mormon describes a supposed migration of Jews to Meso-America hundreds of years before Christ was born. There is no archeological evidence of this ever occurring. However, Mormons are taught to believe the truthfulness of the tale in spite of the facts.

In *The Book of Mormon*, the Mormon Jesus brought death and destruction with him to the Cross. In Third Nephi, Chapters 8 and 9, *The Book of Mormon* details the events surrounding Christ's crucifixion as they were experienced by the people of this new-world, Book of Mormon lands. Judge for yourself if it is the same Jesus.

These *Book of Mormon* chapters describe the desolation at Christ's death of the great city of Zarahemla by fire. It states that the city of Moroni:

> ...did sink into the sea and the inhabitants thereof were drowned...the earth was carried up upon the city of Moronihah...there was great and terrible destruction in the land southward.... Terrible destruction in the land northward.... The highways were broken up.... Many great and noble cities were sunk and many burned and many shaken till the buildings thereof had fallen to the earth.... All these great and terrible things were done in the space of three hours.

Third Nephi 9 tells of further wrath as the Lord also destroyed the cities and inhabitants of Gigal, Onihah, Mocum, Jerusalem, Gadiandi, Gadiomnah, Jacob, Gimgimno, Jacobugath, Laman, Josh, Gad, and Kishkumen (a total of 16 major cities).

Who did all this killing to testify of the Lord's atonement on Calvary? Third Nephi 9:15 reveals the murderer of approximately 2 million innocent inhabitants of *The Book of Mormon* lands:

"Behold, I am Jesus Christ the son of God. I created the heavens and the earth and all things that in them are." He adds (in verse 21), *"Behold, I have come unto the world to bring redemption unto the world to save the world from sin."*

It appears that the easiest way to bring redemption was to kill the vast majority of the people in those lands, the very people Mormons believe are Jesus' "other sheep...which are not of this fold," referred to in John 10:16. This Mormon Jesus was a god of wrath. Could this truly be the act of the One Who was supposed to be the end of the law (Romans 10:4)?

Compare that Mormon Christ to the Biblical Jesus who compassionately cried out to His Father, *"Father, forgive them, for they do not know what they are doing"* (Luke 23:34).

In another case, when the disciples would call down fire on a Samaritan village, Jesus rebuked them and made it clear that he brought peace and restoration, not the kind of retribution evidenced by the Mormon Jesus of *The Book of Mormon*.

> *Now it came to pass, when the time had come for Him to be received up, that He steadfastly set His face to go to Jerusalem, and sent messengers before His face. And as they went, they entered a village of the Samaritans, to prepare for Him. But they did not receive Him, because His face was set for the journey to Jerusalem. And when His disciples James and John saw this, they said, "Lord, do You want us to command fire to come down from heaven and consume them, just as Elijah did?" But He turned and rebuked them, and said, "You do not know what manner of spirit you are of. For the Son of Man did not come to destroy men's lives but to save them." And they went to another village.* (Luke 9:51-56)

Simply put, there are two different Jesuses at work here. The Christ of Mormonism is not the Christ of the Bible. Second Corinthians 11:1-5 tells us that there will be those who would teach a different Christ. Paul says of them, *"For such men are false apostles, deceitful workmen, masquerading as apostles of Christ"* (2 Corinthians 11:13). There is a biblical warning about those who would bring the doctrine of another Jesus, plus a simple test. Do the Mormons and *The Book of Mormon* pass that test? No, they do not and never will.

Power in the Blood

The Mormons have a difficult time understanding what actually happened at Calvary. In the LDS pamphlet, "What the Mormons Think of Christ," we see the problem. In the section, The Blood of Christ (page 22 in the 1976 edition), it reads:

> Christians speak often of the blood of Christ and its cleansing power. Much that is believed and taught on this subject, however, is such utter nonsense and so palpably false that to believe it is to lose one's salvation. For instance, many believe or pretend to believe that if we confess Christ with our lips and avow that we accept him as our personal savior, we are thereby saved. They say that his blood, without any other act than mere belief, makes us clean.
>
> What is the true doctrine of the blood of Christ? Salvation comes because of the atonement, and the atonement was wrought through the shedding of the blood of Christ. In Gethsemane Christ sweat great drops of blood from every pore when he condition-

ally took upon himself the sins of the world, and then the shedding of his blood was completed upon the cross.

In Article 3 of its "Articles of Faith," the Mormon Church teaches and professes:

We believe that through the atonement of Christ, all mankind may be saved, by obedience to the laws and ordinances of the gospel [the laws and ordinance of the gospel, according to the LDS prophet].

The Bible clearly teaches another Christ—and another gospel:

And you, being dead in your sins and the uncircumcision of your flesh, hath he quickened together with him, having forgiven you all trespasses; Blotting out the handwriting of ordinances that was against us, which was contrary to us, and took it out of the way, nailing it to his cross; And having spoiled principalities and powers, he made a shew of them openly, triumphing over them in it. (Colossians 2:13-15)

But now in Christ Jesus ye who sometimes were far off are made nigh by the blood of Christ. For he is our peace, who hath made both one, and hath broken down the middle wall of partition between us; Having abolished in his flesh the enmity, even the law of commandments contained in ordinances; for to make in himself of twain one new man, so making peace; And that he might reconcile both unto God in one body by the cross, having slain the enmity thereby: And came and preached peace to you which were afar off, and to them that were nigh. (Colossians 2:13-17)

In the early LDS church, a more orthodox Christ was preached. But when Joseph Smith began to teach the strange doctrines of this different Christ, the church could no longer embrace the reality of the blood of Calvary and its full redemptive work. That was when the church removed the red wine from the communion table and began using water. This act literally washed away the reality of the blood from its Christian converts. The same holds true today. The cross and the blood have become strangers to the Mormons. The Cross of Christ is absent from every single one of the many thousands of Mormon Churches. And so is the Christ who went to it willingly for us all.

I remember the day of my own salvation in January of 1975, when the little church my wife and I were visiting served Christian communion. I held the elements of that communion in my hands and looked down at the red grape juice. I knew it represented the blood that was shed for me, and as I took it to my lips, I wept, knowing that I was lost and separated from God by the works of my own flesh. I had been taking communion with water and Wonder Bread for 20 years, and it had washed away the reality of His shed blood. But, no more. That night I went forward and prayed for forgiveness and gave my life over to the real Lord Jesus Christ.

The Pearl of Great Price

Throughout this book I have quoted many references from the *Doctrine and Covenants*, which is a compilation of doctrines put forth by the Church's prophets. No discussion of LDS scripture would be complete, however, without touching upon *The Pearl of Great Price*, and in particular, that part known as *The Book of Abraham*. Joseph Smith supposedly translated *The Book of Abraham* from some papyrus fragments that the Smiths had purchased from a man claiming to be an Egyptologist. At the time, with several mummies on display, he was traveling through the area in which the Smiths lived.

Using several of the facsimiles (Egyptian pictures found with the mummies) from the papyri, Joseph Smith demonstrated that these were representations of Father Abraham in Egypt and then proceeded to "translate" the papyri fragments into English. This was done prior to the general understanding of the Rosetta Stone decoding of the ancient Egyptian language.

In a recent comparison of the papyri to Joseph's notes, it was apparent that the thirteenth and fourteenth verses of Abraham 1 were translated from one single character resembling a backward E. Yet, in fact, Joseph Smith translated this into 76 words, with nine proper names and eight other nouns. The character for the Egyptian god, Khonso, was translated by Joseph Smith into 177 words in Abraham 1:16-19.

16 And his voice was unto me: Abraham, Abraham, behold, my name is Jehovah, and I have heard thee, and have come down to deliver thee, and to take thee away from thy father's house, and from all thy kinsfolk, into a strange land which thou knowest not of;

17 And this because they have turned their hearts away from me, to worship the god of Elkenah, and the god of Libnah, and the god of Mahmackrah, and the god of Korash, and the god of Pharaoh, king of Egypt; therefore I have come down to visit them, and to destroy him who hath lifted up his hand against thee, Abraham, my son, to take away thy life.

18 Behold, I will lead thee by my hand, and I will take thee, to put upon thee my name, even the Priesthood of thy father, and my power shall be over thee.

19 As it was with Noah so shall it be with thee; but through thy ministry my name shall be known in the earth forever, for I am thy God.

One well-known scene, copied from the Osiris mysteries, shows Anubis, the jackal-headed god on the left, ministering to the dead Osiris on the bier. The penciled restoration (by Smith) is incorrect. Anubis should be jackal-headed. The left arm of Osiris is in reality lying at his side under him. The apparent upper hand is part of a second bird which is hovering over the erect phallus of Osiris (now broken away). The second bird is Isis and she is magically impregnated by the dead Osiris and then later gives birth to Horus, who avenges his father and takes over his inheritance.[7]

Egyptologist Klaus Baer basically repeated the same description in his translation of the papyri as the "Breathing Permit of Hor." He stated:

> The vignette of P. JS I [Joseph Smith papyri] is unusual, but parallels exist on the walls of the Ptolemaic temples of Egypt, the closest being the scenes in the Osiris chapels on the roof of the Temple of Dendera.

He specifically described Facsimile 1:

There are some problems about [Smith] restoring the missing parts of the body of Osiris. He was almost certainly represented as ithyphallic, ready to beget Horus, as in many of the scenes at Dendera.[8]

In other words, the picture was a known pagan image. It meant something. It wasn't even remotely close to what Joseph Smith claimed in his Father Abraham fraud. All three Egyptologists confirmed that the Joseph Smith papyri dealt exclusively with pagan rituals, pagan gods and the Breathing Permit of Hor. Again, the Mormons are free to cling to their unfounded delusions, which certainly fit the occult background of the founder of Mormonism!

Dr. Edward H. Ashment, an LDS Egyptologist working with the translation department of the LDS Church, published one of the most revealing and honest "in-house" appraisals of this document. Throughout Ashment's appraisal of the facsimiles, he dealt with pagan rituals and pagan gods. At no time did he make a connection to Abraham, Abraham's God or Abraham's religion—just paganism. While Ashment went far out of his way to soften any blows against Mormonism's founding prophet, no one can read his work and not see the totally illiterate definitions given the pagan works by Joseph Smith.[9]

How can any intelligent Mormon hold these pornographic drawings in *The Pearl of Great Price* as the sacred Word of God? This is blasphemy and blindness at its highest.

Previously, I described the Mormon scriptures as similar to a pickup truck filled with tangled fishing line. We are still standing in that pickup truck, up to our waists, almost incomprehensibly looking all about us at the unbelievable mess. Where do we go from here? We have hardly begun to clear up the twisted ends.

Our God is not the author of such confusion. I have taken you far enough so that you may never doubt what Proverbs 30:6 means when it says, "Add thou not unto His words, lest He reprove thee, and thou be found a liar." You have seen only the beginning of an endless series of lies built upon lies, so compounded that it is an impossible task to work your way back to truth.

CHAPTER TEN

Fundamentally Mormons

Why the Mormon Fundamentalists are living out the real LDS Doctrines.

Joseph Smith, the self-proclaimed prophet of God and founder of the Mormon Church, used the doctrine of divine revelation to legitimize his polygamous marriages to many wives at the same time. He spiritualized the immorality of his plural marriages and declared it to be "a New and everlasting Covenant; and if ye abide not that covenant then are ye damned; for no one can reject this covenant and be permitted to enter into my glory."[1]

Polygamy was an essential doctrine of the young Mormon religion and still remains a requirement for godhood. The promise of eternal increase and glory still awaits the true believers:

...they shall pass by the angels, and the gods, which are set there, to their exaltation and glory in all things, as hath been sealed upon their heads, which glory shall be a fulness and a continuation of the seeds forever and ever. Then shall they be gods, because they have no end; therefore shall they be from everlasting to everlasting, because they continue; then shall they be above all, because all things are subject unto them. Then shall they be gods, because they have all power, and the angels are subject to them. Verily, verily, I say unto you, except ye abide my law ye cannot attain this glory.[2]

In addition to his first wife Emma, Joseph Smith appears to have actively enjoyed numerous other wives, ranging in age from 15-year-old Helen Mar Kimball to 59-year-old Rhoda Richards. Writer Fawn Brodie (while at the time, still a member of the Mormon Church) counted 49 women, most of whom he married during 1843 and 1844. Of that list, at least twelve were married women with living husbands.[3] His first plural wife was Fannie Alger, a barely pubescent teenager who was living in the Smith home at the time.[4]

Brigham Young, successor to Joseph Smith, and second prophet of the Mormon Church, vigorously proclaimed that "the only men who become gods, even the sons of God, are those who enter into polygamy."[5] Brigham Young took his own words enthusiastically to heart and maintained a polygamous household of over several dozen wives.

The God of Judeo-Christianity is clearly opposed to the taking of more than one wife. Yet, today's social climate is inclining more and more towards permitting groups of different cultural and religious persuasions to have freedom to exercise their various beliefs. Laws restricting plural marriage today may soon change if they are challenged in our liberal courts, thereby accommodating the multinational influx of polygamous religions and cultures that currently exist in America.

In Utah, numerous polygamous offshoots of the LDS church still live "The Principle" (of plural marriage) with impunity. Mormons are not the only group with this kind of doctrine. There are now millions of Muslims living in America alone, many of whom currently consider plural marriage as an orthodox right of their faith.

In 1890, under orthodox Christian and government pressure, the Mormon Church was forced to re-evaluate the divine commandment of polygamy. Fighting for statehood, Utah was confronted with the need to shed this doctrine, which the rest of the country viewed on a par with white slavery. Confusion and anger resulted when the then President and prophet, Wilford Woodruff, revoked the "new and everlasting commandment" spoken by God's first two latter-day prophets.[6]

Many Mormons who had embraced this eternal promise of glory rebelled. To deny "The Principle" would be to reject the very structure and function of their family units and their spiritual lives. After all, Brother Joseph warned them that if they did not live the Covenant, they would be damned. Many of the polygamists fled to Mexico and Canada. Others, less affluent, removed themselves to the outer edges of the Mormon kingdom, settling in such places as Southern Utah, Idaho and Northern Arizona. Many others considered President Woodruff's action such an evil act of political expediency that it caused the anointing of God to be lifted from the Church. They defected, forming their own offshoots of Mormonism. False leaders in Salt Lake City would not draw them away from the true faith.

Today's Fundamentalists

Generally known as Fundamentalists, many of these groups function today, still believing that the doctrines taught by Joseph Smith and Brigham Young were divine truth, still holding to *The Book of Mormon*, the Melchizedek priesthood, Temple garments and other evidences of their faith. They stand convinced that the LDS church is lost in total apostasy and that their particular group now holds the divine keys to this last dispensation of time.

While the actual numbers involved are hard to pinpoint because of the clandestine nature of such groups, today, one recent article estimated there are 40,000 to 50,000 polygamists who live in and around Utah.

"They are all over the place," Washington County, Utah, Sheriff Kirk Smith said. "We have them in every county in the state of Utah. It is not uncommon in the western United States.[7]

Groups' sizes vary from small, single-family units to entire rural communities. Most of the plural wives come from within the ranks of the polygamous groups themselves. There are always young girls available from the many large families that the practice of plural marriage seems to produce.

Such close interbreeding has its own problems, however. *USA Today* recently reported that:

> Incidents of a rare birth defect are increasing in a polygamous community on the Utah-Arizona border, according to a doctor who is treating many of the children. Intermarriage among close relatives is producing children with a condition called *"fumarase deficiency."* It causes severe mental retardation and epileptic seizures. (*USA Today*, February 10, 2006, p.11A)

Polygamy in Utah is an embarrassment to the Mormon Church, especially at a time when they want to quietly sidestep into the general ranks of ecumenical Christianity.

However, the Mormon Church will not officially recognize it as a *Mormon* problem and deal with it as such. I am convinced that unless the LDS Church openly confronts the issue as a product of its past and pulls back the curtain of silence in the matter, it will *never* be dealt with appropriately. It is a strong branch of the family tree that will not go away without some very serious husbandry.

Margaretta Spencer is a former Mormon and the wife of Jim Spencer. Jim is also a former Mormon and was a pastor in Idaho when he founded Through the Maze, now his full-time ministry to the Mormons. Jim is the author of a number of excellent books on the subject of Mormonism and Evangelism. Margaretta told us about having to deal with polygamy in her childhood:

> I was born and raised in the Mormon Church, and I can remember, because of my heritage, going to my cousin's family re-union, and we had to wear nametags with the wife's name on them, so that we could recognize which family we were descended from.[8]

Jim Spencer summed up the core of the issue for us when he said, "Those who take their religion most seriously return to polygamy, because it has not been expunged from Mormon scripture. In fact, if a Mormon is very honest, he probably needs to be a polygamist. However," he added, "Polygamy is a horror. *The history of polygamy is a history of women who shared their men.* And it's a history of power, abuse of women and children, and spiritual manipulation.[9]

The late Thelma "Granny" Geer was an ex-Mormon who had an LDS family tree that went back to the pioneer days in Utah. She was a descendant of John D. Lee, a Mormon Bishop who was involved in the infamous Mountain Meadow Massacre near St. George, Utah, in 1857, "in which more than 120 emigrants were ambushed and slain."[10]

On August 14, 2007, the movie *September Dawn* opened to wild reviews as it revealed the brutal slayings there in St. George of 120 innocent men, women and children at the hands of the LDS Church, under the orders of the prophet, Brigham Young. The film is a brutally honest rendition of true historic facts the LDS Church has tried unsuccessfully to separate itself from.

Lee was eventually executed for his part in the massacre. Granny was the author of the best-selling book *Mormonism, Mama and Me*. She was also a dedicated Christian witness to untold thousands of Mormons. She shared her thoughts about polygamy in an interview for "The God Makers II" film.

> My great grandfather, John D. Lee, was a polygamist. He served under Joseph Smith and Brigham Young. He had nineteen wives and sixty-four children, so that he could become a god as God is now. He really

believed that God and Jesus are polygamists, and that every Mormon man would have to have a lot of wives. There is also the warning that any person who will not believe this, and enter into the polygamists temple marriages, they shall be destroyed.[11]

When we were in Utah doing some of the shooting for "The God Makers II" film, Pat Matrisciana, president of Jeremiah Films, struck up a conversation near Temple Square with Art Buella, a bystander who turned out to be a Mormon Fundamentalist and a practicing polygamist with a "calling as a prophet." Art volunteered to be interviewed for the film and told us the following:

> I was in the Mormon Church for eleven years, never missed my tithing once, I had a temple recommend. And then the [Mormon] Lord showed me that they [the Mormons] had departed from the original track that Joseph and Brigham had set out. They passed a law that a man could have only one wife, and actually, it is the order of heaven for man to have more than one wife.[12]

Lillian's Story

Lillian Chynoweth, an attractive tall, dark-haired woman, cautiously approached Jeremiah Films late in the summer of

1988. Following the recent murder of her husband, Mark, she had been in hiding from her Fundamentalist family group in fear for her own life and the lives of her children. She told Pat Matrisciana that she didn't know how long she could stay out of harm's way, but before something *did* happen to her, she wanted to tell her story on camera. She wanted the world to see what was really going on behind the secret curtain of Mormon Fundamentalism. It was obvious to Pat that she did not expect to escape detection much longer.

From first-hand experience, Lillian revealed some of the horrors of the fruits of this branch of hard-core Mormonism. She knew the depths of its poison because she had lived in the midst of its tenets all her life. She was witness to the murders, the cheating and stealing and lying, and the degradation that its women and children went through every day of their lives—all justified in the name of their polygamous, vengeful god and declared through the mouth of his prophet, Ervil LeBaron, Lillian's own father.

Her story centered around her psychotic father, who had ordered her husband killed, and the intrigue surrounding the deaths and suicides of twenty-seven members of her family unit since 1972. Her father was the prophet and leader of a large Fundamentalist group called The Church of the Lamb of God. The LeBaron family had been polygamists for a number of generations.

After the 1890 manifesto which outlawed polygamy, Lillian's grandparents left the state of Utah for Mexico to continue to practice their beliefs. Her grandfather, Alma Dayer LeBaron, founded the town of Colonia LeBaron, Mexico, where Lillian was born in 1955 as the fourth daughter of Ervil M. LeBaron.

Lillian was raised in this small colony in Mexico, tucked away in a beautiful valley setting in the Sierra Madre Hills. The people she grew up with were mostly the LeBaron brothers (her father and her uncles) and her cousins, but the town grew as people were converted. Lillian confided that the group today had the most sophisticated forms of weapons available and that they are all trained to kill.[13]

Lillian remembers her father as someone who studied biblical law and Mormon doctrine and who wrote many pamphlets. She was his secretary for ten years and worked closely with him until she realized that, in her own words, he was not only a "pervert" but also "demon possessed." She recollected her earliest childhood memories "of secret meetings" and "a lot of things going on behind closed doors, including wife swapping."

As a youthful child, Lillian "was groomed to marry very young." She said that she "was taken aside and told that it was the Lord's will that we marry such men [polygamists], that we would gain our crown of exaltation, and that we would be priestesses unto the most high god." She explained that among the men there was a network of trading daughters. They would choose and try to gain favor to get the wives of their choice.

Lillian sadly recalled the sorrow and suffering that polygamy caused her mother who "wanted to do what was right...all the wives tried to do what was right, but there were problems, jealousy being the primary one." Lillian promised herself while still a child, and after hearing her mother weep many a night, that she would never get involved with polygamy.

She had a curious childhood bathed in the "Law of Consecration," which is the sacrifice of all things:

> "...the right to our own husband exclusively, the right to have property, or money, all of it belonged to the kingdom. My father taught us that the means justifies the end for the cause of the kingdom of God. There was a lot of auto theft; everyone was involved in shoplifting and stealing food and clothing. We all worked and we gave a hundred percent of everything to my father for his cause. Even when he was in prison, he required all of our money to pay for his attorneys. We usually subsisted on very little. We ate out of dumpsters; we took clothes out of the goodwill collection boxes to cover ourselves. As a child, a very young child in the cult, I was subjected to a lot of suffering because we were sometimes undernourished, we didn't always have the proper clothing, or shoes."

Because of her promise to herself, Lillian chose her own husband, Mark Chynoweth, and they were married. However, after their marriage, Lillian's father was continually after Mark to take on more wives, because, Lillian contends:

> "...that was one way that he, my father, could control men, but my husband never took the bait. My father offered him a lot of my sisters, over and over. He told him to just sleep with them; finally he offered him my eleven-year-old sister to wife, at that age. That's when I stood up and said, 'No, that is sick!'"

Lillian and her husband left her father's group when they refused to bring another wife into the marriage. They left the area and started a new life for themselves, hoping and praying that her father would not seek retribution for their so-called apostasy, under the Fundamentalist doctrine of "Blood Atonement."

Lillian and Mark had a very loving relationship for fifteen years until he was murdered, in Lillian's words, by "one of my half-brothers and one of my half-sisters" in the process known as blood atonement.

A Bloody Doctrine

This doctrine is the second side of the grotesque Fundamentalist coin. It teaches that there are certain sins for which the blood of Christ cannot cover the sinner. The sinner must have his or her own blood shed to atone for that sin. In Fundamentalist groups, those sins were as many and as varied as the warped imaginations of the leaders would allow.

When Lillian and her husband found the real Christ, they dreamed about spreading the Christian gospel together. They attended seminary to study the Bible and had a desire to enter a pastoral ministry one day. They hoped to start a home school to further the teaching of biblical principles. However, their hopes and aspirations were short lived.

On June 27, 1988, their dreams ended in a bloody explosion of horror. That was the date assassins from The Church of The Lamb of God paid them a visit at their place of business in Houston, Texas, and executed Lillian's husband. The slaying of Lillian's husband Mark, in Houston, coincided with the murders of three other so-called traitors to the cult in Irving, Texas. They were Lillian's brother-in-law, Duane Chynoweth, his young 10-year-old daughter Jennifer and Eddie Marston, 32, one of Ervil's stepsons.[14]

Little Jenny's only crime was that she was with her father and therefore was an eyewitness to the brutal execution. My wife and I saw the news coverage on TV, and ours eyes were riveted to the sneaker sticking out from under the blanket covering her small body on the Coroner's gurney. A life of promise and happiness had been wiped out to satisfy some wicked, shameful doctrine of darkness.

The execution date of June 27 was no accident. The significance of the date and time of the shootings (4.00 P.M.) was that they fell on the 144th anniversary of the martyrdom of the prophet, Joseph Smith. The importance of the murders taking place on the very hour and date of the anniversary of Joseph Smith's killing is part and parcel of the bizarre ritual of blood atonement. All the premeditated ceremony surrounding these consecrated killings was part of the offering, a sweet-smelling sacrifice to the god of Mormonism, a plea bargain for the unwashed sins of mortal men. Early Mormon prophets and leaders set the tone for these murders over a hundred years ago, their voices still echoing across the decades to take yet more innocent life:

...and you who have committed sins that cannot be forgiven by baptism, let your blood be shed, and let the smoke ascend, that the incense thereof may come up before God as an atonement for your sins and that the sinners in Zion may be afraid.[15]

> ...I could refer you to plenty of instances where men have been righteously slain in order to atone for their sins.... I have known a great many men who have left this church for whom there is no chance whatever for exaltation, but if their blood had been spilled, it would have been better for them.... *This is loving our neighbours as ourselves; if he needs help, help him; and if he wants salvation and it is necessary to spill*

his blood on the earth in order that he may be saved, spill it. (Emphasis added.)[16]

These are not radical Fundamentalists prophet like Ervil LeBaron speaking. These words come from the mouths of two of Mormonism's leaders: J.M. Grant and Brigham Young. How can Mormon Church leaders pretend to be separate from the evils of blood atonement? How can they deny it? It's all around them. Until recently, even the death penalty in Utah was by firing squad so a murderer's blood would be spilled and the sin atoned for properly.

Mormon Church officials are concerned that the concept of blood atonement is perceived by many Utahans as official church doctrine. Noting that the church's stance on blood atonement and capital punishment has changed over the years, Buckley Jensen, an anti-capital punishment activist, said, "Church officials did promote blood atonement as late as 1961. And in 1978, the church stood behind capital punishment, but not blood atonement. Now, the church is neither for nor against the death penalty and is definitely opposed to the idea of blood atonement."

In a 1954 writing, the late Mormon Church President Joseph Fielding Smith stated, "If then he would be saved he must make sacrifice of his own life to atone – so far as in his power lies for that sin, for the blood of Christ alone under certain circumstances will not avail." However, in a 1978 letter, Bruce R. McConkie stated that blood atonement "was advocated by the church only within the setting of a theocracy."[17]

Of course, McConkie knew that the prophetic goal of Mormonism is that someday this country will become a Mormon theocracy, operating under a Mormon prophet. Then, all these *spiritual laws* such as polygamy and blood atonement will be openly reinstated for the good of the "Kingdom." Do you wonder now where these strange, brutal doctrines of the LeBarons come from?

During our videotaped interview, Lillian's face radiated with joy in her relationship with a God whom she knew and loved. She spoke with enthusiasm of future expectations, her longings for her children, and her aspirations to lead her entire extended family to the truth of real Christianity. All the statements by Lillian come from that video session.[18]

The cameras were rolling as Lillian recounted shocking stories of the past, and a thrilling story of the present. She had now found a precious relationship with the real Lord Jesus Christ and was learning daily from God's true Word, the Holy Bible. She had a passionate zeal to spread her new message of hope to all her family and particularly hoped her words would reach those many other innocent victims still trapped in her now dead father's cult. However, she was not naive about the malevolent physical and spiritual dangers that surrounded her mission. She spoke openly about the arsenal of sophisticated weapons that were stashed away in the cult that she had fled:

They do a lot of trading with the Mexican government. They steal vehicles from the US and trade them for weapons, and protection in Mexico, to the Mexican government. Even the nine year olds are trained to kill. They are to be feared... they are fearless.

At that point, Lillian looked into the camera intently and said:

> I would just like you to know that if anything happens to me...ever, or to my children, I believe that the Mormon Church, in general, will be responsible. Because the very doctrine of blood atonement, the doctrine that requires that our blood might be shed, so that we might obtain salvation in the hereafter, stems from Mormonism.

It was sobering to think that there really were people *somewhere out there* convinced that they were bound by blood oath to execute the holy orders of a dead man, to kill that man's own flesh, his own daughter. Yet, our own thoughts on that balmy summer day could not focus on that reality; we could not comprehend the seriousness of Lillian's anticipation of their brutal retribution. The story of Lillian, gleaned from the Jeremiah Films interview, is one of horror, intrigue and shocking murder. It illustrates the results of a family gone wild, fatally poisoned by the fruits of Mormonism.

Sidestepping Responsibility

It may be easy to dismiss the accusations of Lillian, who placed the general responsibility for all the death and destruction in her family at the door of the Mormon Church. Critics and Mormons alike may claim that Mormonism no longer officially practices such atrocities. But, while the Mormon Church may no longer sanction or approve Joseph Smith's original commandment to practice plural marriage, they do still hold him, and his successor Brigham Young, in high and worshipful regard. They still consider these men to have been the mouthpieces of God. The very Section of *The Doctrines and Covenants* that lays out the literal requirement to enter into plural marriage or be damned *is still there today* and still received as holy scripture by every Mormon believer.[19]

In fact, LDS Priesthood Quorums are still being taught that Joseph Smith holds the full authority and all spiritual keys to this last dispensation of times.[20] It goes without saying that there are millions of people out there who believe this with all the fibers of their being. There are obviously some who will not let later church leaders wash out God's eternal commandment for what was obvious political expediency.

On June 27, 1988, the day Mark Chynoweth and the others were executed, Sharon Fryer of Houston's Channel 13 Eyewitness News, interviewed local Mormon Stake President, Bervin Blake, who offered his condolences to the family, and then said that "a connection between the LeBaron group and Mormonism does not exist." The TV reporter added, "The teachings of the splinter group is completely foreign to those of the Mormon Church."[21]

Once again, the Mormons were swift to cast off the child of sin that was birthed in the inner rooms of their past. Bervin Blake's words were a betrayal of truth and came straight of out the dark pit of Mormonism's inner belly. Lillian's story shows that the fundamentalist connection to the Mormon Church still exists. Mormonism birthed these offshoots whose followers number in the tens of thousands and who look to Joseph Smith, Brigham Young and *The Book of Mormon* as their standards of truth.

The many thousands of people caught up in polygamy and Mormon fundamentalism still esteem the original teachings of Joseph Smith and Brigham Young. They still use *The Book of Mormon* and the speeches and writings of early Church leaders as their rod of truth, and they still wear the old style temple garments that were worn in Brigham Young's day instead of the fashionable, shorter style of modern-day Mormonism.

Instead of the Mormons dismissing their relationship with these groups, Mormons should recognize that the fruits of Mormon teaching at its purest level logically lead to these consequences. These sins stem from the hard-line doctrines of Mormonism that were God's inviolable word to man before the repackaging of Mormonism began and its Public Relations Department stepped in to help The Brethren clean up the Church's image. The Mormon hierarchy should be challenged to confront the errors of the teachings of their prophets and get involved in being part of the solution instead of part of the problem. Mormonism needs repentance and restoration to orthodoxy, not continual revision.

Lillian talked about the bedrock LDS doctrines that controlled the LeBaron clan.

> "We were raised with the basic tenants of Mormonism, including polygamy, which was openly and freely practiced in our community.... My father had a total of eleven wives, my mother being the first. We were very sincere about all the aspects of Mormonism. We used *The Book of Mormon* as one of our main sources of knowledge.... It is a requirement in Section 132 of the *Doctrine and Covenants*; it is clearly stated that if we are to attain the highest degree of glory, that we must do the works of Abraham. Therefore, we were taught that in order to attain the celestial glory, a man must take more than one wife."

But, for the LeBarons, spiritual guidance didn't stop with the LDS standard works. It extended to whatever Ervil LeBaron wanted, whenever he wanted it.

> "My father constantly claimed revelation for every last thing that we did, and controlled every-

thing that we did, as much as he could. And I came to find out what a perverted thing he was really involved in. He would actually take several of his wives to bed at once. And he was very involved in marrying other men's wives. So, the pressure was on always for men to marry several women.

The youngest girls were reserved exclusively for the older men who would have a harder time securing more wives, so that's how they worked it. And my father, he got most of his wives by bribing other men with his daughters. I was one of the ones that refused to fall into that, and I chose my own husband, and married, and had a very loving relationship for fifteen years…until I lost him, through this blood atonement process."

When we finished with the videotaping, we knew that we had been in the presence of someone who was truly living in the center of the 23rd Psalm. There was an anointing on Lillian's life and a strength she demonstrated that came from knowing that she was willing to lay down her life.

Shocking News

Not long after that, Lillian returned to her home in Houston, to pick up the pieces and get on with her life. She returned her children to what she hoped would be a normal life again. Things quieted down.

Then, four months later, came the shocking news. On January 28, 1989, Lillian Chynoweth was found dead. One of the children found their mother lying dead on the floor of the den, a revolver at her side. The official police report said that it was suicide. Others deeply questioned that, knowing that Lillian felt she had work to do before her family caught up with her, knowing it would have been a small matter for her brothers to gain access to her home and execute her in a way made to look like suicide.

Did several of her brothers come to the house and did she let them in? Or, did Lillian really commit suicide? Only the Lord can answer those questions. We would never know until heaven, unless some LeBaron clan member would claim responsibility for it.

What we did know was that Lillian was dead, her children left behind without a mother or father. A sparkling light had been extinguished. The intrigue and police investigations that encompass that polygamous sect continued.

On January 20, 1993, three members of the LeBaron clan were convicted in the slayings, on the testimony of a fourth member who turned State's evidence against them.

Three members of a polygamist sect were convicted of civil rights violations in the slayings of a child and three former adherents who prosecutors said were shot for leaving the church. The jury was to continue deliberating today on conspiracy and murder for hire charges. The verdict Wednesday means the defendants—William Heber LeBaron, 28; Patricia LeBaron, 27; and Douglas Lee Barlow, 31— could receive life in prison without parole, plus 25 years.[22]

Deeper into the Dark Pit of Blood Atonement

I know that this doctrine of Blood Atonement sounds just too strange to be true. Could people really kill family members under some delusion that God was blessing it as an act of spiritual love? It's impossible for reasonable people to comprehend. Yet, it was true with the LeBarons.

Lillian gave us a special insight into the underbelly of blood atonement.

> "At the same time [she and Mark left the cult], our names were on the list to be atoned for. My father believed that we were traitors to God's cause and that our blood must be shed to atone for the sin of turning against light and knowledge, as he supposed. And so he set about having many killed. Twenty-seven, mostly our family, have been killed, since 1972. Yet I don't regret it all. My hope and prayer is that many will come to the True knowledge of the Lord's goodness, and will not be deceived; that my testimony will be used primarily to help the Mormon people to realize the deception that they have fallen into—

because my father's teachings are directly connected with what Mormons believe as core doctrine."

As a child, Lillian knew of the secret goings-on in meetings because they took place in her home. Sometimes she was allowed to come into meetings and listen. She believed that the vows taken were holy,

> "...considered to be very sacred; namely, the covenant of blood atonement, which is a ritual they go through if someone "turns against the light and knowledge" the gospel that Joseph Smith taught. They make specific signs, and ask that their blood might be shed, that they may have salvation in the hereafter."

We asked Lillian to describe her experiences with the doctrine of blood atonement, and it was as though we had opened a dark door to the past.

> "My father was the patriarch of the church of the First Born of the Fullness of Times, and my uncle Joel was the prophet and grand head of that same church. In 1972, my father had my uncle Joel murdered because my father, who had started taking other men's wives, was released of office. In a vengeful sense, my father arranged for the murder of his own brother."

During her interview, Lillian was convinced that:

> "...this blood atonement process is still going on in the Mormon Church, and my father practiced it openly. He felt that the Mormons were real hypocrites. He exposed Mormons all the time for being hypocrites because they hid the true beliefs of Mormonism. I am convinced beyond a shadow of doubt, that my father was murdered in the Utah state prison (in 1981) by the Mormon Church. He was a very charismatic man, and had control of his cellblock. He had most people working for him, and the Mormons feared him greatly, so I believe that they killed him."

Did the Mormon Church have a vendetta with the LeBarons? Lillian's brother, Isaac, paid his tithes to the official LDS church and attempted to "redeem his generation" by returning to the true church, but the Mormon Church wouldn't allow him to repent; it wouldn't even show him forgiveness. In Lillian's words,

> "My brother Isaac LeBaron was a devout Mormon. His friends knew him as one of the most Christ-like people they'd ever known. He very much wanted to have the priesthood. He did everything he could to qualify to receive his ordinances. He went before the bishop in Houston, Texas, to try to gain

his qualifications. There was a list of things he had to do and accomplish before he could receive the ordinances of the priesthood. The last time, they said that they could not give him the priesthood, because he was Ervil LeBaron's son. Shortly thereafter, on June 18th, 1983, he committed suicide in my home. My brother felt like his life was worthless and hopeless because he couldn't obtain the priesthood. He had everything in the world to live for, yet he felt like his life was over because he could not obtain what he most wanted, and that was the priesthood that the Mormons talk about, and preach about.

Some people say that blood atonement is a direct murder, but I think that it's carried out often times in a different way. Where the Mormons will make somebody feel so bad, and reject the priesthood to them, and they know that they will commit suicide, because if the priesthood is not granted to them, their life is not worth living."

Lillian looked away for a few moments, a sorrowful look fixed upon her face. Then she turned back to face the camera.

"The ones that murdered my husband and my family, my brother and my sister, I forgive them entirely. I love them, they are my own family. And they truly, sincerely feel like they are doing what is right. I am praying that somehow, through all of this, that I get the opportunity to witness to them, and to show them how the Lord has worked in my life. Because, but for the grace of God, I could still be involved in that too.

And so, there is nothing but compassion in my heart for them, and we are not bitter, and we are not vengeful, and we do not seek to condemn them, but to bring them to the knowledge of the redeeming power. When they realize what they have done, I pray that they will repent, and I know there can be forgiveness for them.

Although this has been such a big tragedy and loss to our family, and to many people, there has been a lot of good come out of it. It has drawn me and my family close to the Lord, my life is in His Hands. And through all this tragedy that's one thing I have gained, an abiding love for the truth. And my children have also been able to go through this, knowing that all things work together for good, to those of us who love the Lord—*and we love the Lord.*"

What a tragedy! What a waste of precious life! What a mockery of Christ and His redemptive act of sacrificial love at Calvary! Mormonism will never shake the fruit from this vine. This doctrine is still so entwined in their theology that they will never escape its tentacles. They may deny it loudly in one breath, but in the very next, breathe it back into their corporate soul.

For example, the late Mormon apostle Bruce R. McConkie, in his definitive book on LDS theology, *Mormon Doctrine*, denied that the church ever practiced or taught blood atonement. Yet, on the same page, stated that because the blood of Christ is not sufficient to forgive certain sins, the Mormon god requires man to have his own blood spilled.[23]

Art Buella, the polygamist-Fundamentalist leader we met in Salt Lake City, explained it this way:

> "Blood atonement is, that if you have charity enough for someone to save them, the shedding of their blood is the only way that they can atone for certain sins. Jesus shed His blood as an infinite sacrifice, but there are some sins that the blood of Jesus cannot atone for, and therefore it requires the shedding of that man's blood to atone."[24]

"Adultery, apostasy, marriage to a Negro, for not receiving the gospel, for lying, for any of the other offenses, they would have to have their own blood shed to have forgiveness of sins" added Thelma "Granny" Geer.

"People really thought they were doing a favor, in my great grandfather's day, to shed the blood and save their soul, and it's still taking place today.

My great grandfather, John D. Lee, was one of the Mormon men who were called the Avenging Angels, or Destroying Angels. It was their duty, their obligation, to cut the throats, shed the blood of people who are apostate Mormons, who were guilty of speaking against the authorities.[25]

Meanwhile, back on Temple Square, in our interview with the man who claimed to be a polygamist, Art continued to justify his theology based on the teachings of Joseph Smith:

The original doctrine that Joseph Smith and Brigham Young taught is exactly what I believe. I am now, at present, baptizing people, and I have five apostles now, and we are out teaching and preaching the gospel, trying to get the Mormons into the original doctrine that Brigham and Joseph had the church set on. And I refuse to give it up, so I have been cast out of the Mormon Church because of it.[26]

There is the rub. Polygamy and blood atonement, the arcane curse of early Mormonism has never been far below that shiny thin veneer of the pretty face of the "families are forever" Mormon Church. It was standing right there on Temple Square.

Living with the Residue of Polygamy

Michelle Grimm has worked with Saints Alive for over ten years. Her unique background as a former Mormon from a polygamous family with a burning zeal for souls has made her the perfect counselor to the many hundreds of LDS women who have reached out for help over these years. This is her own story of her heritage, bondage, guilt, and finally, the freedom she found in Christ:

"As I sat reading the headlines of the *Ogden Standard Examiner* that first Saturday in June of 1978, I began wondering what type of god would keep changing his mind in regards to my salvation. It was the second of four signs to me from the Lord that my life as a Mormon would one day end. I was fifteen years old and convinced that sex, incest and Mormonism were synonymous. They were all an integral part of what God expected of me and the myriad of other women living in polygamous families. But now this newest revelation just complicated matters even more so!

Growing up as a multi-generational Mormon in Utah is complex. There are standards to uphold to make it look as if the family is temple worthy, even while the inside may be a disaster. I wanted so badly to fit into the group that had temple-worthy parents, but that was never meant to be, so I resolutely made the decision to be worthy alone. The bishop would drive me to do baptisms for the dead on my appointed Saturday mornings at the Ogden Temple. Because my family had belonged to the Church for four to six generations on either side, there were no more dead relatives to be baptized for by the mid seventies. I ended up being baptized for people I didn't know and often wondered if my work would be in vain.

I suppose being a female in Utah in the seventies wasn't much different than it was when my grandmother went through her rites of passage in the forties. By the time I was in junior high, I had planned to be married in the temple to a returned missionary, have seven to ten babies and be my husband's first wife. I often wondered whom he would choose one day to share eternity with us or what color of hair she/they might have.

It was understood from the teachings at church that the 'everlasting covenant' would one day return. For now, it was suspended because of the 'Gentiles' decision to make it illegal, so we found comfort in knowing we would one day institute our Heavenly Father's divine law again. I can remember my grandmothers and aunts reciting stories of what it was like 'back in the good old days.' Stories of the sister wives, how wonderful it was to have a house full of children running under foot and the way 'everyone would join forces to get things done.'

For many years, it seemed ideal. I would imagine that no one would ever be lonely and we'd all sit by the fire listening to the heroic battles spoken of in *The Book of Mormon*. In reality, the descendants of the 'everlasting covenant' could only romanticize what it must have been like as we worked and argued in the orchards to gather the harvest and prepare the jams for the upcoming winter. It never occurred to me there would probably be more infighting than what was already at hand!

One of my favorite activities while growing up was to attend family reunions after harvest time. If I were to go to my father's family reunions, I could count on visiting with anywhere from one to two hundred people. If it was my mother's side, it was at least double those figures. My mother's side of the family held a longer pedigree chart with the 'true Mormon' heritage. In other words, they were polygamists. While polygamy was outlawed in 1890 through the Edmunds-Tucker Act, it did not seem to have much influence upon a portion of my mother's family until the early twentieth century.

My great-great grandfather was the last polygamist in my family. From what my 'pedigree charts' say, he married two sisters from England, and had three other wives, one of which was my great-great grandmother.

At the home of one of my aunts, a wall housed dozens of large framed pictures of relatives. In addition to the pictures, she had made little frames between each generation that explained the numerical place of order for that wife. For example, my great-great grandfather had five wives.

His first wife was my grandmother, but we still paid homage to the other wives because of the children who would be siblings to my aunts and uncles. Two of those extra wives were sisters though, and it can get a little confusing! The wives were both having children with him at the same time, so do the children become siblings or cousins to each other? They are suddenly related to themselves with this scenario.

I had always wondered at the reunions why we would wear our nametags with our grandmother's name on it, instead of our grandfather's name. It was not until after I got out of the Church when an ex-polygamist answered my question! We all had the same grandfather; the only way to distinguish the bloodline was through the grandmother!

It took lots of intense prayer and Bible study after I got out of the Church before I felt totally healed from the destruction of my polygamous heritage.

While the mainstream church no longer practices this, the residual effects last for several generations thereafter. Never mind the fact that they are still teaching the doctrine out of *D&C* 132—the covenant of polygamy and eternal marriage.

I grew up thinking that I was just a commodity needed for nothing but producing babies. I truly believed having babies was what I needed to do to get into heaven and to be willing to include sister wives in eternity to become a goddess with my husband, the god of our new world. I never could wrap my mind around the goddess idea, but submitted myself spiritually to the concept of being "just one of the wives." Therefore, my understanding of everything from God to grass was totally warped!

Through the church and the women in my family, I was taught the essentials of submitting to the 'truth' while being told, 'We'll learn the answers in heaven to the unanswered questions here on earth.' I was in a perpetual state of confusion about the Celestial Kingdom and who would be spending eternity with whom.

The main lesson I got from the teachings on that subject was how to prostitute myself for the things I deemed necessities while here on earth. What difference did it make in the long run anyway? I was only going to be one out of hundreds of women my husband would be with in eternity. I felt totally numb from the contradicting 'scripture' and teachings. One day we were taught that we were a chosen people and therefore privileged. The next day I was just one of millions of other wives and, to complicate the matter, I wasn't exactly 'white and delightsome.' If I showed any emotion by the time I left Utah, it was typically anger.

One afternoon when I was about 12 or so, my mother took me with her to visit a widow in our ward. This woman's husband had died a few years prior, and she was worried about her eternity. Her late husband had not been active, if he had been a member at all. I recall my mother asking her if she was going to be sealed to bishop 'Smith' to ensure that she would go to the Celestial Kingdom. I can still hear my mother's voice with a sense of pride when she told me 'how comforting it is to know the Church takes care of its own.'

I thought about that scenario countless times from then until I got out of the Church, wondering just what in the world my mother meant that day; it had seemed so odd to me knowing that the bishop was already married! In other words, for my mother, it was comforting to know that in heaven you as a woman would be promised that you'd be saved by being one of many wives in your new heaven.

The effect of polygamy whether it be a physical polygamy or spiritual is devastating to everyone involved, not just the females. It produces a theocratic vacuum that sucks in any new idea to be incorporated at personal will, while eating away at your soul, creating disaster in all areas: spiritual, physical, emotional, financial, and mental. It is abusive, encourages sexual perversions and holds the members in a death grip of fear.

There is no sense of who you really are, how you really became a human being on earth or what your purpose is for life. And all that without even mentioning the fact that nothing in their doctrine is correct about the God of the Bible!

By the grace and endless mercy of the Lord Jesus, I have been healed from the destruction of polygamy. He showed me through the story of Ruth how Jesus became my Kinsman Redeemer, how He purchased me and gave me a new heritage! Ironically enough, Ruth being from the tribe of Moabites was in a similar situation thousands of years ago when her kinsman redeemer purchased her. Boaz redeemed her from her incestuous lineage of Lot and gave her a new identity in which she became the great-grandmother of Jesus Himself!

While Mormonism may seem pleasing in appearance now that polygamy is 'over with,' one only need to take a closer look under the facade of the average Utah Mormon and the evidence of how destructive polygamy was and still is an unhealed abscess of evil."[27]

The Elizabeth Smart Affair

The world was thrilled knowing that Elizabeth Smart beat the odds and was actually returned to her family. The movie, *The Elizabeth Smart Story,* about her kidnapping and return shown on TV, November 9, 2003, had little in common with the actual facts in the case. I am convinced that the LDS Church exercised some influence on the script. Someone had to, because it was pretty hard to pick up the real facts. You had to read between the lines to understand that this kidnapping had *anything* to do with the Mormon Church, its tainted history and its very active murky secret of polygamy.

The film shows Brian David Mitchell walking through the house with a flashlight, stopping to 'talk to god' in the entry area, inferring that he is some delusional "messiah-god" figure. He kidnaps Elizabeth, flashing the light around her room, her sister sleeping at her side and takes her away to be his "follower." Nowhere did we learn that he sexually abused her during the nine months of captivity.

Nowhere did we see that their attire drew little interest as they walked among the predominately Mormon population because they are just one such fundamentalist "family" among hundreds of others just like them roaming the streets of Utah any given day.

Nowhere did we learn that he was a former Mormon Bishop, that he did not believe he was god or the messiah, but believed he was the prophesied *"one mighty and strong"* and the true "Mormon" prophet who was to take other wives in the fundamental LDS manner.

Nowhere did you see the parallel to Brigham Young and Joseph Smith and their taking of many polygamous wives. Nowhere do we see that the 40,000 or more people in Utah freely involved today in polygamy do so using LDS scripture and doctrine to support their lifestyle that feeds off the sexual abuse of young girls.

*Nowhere did we learn that Elizabeth was just one of over 1,000 such young girls taken over by so many other Brian David Mitchells **each year** in the many Mormon-bred polygamous groups.* Most of them are given to these men by their own fathers, who in turn take other men's children to their beds.

The fact is that these men are theologically justified by current LDS scripture to violate these young girls. It is in the *current* edition of the LDS Scripture, *The Doctrines and Covenants*. I have copied a few of the polygamy verses for you below. Read them *very* carefully. *LDS Scripture clearly says that those who do not abide in it are damned and any wife that does not agree to it shall be destroyed.* The LDS Church can smile and say they are not involved with what happened to Elizabeth Smart, but they stand condemned by their history and own scripture:

The Law of the Priesthood: Polygamy

Doctrine and Covenants 132:

4 For behold, I reveal unto you a new and an everlasting covenant; and if ye abide not that covenant, then are ye damned; for no one can reject this covenant and be permitted to enter into my glory....

61 And again, as pertaining to the law of the priesthood—if any man espouse a virgin, and desire to espouse another, and the first give her consent, and if he espouse the second, and they are virgins, and have vowed to no other man, then is he justified; he cannot commit adultery for they are given unto him; for he cannot commit adultery with that that belongeth unto him and to no one else.

62 And if he have ten virgins given unto him by this law, he cannot commit adultery, for they belong to him, and they are given unto him; therefore is he justified.

63 But if one or either of the ten virgins, after she is espoused, shall be with another man, she has committed adultery, and shall be destroyed; for they are given unto him to multiply and replenish the

earth, according to my commandment, and to fulfil the promise which was given by my Father before the foundation of the world, and for their exaltation in the eternal worlds, that they may bear the souls of men; for herein is the work of my Father continued, that he may be glorified.

64 And again, verily, verily, I say unto you, if any man have a wife, who holds the keys of this power, and he teaches unto her the law of my priesthood, as pertaining to these things, then shall she believe and administer unto him, or she shall be destroyed, saith the Lord your God; for I will destroy her; for I will magnify my name upon all those who receive and abide in my law.

Even the Secular Press Knew the Truth About the Smart Affair

In his November 7, 2003, TV review article, "Two movies show how low TV, and viewers, have sunk," *Philadelphia Inquirer* writer Johnathan Storm wrote, in part:

> It's a stunning moment in TV vulgarity. A fake John Walsh tells a fake Larry King on a fake television show something that everyone in America already knows is true: A religious zealot may be the one who kidnapped Elizabeth Smart.

Elizabeth and the nation's other blond sweetheart of 2003, Jessica Lynch, square off at 9 p.m. EST Sunday in dueling docudramas. Each is an indictment of network TV for pandering and abandoning creativity. Together, they demonstrate beyond the shadow of doubt that commercial desperation can strip away decency and truth on television. On so many levels, CBS's "The Elizabeth Smart Story" and NBC's "Saving Jessica Lynch" are lies.

Hiding Elizabeth's parents' religion while glorifying their religious faith, CBS spins them into saints. Author Jon Krakauer, in his well-researched book, *Under the Banner of Heaven*, concludes that Elizabeth's ordeal was unlikely to have happened outside the edifice of Mormonism.

Elizabeth's abduction and her family's suffering were horrendous, and surely, neither they nor their church is to blame. But to remove the sexual and religious context is not to tell the Elizabeth Smart story at all. And that's what CBS should have done.

The Church of Jesus Christ of Latter Day Saints is never mentioned in "The Elizabeth Smart Story." Nor is the fact that the Smarts are Mormons, as members of that faith are known, though they are faithful church members, and that the alleged kidnapper, Brian David Mitchell, has claimed he is the "one mighty and strong" who church founder

Joseph Smith said God told him would be sent later to "set in order the house of God."

The List of Abuses Never Seems to End

In an article, "Utah Remains Haven for Older Men Seeking Teen Brides," writer Greg Burton reported about a young girl named Sherrie:

> The pigtailed girl walked into Sherrie Swensen's office three days after snuffing the candles on her 14th birthday cake. On one side was her smiling mother – who gave the obligatory parental consent. On the other was a 56-year-old Texan, four times divorced and eager to remarry.
>
> "The girl stood there and hung her head," says Swensen, who took office as clerk of Salt Lake County two months before the 1991 nuptials. "I couldn't even do a regular ceremony. My God, I thought, this child was being sold."
>
> The marriage so upset Swensen she urged lawmakers to change the law and in 1992 Utah adopted a provision requiring the review of a juvenile-court judge, along with parental consent, before 14-and 15-year-olds could marry.
>
> But while judicial review allowed Utah to dampen slightly its reputation as a haven for out-of-

town lechery, homegrown teens—mostly females—continue to wed at alarming rates.

Last year alone, nearly 1,000 teen-agers 14 to 17 years of age were married in Utah, including a 14-year-old girl who slipped a wedding ring on a man of 37 and the marriage of a 15-year-old girl to a groom older than 45. Of the girls ages 14 to 17, 37 percent married men who were at least four years their senior.

Statistics show Utah girls under 16 long have been more likely to marry than boys. A decade ago, only 39 boys ages 15 and 16 took brides. One married a 29-year-old woman. That same year, however, 431 girls ages 16 and younger married. Fifty-six of the girls were not yet 15 years old, and one 14-year-old married a 44-year-old man.

State statutes are failing to protect the hundreds of children who marry because of the strict limitations on what a judge can consider, say a growing number of county clerks and judges. Clerks are responsible for granting marriage licenses and also can perform marriage ceremonies.

"One of the questions I always ask is, 'Gee, are you in love with this person?' and they never fail to answer, 'Yes,'" says 2nd District Juvenile Court Judge Kent Bachman. "If they say they are not being coerced, I have no other course than to say the law permits it and you have the permission of the court to consider marriage of your own free will."

The situation in Utah was questioned earlier this month when state Rep. Carl Saunders, R-Ogden, proposed and then withdrew a bill that would raise the minimum age to marry from 14 to 16. Saunders said requiring teens to wait until age 16 would help reduce promiscuity – a stay-out-of-the-sack-or-you-will-be-a-single-parent warning.

He backed away, he says, after learning children younger than 16 needed a court order to be married. But, now, weeks before the 1998 legislative session, Saunders says he may yet draft the bill.

"There's a lot of us that would like to see [the age] raised to 18," he says. "But who knows what is practical and possible? I gather most of the judges would like to see the changes, but even a greater problem exists: If these kids don't get married, they just go out and cohabitate anyway."

What should be more troubling, clerk Swensen says, is kids falling into the hands of older, manipulative spouses.

"I'll never forget watching one girl skip down the hall in her wedding gown—literally skipping," she says. "Something is wrong with this picture." What's wrong, says Don Strassberg, professor of psychology at the University of Utah, is that most young teens have a romantic notion, not a realistic notion, of marriage.

"They see marriage as a way to solve other problems — unplanned pregnancy, trouble at school or home," he says. "They don't know what they're getting into, they don't realistically know what they want in a partner and they're really doing it for the wrong reason."

Prior to 1992, Utah was one of only three states where 14- and 15-year-olds could marry without a court order. The judicial provision clearly decreased the number of child brides. Last year, 258 girls and 33 boys ages 14, 15 and 16 married in Utah.

"But now we see more of these girls are coached, their mothers are sitting outside the office," Swensen says. "I've got so many stories of these kids being sold or bartered or whatever—I guess it's hard to believe a mother or father would sign off on that—but they do." Indeed.

In April, a 13-year-old girl described to a Utah jury the horror of her father marrying her off to a 48-year-old man, when a prosecutor asked if she could have fabricated having sex with older men.

"There's no way my imagination could make up what I went through," she answered, while clutching a teddy bear.

Her father, John Perry Chaney, who impregnated a 15-year-old girl, ran afoul of, among other things, Utah's law forbidding girls younger than 14 to marry.

If Utah continues to allow 14- and 15-year-olds to marry, Swensen believes the judiciary should at least consider the appropriateness of the marriage. But Rep. Gene Davis, (D) Salt Lake City, resists the urge to thrust a judge into the marriage contract.

"There are a lot of reasons youngsters get married, some of them are genuinely in love – a number of child brides and grooms have had successful marriages," says Davis, who introduced the 1992 judicial-review bill. "We fixed the law in 1992 of people coming into the state and I think the law is tight enough right now. We aren't going to stop teen pregnancy by preventing them from getting married."

Rep. Bill Wright, (R) Elberta, one of only five representatives who voted against the 1992 bill, believes the majority of married teens have found bliss, not burden.

"I would be opposed to raising the age, it's totally unnecessary," he says. "I can think of two or three of the best families I know that married when they were 15. So a young man or young woman makes a mistake, you're going to condemn the whole society?" Wright says the vast majority of teen marriages are "lifestyle choices."

Every time clerk Swensen hears that argument, she pictures the little girl from New York who walked into her office to marry her stepfather's brother. "It's just sick," she says. "But there's not a lot any of us can do to stop it."[28]

Teens Defend Polygamy at Utah Rally

Calling their lives blessed, more than a dozen children and young adults from polygamist families in Utah spoke at a rally Saturday, calling for a change in state laws and the right to live the life and religion they choose.

"Because of our beliefs, many of our people have been incarcerated and had their basic human rights stripped of them, namely life, liberty and the pursuit of happiness," said a 19-year-old identified only as Tyler. "I didn't come here today to ask for your permission to live my beliefs. I shouldn't have to."

> Polygamy is banned in the Utah Constitution and is a felony offense. The rally was unusual because those who practice polygamy typically try to live under the radar.
>
> "It drew about 250 supporters to City Hall," said Mary Batchelor, co-founder of Principle Voices of Polygamy, which helped organize the event.[29]

Polygamy's Lost Boys

With the Fundamentalists' ever-growing need for young girls to fill the beds of the Elders of the groups, young men within the polygamous communities have a hard time finding their first wife from among those already being bartered or passed out to the worthy senior men. Armed with no skills and the barest educational training, many are cast out into the world they were raised to fear and shun.

Gathering puts focus on polygamy's "lost boys"
By Joseph A. Reaves, *The Arizona Republic*

SALT LAKE CITY—Dozens of young males, many of them timid teenagers, gathered on the steps of the Utah Capitol on Saturday in an unprecedented effort to tell the world the horrors they suffered growing up in the nation's largest polygamous community.

The young men and boys were raised in the Fundamentalist Church of Jesus Christ of Latter-Day Saints, which has its headquarters in the twin-cloistered communities of Hildale, Utah, and Colorado City, along the remote Arizona Strip 120 miles northwest of the Grand Canyon. All said they either were excommunicated from the church or pressured into leaving by Warren Jeffs, the self-proclaimed prophet and unchallenged ruler of the FLDS.

They stressed they were but a fraction of more than 400 males ages 13 and older who have been banished from the communities since Jeffs gained supreme power. All have little education and no preparation to survive in the outside world.

"We just want everyone to become aware this is really happening in the United States," Richard Gilbert, 19, said. "I was excommunicated by the prophet Warren Jeffs at the age of 16 because I decided I wanted to go to public school."

In July 2000, while controlling the church for his dying father, Jeffs ordered all FLDS disciples to pull their children out of the Colorado City Unified District schools and educate them at home.

Gilbert's desire to attend public school was sin enough to get him kicked out of church and community. But it could have been a million other things: from playing games to watching TV or ogling girls.

"I was excommunicated by the prophet Warren S. Jeffs approximately two years ago (for) associating with non-members of the church and watching three different movies," Tommy Steed, 19, said.

The worst sin, though – the one for which most are banned – is simply becoming a mature young man in a society where older married men are seeking younger brides. (Emphasis added.)

"People from outside this region are amazed that this has gone on for so long," said Jonathan Krakauer, author of

Under the Banner of Heaven, a book that brought national attention to the FLDS lifestyle. "This is a pocket of an absolute tyrant who rules the lives of 10,000 people and seems to take pleasure in destroying families."

Not only are families ripped apart by the shock expulsions, but the young men and boys have little chance of ever getting their lives back on track.

Hardly anyone in Colorado City-Hildale, male or female, has more than eighth-grade education. Everyone is taught from early childhood that the outside world is evil, the prophet is God's representative on Earth, and his decisions and decrees are beyond reproach. Anyone who leaves the church is damned not only in the afterlife but will be ground to dust in this life.

The combination of isolation, indoctrination and little education leaves young men and boys virtually incapable of surviving in the outside world. Several have committed suicide. Scores turned to drugs and alcohol, and many are homeless, they said.

"When I was excommunicated, my hope for salvation vanished," said Steed, who still has the shy, high-pitched voice of a much younger boy. "It took me a year to get over contemplating suicide" [30]

Warren Jeffs and the FLDS

Warren Jeffs is the Polygamous Cult leader that had been on the FBI's Most Wanted List until the car he was a passenger in was stopped in Southern Utah. The Associated Press reported (in part) on August 29, 2006:

> After more than a year on the run and three months on the FBI's Most Wanted List, the charismatic leader of a polygamous sect was captured during a routine traffic stop and now faces charges he arranged marriages between underage girls and older men.
>
> Warren Steed Jeffs, 50, was arrested without incident just outside Las Vegas late Monday, the FBI said Tuesday. No weapons were found, but the 2007 red Cadillac Escalade he was riding in was filled with items including three wigs, 15 cell phones, $54,000 in cash and $10,000 in gift cards, authorities said.
>
> Jeffs leads the Fundamentalist Church of Jesus Christ of Latter-day Saints, a group that broke away from the Mormon Church a century ago. He is said to have at least 40 wives and nearly 60 children. Church dissidents say that underage marriages – some involving girls as young as 13 — escalated into the hundreds under his leadership.

Warren Jeffs: Holy Prophet or Sexual Pervert

Warren Jeffs is the prophet of the Fundamentalist Church of Jesus Christ of Latter-day or FLDS. His power and control and the following destruction over the lives of thousands of polygamists has seemingly come to an end of sorts. Here are several reports regarding his organization.

Excerpted from *NPR.org,* May 3, 2005:

Upon the death of his father, 49-year-old Warren Jeffs took over as prophet of the FLDS, or Fundamentalist Church of Jesus Christ of Latter-day Saints, in September of 2002. Jeff's father, Rulon T. Jeffs, had been the group's prophet for the previous 15 years. He died at the age of 92, leaving an estimated 75 widows and 65 children to mourn him. The nearly two-decade tenure of father and son has split the polygamist community on the Utah-Arizona border. After taking power in 1986, Rulon Jeffs slowly abolished the seven-member Priesthood Council that had previously governed the sect. Rulon Jeffs eventually claimed a "One Man Rule" and as a result, part of the group split away and founded their own polygamist settlement nearby.

According to former followers, the prophet is considered to be God's mouthpiece on earth. It is believed that God speaks directly to Warren Jeffs to reveal His will. And through the prophet, God directs which male members are worthy of entry into heaven (females are invited into heaven by satisfied husbands). Jeffs is also the only person who can perform marriages, and it is through him that wives are assigned to their husbands. Pleasing the prophet can result in loyal members being rewarded with one or more wives. Wives are considered to "belong" to their husbands for eternity.

In order to reach the highest degree of glory in heaven, members of the FLDS believe that each man must have at least three wives. A significant means of prophet power is derived from his ability to punish followers by reassigning their wives, children and homes to another man. Obedience is highly valued, and it is rare for wives to resist reassignment.

The group takes its theology regarding "plural marriages" from the teachings of Joseph Smith, Brigham Young and the early Church of Jesus Christ of Latter-day Saints, better known as the Mormon Church. But under pressure from the U.S. government, church leaders abandoned polygamy in 1890 so that Utah could gain statehood. Polygamists believe that's when the Mormon Church strayed from the path of righteousness. Likewise, members of the FLDS are not welcome in Mormon congregations, and Mormons who are found practicing polygamy are excommunicated.

Nearly all property in Colorado City, Ariz., and Hildale, Utah, including residential property, is owned by a church trust and controlled by Warren Jeffs. According to former vice-mayor and Colorado City Councilman Richard Holm, the trust is estimated to be worth in excess of $100 million. Holm also estimates that Warren Jeffs has more than 50 wives. But exactly how many wives, or where Jeffs is currently, nobody outside his inner circle seems to know.

There are widely varying estimates of how many people practice polygamy in North America—20,000 to 50,000 and more—but the secrecy of such groups makes a definitive number elusive.[31]

The online encyclopedia Wikipedia has this about Jeffs and his community:

The Fundamentalist Church of Jesus Christ of Latter Day Saints (FLDS) is a religious group of Mormon fundamentalists, and may be America's largest practitioner of plural marriage. The church is not affiliated with the larger Church of Jesus Christ of Latter-day Saints, from which it split in the early 20th century after the latter renounced polygamy.

Since 2002 Warren Steed Jeffs has led the church, succeeding his father, Rulon Jeffs. Its headquarters have been, for nearly the last century, in Hildale, Utah, which is a twin city with Colorado City, Arizona, although recent news reports indicate a shift of the church's main headquarters to Eldorado, Texas, where a temple has been built.

Warren Jeffs, the leader of the FLDS, was arrested in southern Nevada on the evening of August 28, 2006, though news of his arrest wasn't broadcast until the following day. According to FBI spokesman David Staretz, Jeffs was taken into custody after he, one of his brothers, and one of his wives were pulled over shortly after 9 p.m. PDT by a Nevada Highway Patrol trooper on Interstate 15 just north of Las Vegas. The leader of the Fundamentalist Church of Jesus Christ of Latter-day Saints was wanted for the alleged sexual assault of a minor in 2002 and for one count of conspiracy to commit sexual assault with a minor that same year, as well as federal charges of flight to avoid prosecution. The alleged offenses took place in the vicinity of Colorado City. Additionally, Jeffs is wanted in Utah as an accomplice to rape. For nearly two years Jeffs had been a fugitive and from May of 2006 until August 28, 2006, he was on the FBI's Ten Most-Wanted list, with a $100,000 reward offered for information leading to his capture.

The End of His Reign

ST. GEORGE, Utah, Sept. 25—The polygamist Warren S. Jeffs, hailed by his followers as a prophet but denounced by critics as a tyrannical cult leader, was convicted here on Tuesday of being an accomplice to the rape of a 14-year-old church member. Mr. Jeffs, 51, faces up to life in prison.[32]

Distinctive Doctrines

The FLDS church teaches polygyny, a type of polygamy that allows marriage of more than one woman to a man (it does not permit polyandry). In the Church's teachings on the plurality of wives, women are required to be subordinate to their husbands as a general requirement for the highest eternal salvation of men, Godhood. It is generally believed in the church that a man should have three wives to fulfill this requirement.

Both men and women must abide by a strict dress code. Women are generally forbidden to wear makeup, pants or any skirt above the knees, or to cut their hair. Men are usually seen wearing plain clothing, usually a collar shirt and pants, and do not have any tattoos or body piercings. In Colorado City, Arizona, women and girls usually wear homemade dresses and long stockings, keeping their hair coiffed.

The church currently practices the "Law of Placing" under which all marriages are assigned by the prophet of the church. Under the Law of Placing, the prophet elects to give or take wives to or from men according to their worthiness.

The FLDS Church also commonly prevents its members from owning property, instead being entirely held by the church itself. Within their doctrine, the Church views this as a form of the "Law of Consecration" or "United Order." This is most notable in the United Effort Plan (UEP) which held all FLDS church members' property, homes, and most businesses and therefore most jobs in the Colorado City and Hildale area.[33]

I have often said that if I were a Mormon again and believed that both Joseph Smith and Brigham Young were true prophets of God, I would have to accept the LDS scripture found in the present day *D&C* 132 that insists that polygamy is the "new and Everlasting Covenant of God" and know that without this covenant I could not gain celestial glory and godhood. I would have to be a polygamist.

Polygamy is the ugly underbelly of the Mormon Church. The wretched lives of the tens of thousands of women and young girls enslaved by it are the testimony of the true evil that lies behind the doors of the LDS temples and in the hearts of its leaders. There will be no end to it until The

Brethren stand up and take responsibility for its creation, preservation and truly force its demise, openly and publicly, as honest men should.

CHAPTER ELEVEN

The Devil is in The Details

Satan has his claws entwined throughout the doctrines and practices of Mormonism, especially throughout the temple ritual and even sewn into the temple garments.

On October 25, 1991, just in time to spoil Halloween, a secret, internal report from the Presiding Bishopric of the LDS Church surfaced. It alleged that satanic ritual child abuse (known as SRA) was being perpetrated by both members and leaders of the Mormon Church in Utah, Idaho, California, Mexico and elsewhere.

SRA is defined as abusive acts of emotional, psychological, sexual or physical battering done in a religious or occult context. These acts are designed to subjugate the children involved and brainwash them into a satanic mindset. SRA is usually done by parents, grandparents or other adults who have access to the children and perform these evil deeds in the sadly misguided hope of gaining occult power from Satan.

According to the *Salt Lake Tribune*, the report by LDS Bishop Glenn L. Pace stated that members *and* officials of the Church were deeply involved in such abuse. Even temple workers and Tabernacle choir members stood implicated of SRA in Church meetinghouses and possibly even in the temples.

In the report, Pace testified that:

I have met with sixty victims. That number could be twice or three times as many if I did not discipline myself to only one meeting per week.... I don't pretend to know how prevalent the problem is.... Assuming each [victim] comes from a coven of 13, we are talking about the involvement of 800 or so right here in the Wasatch Front. Obviously, I have seen only those coming forth to get help.[1]

My ministry, Saints Alive, had received a copy of the report in late summer. We opted to refrain from publishing it without further substantiation, since it would be difficult to believe on its own merit. (Saints Alive has been accused, in the past, of publishing sensationalistic or occult information about the LDS Church, and wished to be careful in the matter.) However, while similar information had been emerging for years about this kind of practice within the church, this was the first time the Church itself had in any way acknowledged its existence.

At the 1990 Capstone Conference, in Salt Lake City, Jeremiah Films showed video preview clips of some of the footage they had taken for the film, "The God Makers II." These clips included an interview with one man who testified that he was involved with others in satanic rituals within the LDS Church and on LDS property. The stories they had been gathering closely matched those reported by Bishop Pace a year later. In fact, I suspect that the Church interviewed several of the same people.

That was not the first time we reported on the diabolical core of the LDS theology. We exposed the Church's satanic roots three years earlier with my teaching, The Sure Sign of the Nail, in Salt Lake City in 1987.[2] The late Dr. Walter Martin happened to be ministering with me that night, and he commented that I had better be prepared for the heat I was going to take from all sides for opening up that bag of demons. It was a strong prophetic word.

Even before that meeting, Saints Alive had published information from a former Satanist and temple Mormon, Bill Schnoebelen, who had joined the staff at Saints Alive. Bill testified that he had converted to the LDS Church under the direction of his occult leader and compared the numerous parallels between witchcraft and LDS temple rituals.

His testimony later evolved into the books, *Mormonism's Temple of Doom* and *Whited Sepulchers: the Hidden*

*Language of the Mormon Temple,*³ which he co-authored with Jim Spencer, Idaho pastor and former Mormon. This information chronicled the precise corollaries between LDS temple practices, Freemasonry and Witchcraft, both past and present.

With the release of *Mormonism's Temple of Doom* during a Saints Alive Capstone conference in Utah in 1987, a great deal of controversy arose over the authors' linking Mormonism with the occult. Walter Martin, America's "Bible Answer Man," author of *Kingdom of the Cults* and President of Christian Research Institute (CRI), came to the rescue.

Jim Spencer shared this about Martin's involvement:

> From the moment *Mormonism's Temple of Doom* was first published in 1987, it has had an impact on its readers. I gave a copy of it to Walter Martin at the 1987 Capstone Conference which was held at Park City, Utah, in the summer of 1987. Walter had been the keynote speaker at the conference. Ed Decker and I drove him to Salt Lake City Airport for his flight home.
>
> Sometime late that night, the phone in my hotel room rang. It was Walter. He said, "Send me a hundred of those books and give me your best price!" He said he had talked to a group of Baptists that evening and wanted to get them some copies.

A few months later, however, some well-meaning Christians decided the book was "too hard." They came against it and against the authors (and—God only knows why—Ed Decker as well). At one point, even prominent members of Walter Martin's own Christian Research Institute were against the book.

In December, Dr. Martin did a seminar at Calvary Fellowship in Seattle. During the question and answer session, a woman asked him about the connection between Mormonism and Freemasonry. Dr. Martin held up a copy of the book and endorsed it and its authors. You can get the actual audio statement at www.mazeminstry.com.

In the midst of all this wrangling, I called Dr. Martin and asked him to set the record straight. I told him I would print his final word on the subject inside the front cover of the book. The text of his letter to me is reprinted there to this day.

Walter Martin confirmed his endorsement in writing to author Jim Spencer on January 6, 1989, stating:

> Controversy has arisen over the book in that some people have understood the authors to be saying that Mormonism is a lineal descendant of specific occult organizations (i.e. Freemasonry). I can understand how that conclusion could be reached. The authors,

however, have—on many occasions—stated that their position is "remarkable and undeniable similarities exist between Mormonism and other occult organizations." They contend, in *Mormonism's Temple of Doom*, that disciplines such as Mormonism, Freemasonry and Wicca are streams of the same satanic river. This can be substantiated as fact. (Letter from Walter Martin, President CRI, to James Spencer, January 6, 1989)

Even before that, former Temple veil worker Chuck Sackett produced material in *What's Going on in There?* in 1982, which showed that the mysterious temple chant, "Pay Lay Ale" (removed from the temple rites in 1990), was most likely a rough translation from the Hebrew that suggested the chant could easily mean *"Marvelous Lucifer!"* or *"Marvelous (false) god!"*[4] since it is Lucifer who appears in response to the chant. Thus, the satanic connections in Mormonism were by no means news to us who monitored the cults. However, we were all shocked to find that the problem within the Mormon Church was apparently more widespread than even any of us had imagined.

A Different Spin on the Story

However, we were disturbed by the strange spin put on the story by the media. Essentially, the LDS Church was portrayed by some as being *victimized* by evil Satanists who had infiltrated its ranks and defiled its children.

Additionally, the LDS Church issued the following official statement:

> *Satanic worship and ritualistic abuse are problems that have been around for centuries and are international in scope. While they are, numerically, not a problem of major proportions among members of the Church of Jesus Christ of Latter-day Saints, for those who may be involved they are serious.*

That statement could receive a reward of some sort as the bland understatement of the year! If a high-level LDS leader reported over 800 Satanists who are "active Mormons" *in just the Wasatch Front* and between 60 to 180 victims; that *is* a very real problem of "major proportions"—at least anywhere else but in Mormon Utah.

I have prayed with and counseled scores of people who are survivors of one sort of cult activity or another. Each of them is a precious human being who has had incalculable damage done to him or her by this sort of evil. Without the power of the blood of Jesus Christ, such people would have little hope at all. Their personal plights *cannot be* trivialized.

Beyond that, it is historically difficult to characterize the LDS Church as an innocent church which just happened to be *victimized* by invading satanic perversion. Certainly, many churches have had this sort of problem come up in the past few years—though none to the spectacular degree indicated in Pace's report. However, there are some deeper issues here which touch on theology and spirituality, and they must be addressed.

Fruit doesn't Fall far From the Tree

Most reports of the LDS Church's problems with satanic abuse don't mention that Mormonism was originally brewed in a seething cauldron of occultism, sorcery and blood sacrifice. Contrary to the charming, Church-approved tale of the "First Vision," in which Joseph Smith was supposedly visited by two gleaming personages, the actual beginnings of Joseph Smith's spirituality were steeped in witchcraft.

First, Joseph Smith, Sr. and his entire family were casting magic circles and practiced the "faculty of Abrac," according to Joseph Smith, Jr.'s own mother, Lucy Mack Smith![5] Abrac is short for Abracadabra, and is a common, old-fashioned way of saying that they practiced *folk magic*.

Joseph Smith himself practiced "glass-looking," a 19th-century term for crystal ball gazing. He was even convicted of this in a Bainbridge, New York court.[6] In fact, Joseph's annual meetings (on a witchcraft holiday) with the angel "Moroni" on the Hill Cumorah were actually attempts to conjure up a demon spirit through magic and necromancy.[7] There is strong evidence that in 1824 he actually had to dig up the body of his dead brother, Alvin, and bring part of that body with him to the hill to gain the gold plates![8]

Joseph Smith was also well known in his community for using blood sacrifices in his magic rituals to find hidden treasure. One report said that:

> *Jo [sic] Smith the prophet, told my uncle William Stafford, he wanted a fat black sheep. He said he wanted to cut its throat and make it walk in a circle three times around and it would prevent a pot of money from leaving.*[9]

Smith's participation in this kind of occult ritual is born out by several other testimonies.[10] Additionally, after his death, Smith was found to be carrying a magic talisman on his person sacred to Jupiter, and designed to bring him power and success in seducing women.[11]

With unbiblical practices like that at its roots, how could the tree of Mormonism be anything else but sinful and occult? As has been frequently shown, the sacred Temple rituals of the LDS Church are grounded in practices familiar to those involved in both Masonry and Witchcraft. Even many of the icons on the outside walls of older Temples are textbook examples right from witchcraft. This demonic core of Mormonism is hardly hidden from view.[12]

Is it any wonder that Mormons get involved in these sorts of abominable practices when they are submitted to a priesthood that flows right out of the very jaws of demonism? When their founding prophet and his family were sorcerers, how could Mormons resist the blandishments of the occult or Satanism?

Where is the Revelation Power?

If the LDS Church is truly the Church of Jesus Christ and is run by a "Living Prophet," how could such atrocities as SRA even get to "first base"? LDS doctrine teaches that all bishops and stake presidents have spiritual *"keys of discernment"* with which they can tell if church members are lying or living unworthy lives. Yet, many of these Satanists are also card-carrying "Temple Mormons" who must pass the annual muster of stringent questioning from both their bishop and their stake president. *In fact, Pace reported that some of the Satanists were bishops and stake presidents themselves!* Again, quoting from Pace's report:

> ...they [the victims] have told me the positions in the church of members who are perpetrators. Among others, there are Young Women leaders, Young Man [sic] leaders, bishops, a patriarch, a stake president, temple workers, and members of the Tabernacle Choir. These accusations are not coming from individuals

who think they recognized someone, but from those who have been abused by people they know, in many cases their own family members.... We are disturbed to receive reports that a scoutmaster has abused the boys in his troop.... Not only do some of the perpetrators represent a cross section of the Mormon culture, but sometimes the abuse has taken place in our own meetinghouses.[13]

Additionally, Mormons believe that the temples themselves are watched by angels; and that no unworthy person (even if he or she holds a valid temple recommend) can enter. Either the human temple worker at the gate would be *"told by the Holy Ghost" to* refuse them entry or the angel would stop him or her. How much more so would these sentinels stand against the entry of those involved in actual evil rituals, unless they themselves were evil angels? Remember, Pace said that some of the perpetrators were actually temple workers!

In speaking of these Satanists, we are talking about *people who torture children and kill people!* If such perverts can pass undetected by all the protective power of the priesthood authority of the LDS Church and participate in their sacred Temple rites, then what good is there in such a blind and toothless Mormon priesthood?

Mormons quote Amos 3:7, "Surely the Lord God will do nothing, but he revealeth his secret unto his servants the prophets," to prove the truthfulness of the Church and the sure need for a living prophet. However, if even a tenth of Bishop Pace's accusations are true, not only has the Lord been doing things without revealing them to the LDS "prophets," but Satan has also been sliding a lot of evil by them.

Since virtually all the testimonies Pace has gathered are from adult survivors of SRA, this means that these practices have gone on in the LDS Church for at least a generation, if not multiple generations! Yet where were the "prophetic" warnings of these practices 20 years ago? The truth is obvious. These are prophets who do not prophecy in the name of the True God.

Preaching the Devil's Sermons

Another issue which has emerged through the publication of the Pace report is that many of the victims Pace interviewed became aware of the atrocities done to them through their attendance at the Temple. Participation in its rites triggered flashbacks of rites they took part in as children. This was only possible because the LDS Temple rituals were *virtually identical to* those rites being done by the Satanists! As Pace notes:

> I'm sorry to say that many of the victims have had their first flashbacks while attending the temple for the first time. *The occult along the Wasatch Front*

uses the doctrine of the Church to their advantage. For example, the verbiage and gestures are used in a ritualistic ceremony in a very debased and often bloody manner. *When the victim goes to the temple and hears the exact words, horrible memories are triggered.*[14]

But the theory *now* presented by the Mormons and their supporting media is that Satanists had infiltrated the LDS Church. These Satanists stole the rituals of the Temple and deliberately used them in a satanic, blasphemous fashion. Bishop Pace says:

The perpetrators are also living a dual life. Many are Temple recommend holders. This leads to why the Church needs to consider the seriousness of these problems. In effect, the Church is being used.[15]

However, it seems to me that it is difficult for Mormons to say that their most sacred rituals have been blasphemed when they are already so blasphemous that Satanists can use the exact words used in ceremonies, word for word!

It has been long known that the LDS temple rituals were full of occult and satanic symbolism. Many of those portions in "The God Makers" and "Temple of the God Makers" movies are the very same portions subsequently quietly removed from the Temple ritual. Some of those elements had been present in witchcraft and Freemasonry long before Joseph Smith was born!

Whether these modern Satanists and witches stole the rites from the LDS temple (as the Pace report and others suggest) or whether both the Satanists and the Mormons were using portions of the same ceremonies separately cannot be proven. The same core of spiritual evil permeates both. However, along the Wasatch Front, most likely the numerous LDS Temple recommend holders, who have been among the perpetrators, brought much of the temple ritual into the more enlightened liturgy of the dark arts. If this is the case, as Pace suggests, and the LDS Temple ceremonies can be that easily and effortless adapted to witchcraft and Satanism so that the victim "goes to the Temple and hears the exact words...," it plainly shows that the Mormon Temple rituals are already replete with dark, pagan and anti-biblical elements.

According to what we read into the Pace report, the rituals apparently only need minor tinkering to be completely compatible with diabolical theology! As my friend Jim Spencer has said, *"When the devil starts preaching my sermons, I'd better start asking myself where I am getting my material."*

Do You Think We'll Get an Apology?

Since Jeremiah Films and Saints Alive began speaking out on these issues of the occult and satanic core elements in

Mormonism, both have been the targets of steady and severe criticism, not only from Mormons, but also from several other ministries. I have been accused of being psychotic or out of touch with reality for speaking out about the satanic roots of Temple Mormonism.[16]

Jim Spencer and Bill Schnoebelen have had their reputations slandered and their ministries attacked. Bill, as a former Satanist and Temple Mormon, was singled out. Everything possible was done to destroy his testimony of having been a witch who was told to join the LDS Church by high-level witches because it was essentially a safe organization for witches. As early as 1986, he warned about the strong correlations between the Temple rites and occult ceremonials.[17]

These attacks have cost each a great deal! Many people chose to believe what was being said and no longer supported the ministries involved in the revelation of the Satanic tie-ins between Mormonism and Satanism. Yet I chose not to respond publicly, because I felt the Lord did not call me to fight publicly with other ministries, however hurt and justified I felt in the flesh. Bill and I did respond with answers privately, but that only fueled the fires of criticism, and the attacks just continued.[18]

Each of the "accused" quietly but firmly held to our position. Now LDS leaders and news media are speaking openly of the same satanic conspiracy within Mormonism, and I wonder if we will hear any apologies from those who attacked us. Ironically, one ministry that was at the forefront of the attacks over our penchant for seeing devils everywhere was the one to first publish the Pace report, and for that we are grateful. Certainly, these reports have vindicated our position in the strongest possible way on the satanic strongholds within Mormonism.

Ultimately, whether Satanism abused the safe haven of Mormonism or Joseph Smith borrowed freely from Freemasonry, the occult and Witchcraft (or Abrac), the larger point is that the very fact that *all of these religions are tributaries of the same satanic river!*

It should be a cause of deep concern to every Mormon that witches and Satanists can blend so seamlessly and effortlessly into their Church! It should cause their hair to stand on end to realize that Joseph Smith was openly involved in Freemasonry and Witchcraft at the *very same time he revealed the temple rituals.*

It should be even more alarming that Satanists have been freely moving about in the most sacred precincts of its temples, all these years. Since there has never been any statement from The Brethren concerning a purge of these pagans, it should terrify the Mormons that these vile creatures are still moving freely among the faithful, watching over the Saints with the evil, roaming eyes of hungry wolves.

The Brethren would do well to spend a little more time using their revelatory powers and openly casting out the satanic element in the Church and a little less time worrying about the Home Schoolers and Bo Gritz groupies. The truth is they won't because they can't.

The Juggernaut of Sin!

The alleged multi-generational character of these satanic groups within Mormonism brings into stark relief the broader problem within the LDS Church—the sin problem!

Mormonism denies the Biblical doctrine of original sin. Mormons do not believe the Bible when it says *"...all have sinned, and come short of the glory of God"* (Romans 3:23), or *"There is none righteous, no, not one"* (Romans 3:10). They refuse to accept the words of the Psalmist when he declared; *"Behold, I was shaped in iniquity, and in sin did my mother conceive me"* (Psalm 51:5).

Mormons, in keeping with today's prevalent New Age worldview, would prefer to think that humanity is essentially good. This same philosophy is the foundation of all Eastern mysticism. They do not believe the Word of God which teaches us the painful truth that *"the heart is deceitful above all things, and desperately wicked: who can know it?"* (Jeremiah 17:9) They have departed from the revealed Truth of God! Therefore, they cannot understand nor appreciate the enormity of the deep sin in their own lives, nor in the lives of their fellow men and women.

Because of this, the Mormons begin with a faulty premise. They believe that they can, through an effort of personal human will, achieve victory over the sin in their lives—without the blood or the cross of Jesus Christ.

The late Dr. David Breese was the President of Christian Destiny and a renowned author of many books, including the best-selling *Know the Marks of a Cult*. In his interview with Jeremiah Films, he responded to this type of anti-biblical teaching.

The Bible says, "Not by works of righteousness which we have done, but according to His mercy He saves us" (Titus 3:5). How then are we saved? On what basis do we go to heaven? When you believe that Jesus Christ is the Son of God, that He died for your sins on Calvary's cross, and that sacrifice is the sufficient payment for your sins, you are instantly and eternally saved, by the grace of God.[19]

Mormons have turned their backs on the only solution to sin which God provides. They do not understand that in their lives, as in the lives of all unregenerate people (people who have not been born again), there is spiritual *entropy* at work.

Entropy is the thermodynamic law which states that all elements tend to break down and degenerate over time. If anything, this is even truer in the spiritual sense than in the natural. Sin nature—whether in a person, family, or institution—just doesn't get better. Over the years it tends to get worse, unless the completed works of the cross and the blood of Jesus Christ are applied. As the drug addict needs more and more of a dose each time to reach that *power edge* of the experience, so also does the sinner need to reach deeper into sin to attain that same power edge of the sin nature.

Anyone formerly entrapped in sin, whether it is drugs, drunkenness, fornication, pornography or false religion, will readily testify to the implacable power of that particular sin over his or her life! It is a downward spiral of evil that can even spread into their children and grandchildren. It is a spiral from which they were powerless to escape without the grace of Jesus Christ.

The sin problem in the LDS Church and in the lives of individual Mormons cannot *ever* get better until the Church corporately and Mormons individually repent of their idolatry and come to the cross.

Mormons involved in the occult practices found in the standard LDS Temple rites are dabbling in true occult rituals. No wonder they can be drawn in such numbers into the deeper, darker practices described in the Pace report.

You can look back a century and a half and see Joseph Smith practicing necromancy and fornicating with underage girls, committing wholesale adultery. You should not then be surprised to find his spiritual descendants trapped in the same and even worse forms of sin. If Joseph practiced sorcery and animal sacrifice, why should you be shocked if some Mormons today practice sorcery and human sacrifice, as the Pace report documented?

Only people who have come to terms with their own sin nature could be apologetic about the growing momentum of evil growing within the LDS Church. The response of The Brethren has been to turn Bishop Pace into an invisible man and act like nothing was out of balance in having hundreds of Satanists running around the heart of Utah and the Church.

The Mormons are simply following in the footsteps of their "prophets." It is a path of destruction from which they must flee for their very lives. The Bible leaps out in this matter. *"For the leaders of this people cause them to err; and they that are led of them are destroyed."* (Isaiah 9:16)

In the words of Jeremiah, *"For my people have committed two evils; they have forsaken me the fountain of living waters, and hewed them out cisterns, broken cisterns, that can hold no water"* (Jeremiah 2:13).

As Mormon As the Tabernacle Choir

These sins that have come to light are just the logical progression of the chain of events started by Joseph Smith and Brigham Young. Many LDS apologists and even a few in ministries to the Mormons want to portray these alleged crimes as a bizarre aberration. They present it as the result of evil devil worshippers somehow sneaking in and infiltrating the noble LDS Church. Yet, the spiritual reality is that the Mormon people are hopelessly trapped in an increasingly tangled web of occultism and sin.

Looking at the historic precedents set by Joseph the adulterer and sorcerer and Brigham the murderous "Blood

Atoner," one can say that such crimes are as typically Mormon as the Tabernacle Choir. They are just a side of Mormonism, which has been hidden from public view until the story broke through the veil of secrecy. It's a side that, until now, very few people could see and, if The Brethren have their way, will quickly be hidden away as though it never existed. In the years since the Pace report broke out, both Pace and his revelation of corporate iniquity have all but passed into oblivion. The silence of The Brethren has overshadowed the cries of the victims. This ostrich approach has worked time and time again, and has, for the most part, worked again. The scriptures tell us that:

> *...if our gospel be hid, it is hid to them that are lost: In whom the god of this world hath blinded the minds of them which believe not, lest the light of the glorious gospel of Christ, who is the image of God, should shine unto them.* (2 Corinthians 4:3-4)

There is no doubt in our minds but that the god of the Mormon Temple ritual, the god that requires the swearing of bloody oaths, the god whose most sacred rituals are done in secret, the god whose solemn rites are clearly tied to the occult, is that same god who has blinded the minds of the unbelievers who enter those Temple doors.

The only hope for Mormonism is Jesus Christ, God come in the flesh. I praise God that many thousands of Mormons continue to be set free from the power of the priestcraft that controls the Mormon Church and its downward spiral of evil. I praise God that these things of darkness have been exposed to the light of truth. We need to pray that these new revelations will cause many more sincere LDS people to begin to question the roots of their faith and look to Christ instead of Joseph Smith!

Happy Halloween!

While the inner circle of the LDS people and leaders who are enlightened by the power of the occult operate their craft within the shadows of the "Holy of Holies," the regular, unenlightened ones, in the outer courts of the local wards, are given the taste of the occult once a year in the gala festivals of the Halloween night.

In an October 24, 2006, email from LDS Living/Desert Books, they featured the book, *Halloween Family Traditions* by Kimberly Bytheway and Diane H. Loveridge, which promised that:

There's something exciting and even liberating about dressing up, playing games, and eating sweets on this favorite holiday! When we celebrate the time as a family, we learn that sharing that fun and excitement brings us closer together. It's a perfect time to create memories!

I remember the excitement at the local ward level as Halloween approached. One year I played an evil demon in one of the many Sunday School rooms being used to give the kids a good scare.

The Masons talk about the Blue Lodge being the outer court from where the more open members would be recruited to go higher up into the great mysteries of the craft.

Now I can see that Halloween, as a church-sanctioned activity was an open door to new recruits and victims for the many Satanists among the flock. Someone once said, *"The Devil is in the details."* Well, the devil surely is there on Halloween night at your local LDS church.

Run, Don't Walk

I said it clearly and boldly in Salt Lake City in 1987. Let me say it clearly again!

The god of Mormonism is Lucifer (the elder brother of the Mormon Jesus), the instructor of eternal truth for Adam and Eve in the LDS Temple ritual itself.

Dear, dear Mormon people, flee for your very lives from this evil thing!

CHAPTER TWELVE

The Mormon Plan for America and The Rise of Mitt Romney The Man Who Would Be God

The very ethos of the Mormon faith is built around the anticipated return of Jesus to Independence, Missouri, for his thousand-year millennial reign. It is here that he will assign godhood to the worthy. However, it cannot take place until the U.S. Constitution falters and is saved by the LDS church. The nation will become a Mormon theocracy. Mitt Romney has raised Mormon speculation that this may be the time and that he may be the one to lead the way as both U.S. President and LDS high priest.

Almost 30 years ago, the late BYU Professor and LDS author Cleon Skousen founded the Freemen Institute (later to be called The National Center for Constitutional Studies). The name came from *The Book of Mormon*.

> And those who were desirous that Pahoran should remain chief judge over the land took upon them the name of freemen; and thus was the division among them, for the freemen had sworn or covenanted to maintain their rights and the privileges of their religion by a free government. (Alma 51:6-7)

Skousen joined forces with Jerry Falwell's Moral Majority on some major political issues in the late 70s and early 80s, and I was prompted to study out both the public, and the LDS insiders, positions on government, the U.S. that the LDS Church says is a divine document constitution. Using that research, I produced a study called "The Mormon Plan for America."

When George Romney, Mitt's father, made his aborted run for President in 1968, there was a lot of internal LDS talk about prophecies of the last days when the U.S. Constitution would hang by a thread to be saved by the elders of the LDS church. Many felt that the day had finally arrived for the actual "Kingdom of God" to be established.

This pure form of theocratic, prophet-led government would prepare the way for the ushering in of the Millennium, the time when Jesus would return to earth, sit in his temple in Missouri to reign over the earth, with the center of His government operated as the "Kingdom of God" on earth.

The actual background for all these whispered conversations came from much of the historical documents of the church and the speeches of many of the early church authorities. They are being resurrected again, and gaining momentum as his son Mitt appears to be in line for the next GOP candidate for the presidency.

The prophetic plan for an American theocracy goes something like this: Joseph Smith implemented a program called the United Order in the church. It was a plan of sharing everything in common—all properties and wealth turned over and owned by the church and dispersed by the Brethren to the people on an as-needed basis with a requirement for good stewardship or loss of use.

The Kingdom of God

It was called the "Kingdom of God." It was people living as God ordained under the United Order. However, it failed. It was later determined that it could only work when both the secular and ecclesiastic functions operated under one authority, with an LDS prophet ruling over a theocratic government where eternal commandments like the United Order and plural marriage and blood atonement would function within "The Kingdom of God."

That Theocracy would come into existence when the U.S. Constitution would hang by a thread and the Mormon elders would be there to save it and the country, thereby ushering in The Kingdom of God, the prophesied Mormon theocracy.

On December 7, 1968, Elder Hugh B. Brown presided over the groundbreaking of the LDS Washington D.C. Temple. It was dedicated in November 1974 by the prophet, Spencer W. Kimball.

The unique thing about this temple *that struck me as singularly important* was the design and furnishing of a large room on the upper floor. A photograph of this room is in the film, "The God Makers." It was set to house a presiding governing body, led by the prophet.

It is my own personal belief that it was designed as the place where the theocratic government of God would conduct its business, with the prophet in His place of authority.

Now we jump ahead 40 years to 2007…and the 2008 Presidential election. A whole generation has passed, and the son of George Romney has risen to the top of the list of Mormons who would qualify to take that run at the Oval Office and perhaps be in the right place as President or Vice President as the Constitution hangs by that foretold thread… and be there to call upon the elders (The Brethren) to save the nation and soon usher in the "Kingdom of God."

Far fetched? I would agree that I sound like a man shouting fire in a theatre, but, as you will read, I am talking about valid LDS end-times teachings.

You will also see that Mitt Romney has been raised and trained for this day. His family has been in the church for generations. He is the great grandson of polygamists Gaskell Romney and Anna Amelia Pratt.[1] He wears every credential, has held almost every office, and holds both the Aaronic and Melchizedek priesthoods.

The Candidate with the Real God Complex

Mitt Romney is a Temple Mormon, a High Priest, and as such, he has sworn blood oaths of sacrifice, obedience and consecration to the church and the "Kingdom of God." His perfect obedience to these laws will allow him to become a god in the next life, the literal father of the peoples of a new and different earth. He is truly a Presidential candidate with an actual, definable god complex.

On February 12, 2007, as Mitt Romney announced that he would run for the office of President, he commented in a *USA Today*, article, "Will Mormon faith hurt bid for White House?" by Jill Lawrence:

> It is not his job as a presidential candidate to educate people about his church. "I'm running for a secular position," he said in an interview. "I subscribe to what Abraham Lincoln called America's political religion. The Constitution and the rule of law are the highest promises I would make in taking the oath of office."

Mitt Romney's LDS understanding of the U.S. Constitution and its divine role in the end times is not that of the average American.

Mitt Romney is a nice-looking man, successful in the business world, with core values of family, church and faith. He does not smoke, drink or even touch coffee or tea. He has been married to the same woman for decades. He seems like the cure for dealing with the corruption of our national leadership. What could possibly be wrong in having such a man as our President? Let's look at some of the reasons his presidency could be the end of America as we know it.

I recently searched through my files and have resurrected and updated a research paper, "The Mormon Plan for America." That information is part of what I share below.

Some Extremely Grave Questions

Let me re-introduce you to a portion of one chapter in my book, *The God Makers*, co-authored with Dave Hunt.[2] It is a part of Chapter 16: "The Hidden Kingdom." *I suggest that you buy the book and read the entire story. It will shock you even more than what I will reveal here.*

> It is a hidden kingdom that lurks beneath the placid surface of public Mormonism. It is this LDS "Kingdom of God" that former Governor Mitt Romney has sworn blood oaths of obedience to in

the LDS Temple ritual. The Late Apostle and LDS theologian, elder Bruce R. McConkie, described the Mormon temples as *"holy sanctuaries wherein sacred ordinances, rites, and ceremonies are performed which pertain to salvation and exaltation in the kingdom of God....*

There are several purposes to be achieved in the temple by worthy Mormons. First, they learn the secret/sacred signs, tokens, handshakes necessary to pass by the sentinels and enter the Celestial glory where they will become gods and goddesses and people new earths like this one.

Second, they receive sacred undergarments to wear for their protection while on earth, a secret new name by which they will be called from the grave and then swear obedience to certain laws that will govern their membership, obedience to the prophet and their behavior while on earth. Their sacred undergarments are marked with secret talismanic symbols that he believes will keep him protected as he works his way to godhood. *These are the very same markings that Lucifer claims in the LDS Temple ritual are the emblems of his, Lucifer's, power and priesthood.*

Mitt Romney's temple experience was no different than this when he first received his "endowments" in preparation for his service as an LDS Missionary. From his secret name to his blood oaths and sacred garments with Lucifer's marks sewn in, his temple experiences have been the path he has chosen in his quest for godhood.

The Law of Sacrifice

One of several temple oaths was Romney's oath of Obedience to the Law of Sacrifice, in which he vowed:

As Jesus Christ has laid down his life for the redemption of mankind, so we should covenant to sacrifice all that we [I] possess, even our [my] own lives [life] if necessary, in sustaining and defending the Kingdom of God.[3]

The "execution of the penalty" for disobedience at the time Mitt Romney took out his "temple Endowments" was demonstrated by:

...placing the thumb under the left ear, the palm of the hand down, and by drawing the thumb quickly across the throat to the right ear, and dropping the hand to the side.[4]

It is hard to imagine that well-educated Mormon men of such political stature like former Massachusetts Gov. Mitt Romney, Utah Senator Orrin Hatch of Utah, or Senator Harry

Reid of Nevada could bring their thumbs to their throats and swear a blood oath that they will "suffer" their throats slit from ear to ear should they not "sacrifice all that [they] possess, even [their] own lives if necessary, in sustaining and defending the Kingdom of God, as defined by the Mormon prophet.

These LDS oaths are taken directly from the rituals of Blue Lodge Masonry, the source of much of the LDS Temple rituals. It is no wonder, since the first five presidents and prophets of the LDS church were Masons.

These high-level Temple Mormons clearly know that this Mormon "Kingdom of God" is, in reality, a Mormon one-world government, a theocracy, soon coming to America, that will be run by the strong arm of the Mormon Brethren, headed up by the only true prophet of God on earth. It is clear that they did swear such an oath.

The Law of Consecration

The other significant oath Mitt Romney has sworn to obey is the Law of Consecration. In the LDS temple ritual, the officiator says to the temple "patrons":

We are instructed to give unto you the Law of Consecration as contained in the book of Doctrine and Covenants, in connection with the Law of the Gospel and the Law of Sacrifice which you have already received. It is that you do consecrate yourselves, your time, talents and everything which the Lord has blessed you, or with which he may bless you, to the Church of Jesus Christ of Latter-day Saints, for the building up of the Kingdom of God on the earth and for the establishment of Zion.

All arise. *(All patrons stand.)* Each of you bring your right arm to the square.

You and each of you covenant and promise before God, angels, and these witnesses at this altar, that you do accept the Law of Consecration as contained in the Doctrine and Covenants, in that you do consecrate yourselves, your time, talents, and everything with which the Lord has blessed you, or with which he may bless you, to the Church of Jesus Christ of Latter-day Saints, for the building up of the Kingdom of God on the earth and for the establishment of Zion.

Each of you bow your head and say "yes."
PATRONS: Yes.

Now we can see and understand the spiritual positioning of elder Mitt Romney beginning on that first day and reinforced with every temple visit thereafter until it has been ground into his very DNA.

Let's go back to Chapter 16 of my book, *The God Makers*.

Secrets of the Hidden Kingdom

Mormon leaders call their empire the "Kingdom of God." However, their "God" is an extraterrestrial from Kolob, definitely *not* the God of the Bible; and the "Zion" to which their spirit-brother-of-Lucifer Jesus Christ will return to reign is Independence, Missouri.

Most Christians believe, as the Bible declares, that Christ will return to Jerusalem, Israel, to establish His millennial kingdom, whereas Mormons believe that they must establish a worldwide Mormon kingdom dictated from their Missouri base in order to make it possible for Christ to return.

Therein lies a great difference, which is why the Mormon hierarchy, beginning with Joseph Smith himself, has always had worldwide and absolute political power as its goal.

Mormon historian Klaus J. Hansen has written:

The idea of a political kingdom of God, promulgated by a secret Council of Fifty, is by far the most important key to an understanding of the Mormon past.[5]

Mormon writer John J. Stewart has said:

The Prophet established a confidential Council of Fifty, or "Ytfif," (Fifty spelled backwards), comprised of both Mormons and non-Mormons, to help attend to temporal matters, including the eventual development of a one-world government, in harmony with preparatory plans for the second advent of the Saviour.[6]

Let's jump again to the section called: "Some Extremely Grave Questions":

Mormonism seems as American as apple pie, and Mormons seem to be the perfect citizens with their close families, high morals, patriotism, Boy Scout programs, Tabernacle Choir, and conservative politics. A *Los Angeles Times* article implied that Mormons have recently gained the image of "super-Americans... [who] appear to many to be 'more American than the average American.'"[7]

This may explain why such a high proportion of Mormons find their way into government. Returned LDS missionaries have "the three qualities the CIA wants: foreign language ability, training in a foreign country, and former residence in a foreign country."[8] Utah (and particularly BYU) is one of the prime recruiting areas for the CIA. According to BYU spokesman Dr. Gary Williams, "We've never had any trouble placing anyone who has applied to the CIA. Every year they take almost anybody who applies."[9]

He also admitted that this has created problems with a number of foreign countries, who have complained about the "pretty good dose of [Mormon] missionaries who've gone back to the countries they were in as Central Intelligence agents."[10]

This may at least partially explain the reported close tie between the Mormon Church and the CIA.[11] A disproportionate number of Mormons arrive at the higher levels of the CIA, FBI, military intelligence, armed forces, and all levels of city, state, and federal governments, including the Senate, Congress, Cabinet, and White House Staff. Sincere and loyal citizens, most of them may be unaware of the secret ambition of The Brethren. What could be better than having such patriots as these serving in strategic areas of government and national security?

Unfortunately, as we have noticed in every other area of Mormonism, the real truth lies hidden beneath the seemingly ideal image of patriotism presented by Mormons in public service. In fact their very presence in responsible government positions, particularly in agencies dealing with national security, raises some extremely serious questions that were expressed in my following letter mailed to the LDS Brethren in

Salt Lake City. I also published it as an open letter in *The Salt Lake Tribune*.

The Mormon Oath of Vengeance Against This Nation

An open letter to:

The President, First Presidency and members of the General Authorities of the Church of Jesus Christ of Latter-day Saints.
August 21, 1980

Gentlemen:

    I was recently reflecting that although the actual blood oath and the oath of vengeance were removed from the Temple ceremonies sometime after 1930, you gentlemen [listing ten of the above] are of an age to have received your own endowments prior to their removal, and therefore, are still under these oaths.

    I am particularly interested in your personal position on your oath of vengeance against the United States of America. As you recall, the oath was basically as follows:

You and each of you do solemnly promise and vow that you will pray and never cease to importune high heaven to AVENGE THE BLOOD OF THE PROPHETS (Joseph and Hiram Smith) ON THIS NATION, and that you will teach this to your children and your children's children unto the third and fourth generation.

Have you officially renounced this oath? Or are you still bound by it?

If you have not renounced it, how can you presume to lead four-and-one-half [now over six and a half million Americans] million people [US citizens] under item 12 of your Articles of Faith and still be bound to call upon heaven to heap curses upon our nation? ("We believe in being subject to Kings, Presidents, Rulers and Magistrates, in obeying, honoring, and sustaining the law.")

If you have renounced it, how can you justify having sworn such an oath in the most holy of holy places on this earth, before the sacred altar of your omnipotent God, and then renounce it? Gentlemen, I call upon you to repent of this abomination and proclaim to both the Mormon people and to the people of the United States of America that you renounce that oath and all it represents.

I also call upon all members of the Mormon Church who hold office in our government, serve in the Armed Services, work for the FBI and CIA who have gone through the Mormon Temple and sworn oaths of obedience and sacrifice to the church and its leaders (above), to repent of these oaths in the light of the obvious conflict of interest between their pledge of allegiance to the USA and their higher loyalty to a group of men who are sworn to seek vengeance against this great nation.

Sincerely,
(Signed) J. Edward Decker
cc: President J. Carter, Mr. Ronald Reagan

No response was received to this letter. The Brethren are so powerful that they are immune to criticism and feel no need to explain themselves or account to anyone for these actions. The Mormon Church already packs a political punch far out of proportion to its size. *The Wall Street Journal* explained how, in spite of the Constitution separation between Church and State, public schools in Utah are used to instill Mormonism in young minds.

It mentioned political reapportionment, airline deregulation, the basing of the MX missile and the ERA as political issues affected by the power of the Church. For example, when the Church opposed the MX for Utah, those plans were immediately dropped by the federal government. The same *Wall Street Journal* article quoted the following statement from J.D. Williams, a University of Utah political science professor:

> *There is a disquieting statement in Mormonism: "When the leaders have spoken, the thinking has been done." To me, democracy can't thrive in that climate. They [Mormon politicians] don't have to be called to Church headquarters for political instruction. They know what they're supposed to do. That's why non-Mormons can only look toward the Mormon Church and wonder: "What is Big Brother doing to me today?"[12]*

The following is from another section in <u>The God Makers</u>:

A Disturbing Possibility:

[Will It Be the Christians Who Put Romney in Office?]
While the election of a Mormon President seems unlikely, it is highly probable under the present swing toward conventional morality and conservatism that a Mormon could one day become at least a Republican Vice-Presidential nominee. Yet, Romney's increasing

financial support and his headlining poll figures have him looking straight at the Oval Office.

This is especially true when one considers the growing cooperating between Mormons and Christian leaders like [the now deceased] Jerry Falwell and groups like the Moral Majority. With the power, wealth, wide influence, numerous highly-placed Mormons, and large voting block under their virtual control, The Brethren have a great deal to offer a Republican Presidential candidate. Let's assume that a Mormon Vice-Presidential candidate is on the winning ticket, and thereafter the President dies in office or is assassinated, causing the Mormon to succeed him as President of the United States.

As an aside to what I wrote in *The God Makers*, It drives me into a state of severe disbelief and utter frustration to see so many Christian leaders leaping into the Mitt Romney camp. Pat Robertson, who had him as the main speaker at Regent University graduation this year, Jay Sekulow, head of the ACLJ, endorsed Romney and said that Romney would appoint constructionist judges, and that he (Sekulow) had the opportunity to observe Romney and know that he is for real.

Lou Sheldon, a well-known evangelical Presbyterian minister and conservative lobbyist in Washington, is endorsing former Massachusetts Governor Mitt Romney for the 2008 Republican presidential nomination. Sheldon, the outspoken chairman of the Traditional Values Coalition, has agreed to serve as one of the co-chairs of the "Romney for President Faith and Values Steering Committee."

Mark DeMoss is president of the DeMoss Group (an Atlanta-based public relations firm that works primarily with evangelical organizations) and the author of *The Little Red Book of Wisdom*. He also has endorsed Gov. Romney for President of the United States. DeMoss has become a national, unpaid emissary for Romney, making his case before Southern Baptists and other evangelicals. He organized an introductory meeting last October that included Jerry Falwell and Franklin Graham. Last month, he put Romney in front of 100 attendees at the National Religious Broadcasters convention in Orlando.

Continued from *The God Makers*:

> There is every reason to believe that the new President would immediately begin to gather around him increasing numbers of zealous Temple Mormons in strategic places at the highest levels of government. A crisis similar to the one which Mormon prophecies "foretold" occurs, in which millions of Mormons with their year's supply of food, guns, and ammunition play a key role. It would be a time of excitement and zealous effort by the "Saints" to fulfill Joseph Smith's and Brigham Young's "prophecy":

The time will come when the destiny of the nation will hang upon a single thread. At that critical juncture, this people will step forth and save it from the threatened destruction.[13]

Not only does Mormonism predict the "saving" of America, but the precedent for an attempted takeover by force or subterfuge through political means has been set by the founding "Prophet" himself. In 1834 Joseph Smith organized an army and marched toward Independence, Missouri, to "redeem Zion." In spite of a humiliating surrender to the Missouri Militia that proved his bold "Prophecies" false, the "Prophet" later formed the "Nauvoo Legion" and commissioned himself a Lieutenant-General to command it. Lyman L. Woods stated:

I have seen him on a white horse wearing the uniform of a general....

He was leading a parade of the Legion and looked like a god.[14]

Joseph Smith was not only ordained King on earth, but he ran for President of the United States just before his death, at which time Mormon missionaries across the country became "a vast force of political [power]."[15] Today's Church leaders are urging Mormons to prepare themselves for the coming crisis in order to succeed where past "Saints" have failed. A major article in the LDS *Ensign* magazine about being prepared included this oft-repeated warning reminder:

The commandment to reestablish Zion became for the Saints of Joseph Smith's day the central goal of the church. But it was a goal the Church did not realize because its people were not fully prepared.[16]

Going back to our hypothetical crisis, what Mormons unsuccessfully attempted against impossible odds in the past, they might very well accomplish with much better odds in this future scenario. Under cover of the national and international crisis, the Mormon President of the United States acts boldly and decisively to assume dictatorial powers. With the help of The Brethren and Mormons everywhere, he appears to save America and becomes a national hero. At this time he is made Prophet and President of the Church of Jesus Christ of Latter-day Saints and the Mormon Kingdom of God, while still President of the United States. There is no provision in the Constitution to prevent this.

With the government largely in the hands of increasing numbers of Mormon [and Masonic] appointees at all levels throughout the United States, the Constitutional prohibition against the establishment of a state church would no longer be enforceable. Mormon prophecies and the curse upon the United States government in revenge for the blood of Joseph and Hyrum Smith would seemingly have been fulfilled. In effect, the United States would have become a theocracy exactly as planned by The Brethren, completing the first step in the Mormon takeover of the world. LDS President John Taylor boasted of it 100 years ago:

Let us now notice our political position in the world. What are we going to do? We are going to possess the earth... and reign over it for ever and ever. Now, ye Kings and Emperors help yourselves if you can. This is the truth and it may as well be told at this time as at any other. There's a good time coming, Saints, a good time coming![17]

A More Likely Scenario

While the above presents an extremely disturbing possibility, it may seem highly speculative and improbable. There is another scenario, however, which is equally disturbing and much more likely. It arises from the fact that Mormonism is actual part of something much larger.

We have already noted that the "revelations" that Joseph Smith received, far from being unique, were in fact very similar to the basic philosophy underlying many occult groups and secret revolutionary societies. Thus far in history, these numerous occult/

revolutionary organizations have remained largely separate and in competition with one another.

If something should happen to unite them, and at the same time their beliefs should gain worldwide acceptance, a new and unimaginably powerful force for world revolution would have come into existence. There is increasing evidence of a new and growing secular/religious ecumenism persuasive enough to accomplish this unprecedented and incalculably powerful coalition.

It could be the means of creating the one-world government that has not only been the long-standing hope and plan of The Brethren and many other occult/revolutionary leaders, but is increasingly gaining a wide acceptance through New Age networks as the only viable option to a nuclear holocaust and/or ecological collapse.[18]

Let's review this once more from the top before we thread Mitt Romney's bid for the Presidency into the mix.

The Holy Constitution

The Constitution will hang by a thread, to be saved by the Mormon Church.

Will the Constitution be destroyed? No, it will be held inviolate by this people; and, as Joseph Smith said, *"The time will come when the destiny of the nation will hang upon a single thread.* At that critical juncture, this people will step forth and save it from destruction." It will be so.[19]

And when the Constitution of the United States hangs, as it were, upon a single thread, they will have to call for the "Mormon" Elders to save it from utter destruction; and they will step forth and do it.[20]

We shall spread abroad, and the day shall will come – and this is another prediction of Joseph Smith's – I want to remind you of it, my brethren and sisters, *when good government, constitutional government, liberty will be found among the Latter-day Saints, and it will be sought for in vain elsewhere.... The day will come when the constitution and free government under it will be sustained and preserved by this people.*[21]

The Mormons will usher in a Theocracy, or "The Kingdom of God," directed by the Lord's Prophet (LDS).

With the restoration of the gospel and the setting up of the ecclesiastical Kingdom of God, the restoration of the true government of God commenced. Through this church and Kingdom, a framework has been built through which the full government of God will eventually operate.... The present ecclesiastical kingdom will be expanded into a political kingdom also, and then both civil and ecclesiastical affairs will be administered through it.[22]

Brigham Young confirmed that when the LDS Kingdom of God was in control, the American flag would fly above us.

> When the day comes in which the Kingdom of God will bear rule, the flag of the United States will proudly flutter unsullied on the flag staff of liberty and equal rights, without a spot to sully its fair surface; the glorious flag our fathers have bequeathed to us will then be unfurled to the breeze by those who have power to hoist it aloft and defend its sanctity.[23]

The Mormons will possess the whole earth and reign over it. As the Civil and Religious laws become one, the "United Order" will become the "Kingdom of God."

> *VERILY I say unto you, my friends, I give unto you counsel, and a commandment, concerning all the properties which belong to the order which I*

commanded to be organized and established, to be a united order, and an everlasting order for the benefit of my church, and for the salvation of men until I come—[24]

The poor will be exalted and the rich made low. All property, including liquid assets, will be deeded to the "kingdom" (Church), all money turned in. Some property will be conditionally "deeded" back for us to "manage" as is deemed necessary for each man.

This is spelled out in the *Doctrine & Covenants* 42:

28 Thou knowest my laws concerning these things are given in my scriptures; he that sinneth and repenteth not shall be cast out.

29 If thou lovest me thou shalt serve me and keep all my commandments.

30 And behold, thou wilt remember the poor, and consecrate of thy properties for their support that which thou hast to impart unto them, with a covenant and a deed which cannot be broken.

31 And inasmuch as ye impart of your substance unto the poor, ye will do it unto me; and they shall be laid before the bishop of my church and his counselors, two of the elders, or high priests, such as he shall appoint or has appointed and set apart for that purpose.

32 And it shall come to pass, that after they are laid before the bishop of my church, and after that he has received these testimonies concerning the consecration of the properties of my church, that they cannot be taken from the church, agreeable to my commandments, every man shall be made accountable unto me, a steward over his own property, or that which he has received by consecration, as much as is sufficient for himself and family.

33 And again, if there shall be properties in the hands of the church, or any individuals of it, more than is necessary for their support after this first consecration, which is a residue to be consecrated unto the bishop, it shall be kept to administer to those who have not, from time to time, that every man who has need may be amply supplied and receive according to his wants.

34 Therefore, the residue shall be kept in my storehouse, to administer to the poor and the needy, as shall be appointed by the high council of the church, and the bishop and his council....

If a man shall transgress this law, it shall ALL be taken from him, without recourse. *All* this is for the benefit of the Church. He who sins against this shall be cursed and delivered over to Satan. Lands shall be gotten by purchase or by blood when there is a problem in obtaining it. Every Mormon in the world swears an oath of obedience to the Law of Consecration and the Law of Sacrifice...in the Temple rites. They are bound by blood oath to honor their word.

Let's look at the portion of the Revelation, *Doctrines & Covenants* 104, given to Joseph Smith the Prophet, April 23, 1834, concerning the United Order, which set this in its spiritual place:

> *1 VERILY I say unto you, my friends, I give unto you counsel, and a commandment, concerning all the properties which belong to the order which I commanded to be organized and established, to be a united order, and an everlasting order for the benefit of my church, and for the salvation of men until I come—*
>
> *2 With promise immutable and unchangeable, that inasmuch as those whom I commanded were faithful they should be blessed with a multiplicity of blessings;*
>
> *3 But inasmuch as they were not faithful they were nigh unto cursing.*
>
> *4 Therefore, inasmuch as some of my servants have not kept the commandment, but have broken the covenant through covetousness, and with feigned words, I have cursed them with a very sore and grievous curse.*

5 For I, the Lord, have decreed in my heart, that inasmuch as any man belonging to the order shall be found a transgressor, or, in other words, shall break the covenant with which ye are bound, he shall be cursed in his life, and shall be trodden down by whom I will;

6 For I, the Lord, am not to be mocked in these things—

7 And all this that the innocent among you may not be condemned with the unjust; and that the guilty among you may not escape; because I, the Lord, have promised unto you a crown of glory at my right hand.

8 Therefore, inasmuch as you are found transgressors, you cannot escape my wrath in your lives.

9 Inasmuch as ye are cut off for transgression, ye cannot escape the buffetings of Satan until the day of redemption.

10 And I now give unto you power from this very hour, that if any man among you, of the order, is found a transgressor and repenteth not of the evil, that ye shall deliver him over unto the buffetings of Satan; and he shall not have power to bring evil upon you.

11 It is wisdom in me; therefore, a commandment I give unto you, that ye shall organize yourselves and appoint every man his stewardship;

12 That every man may give an account unto me of the stewardship which is appointed unto him.

13 For it is expedient that I, the Lord, should make every man accountable, as a steward over earthly blessings, which I have made and prepared for my creatures.

14 I, the Lord, stretched out the heavens, and built the earth, my very handiwork; and all things therein are mine.

15 And it is my purpose to provide for my saints, for all things are mine.

16 But it must needs be done in mine own way; and behold this is the way that I, the Lord, have decreed to provide for my saints, that the poor shall be exalted, in that the rich are made low.

17 For the earth is full, and there is enough and to spare; yea, I prepared all things, and have given unto the children of men to be agents unto themselves.

18 Therefore, if any man shall take of the abundance which I have made, and impart not his portion, according to the law of my gospel, unto the poor and the needy, he shall, with the wicked, lift up his eyes in hell, being in torment.

Is Socialism the United Order?

In a speech by this title, given at the LDS April 1966, General Conference of the Church, Mormon Elder and one of the governing Brethren of the church, Marion G. Romney, of the Council of the Twelve Apostles [and an uncle to <u>Mitt Romney</u>] had this to say about this United Order that Joseph Smith claimed came directly from God for the administration of properties and possessions:

> Now as to the United Order, and here I will give the words of the Lord and not my words. The United Order, the Lord's program for eliminating the inequalities among men, is based upon the underlying concept that the earth and all things therein belong to the Lord and that men hold earthly possessions as stewards accountable to God.
> On January 2, 1831, the Lord revealed to the Prophet Joseph Smith that the Church was under obligation to care for the poor. (See *D& C* 38.) Later he said:
> "*I, the Lord, stretched out the heavens, and built the earth...and all things therein are mine. And it is my purpose to provide for my saints, for all things are mine. But it must needs be done in mine own way....*"[25]
> On February 9, 1831, the Lord revealed to the Prophet what his way was.[26] In his way there were

two cardinal principles: (1) consecration and (2) stewardship.

To enter the United Order, when it was being tried, one consecrated all his possessions to the Church by a *"covenant and a deed which" could not "be broken."*[27] That is, he completely divested himself of all of his property by conveying it to the Church.

Having thus voluntarily divested himself of title to all his property, the consecrator received from the Church a stewardship by a like conveyance. This stewardship could be more or less than his original consecration, the object being to make *"every man equal according to his family, according to his circumstances and his wants and needs."*[28]

This procedure preserved in every man the right to private ownership and management of his property. At his own option he could alienate it or keep and operate it and pass it on to his heirs.

The intent was, however, for him to so operate his property as to produce a living for himself and his dependents. So long as he remained in the order, he consecrated to the Church the surplus he produced above the needs and wants of his family. This surplus went into a storehouse from which stewardships were given to others and from which the needs of the poor were supplied.

These divine principles are very simple and easily understood. A comparison of them with the underlying principles of socialism reveal similarities and basic differences.

The following are similarities: Both (1) deal with production and distribution of goods; (2) aim to promote the well-being of men by eliminating their economic inequalities; (3) envision the elimination of the selfish motives in private capitalistic industrial system.

Now the differences: (1) The cornerstone of the United Order is belief in God and

acceptance of him as Lord of the earth and the author of the United Order. Socialism, wholly materialistic, is founded in the wisdom of men and not of God. Although all socialists may not be atheists, none of them in theory or practice seek the Lord to establish his righteousness. (2) The United Order is implemented by the voluntary free-will actions of men, evidenced by a consecration of all their property to the Church of God.

One time the Prophet Joseph Smith asked a question by the brethren about the inventories they were taking. His answer was to the effect, *"You don't need to be concerned about the inventories. Unless a man is willing to consecrate everything he has, he doesn't come into the United Order."*[29] On the other hand, socialism is implemented by external force, the power of the state.

What Have We Learned?

Basically, what we glean from Elder Marion Romney is that the United Order is a theocratic form of socialism. That, as a system, it can only operate properly under the Law of Consecration, as a function of the "Kingdom of God" as understood in the context of the authority of the only true church on earth—the Mormon Church.

Mitt Romney understands this as a function of his Mormon upbringing, training, BYU education, Temple worthiness and his LDS Priesthood [both Aaronic and Melchizedek, as an elder and High Priest].

He also is the nephew of the very General Authority and Apostle of the church, Marion Romney, who taught the doctrine from the pulpit to the entire church at the General Conference in 1966.

In his defense, I do not believe that Mitt Romney is overtly plotting such an LDS "New World Order." I am certain it is not even in the back of his mind as he runs for office. However, as you have clearly seen, it is in his spiritual DNA, in his blood, in his roots and in his temple obligations. He knows about it and avoids talking about it under any venue.

In a TV interview the weekend following his 2007 announcement, he said that

...his Mormon beliefs would not handicap his run for the Republican presidential nomination.

"I'm not running for pastor in chief," Romney told ABC News' "This Week with George Stephanopoulos" Sunday. "I'm running for commander in chief." The interview with the candidate and his wife Ann was videotaped earlier.[30]

In the announcement itself, Romney stated that the USA needed transformation.

> Mitt Romney wants transformation. How do we know? The former Massachusetts Republican governor used the word "transform" or a variant no fewer than 13 times in his presidential announcement Tuesday.... So when he said on Tuesday, "If there ever was a time when innovation and transformation were needed in government, it is now," Romney was accurately describing the need to overhaul the doddering status quo in health care, education and homeland security – just for starters.
>
> He was also correct when he added, "I do not believe Washington can be transformed from within by a lifelong politician."[31]

Yet, his Theocratic mindset reveals itself when he talks about some things. Recently, Romney said that the Hezbollah should be a role model for U.S. and urged emulating welfare projects used by terror group against Israel.

JERUSALEM – Republican presidential candidate Gov. Mitt Romney cited the social welfare network of the Lebanese Hezbollah terror group as a role model the U.S. should copy to help promote "goodness" and "freedom" around the world.

Sections of Hezbollah's social welfare network, including schools and camps, are routinely used by the terror group to indoctrinate students in anti-Israel propaganda, instruct in military tactics and promote Shiite Islamic beliefs, including the waging of a final, apocalyptic world battle against "evil."[32]

Remember, Mormonism Teaches That...

When our leaders speak, the thinking has been done. Satan gets a great victory when we disagree or "do our own thinking."[33]

The Church Prophet has the right to identify how the Lord would have us vote and who would dare disobey?

Now, does the office of the President of the Church embrace the right to identify for the whole membership of the church, and all the peoples of the world for that matter how the Lord would desire that we vote on certain matters? Certainly it does! Who would dare to proscribe God?[34]

> When the prophet speaks, the debate is over.[35]
>
> All LDS administration is done by direct Revelation from God.[36]
>
> When the Mormon leaders speak, we are to obey and believe, even if our scientific knowledge says otherwise.[37]
>
> God can (and often does) change his mind from revelation to revelation.
>
> > *That is modern revelation. May I repeat? Modern revelation is what President Joseph Smith said, unless [then] President Spencer W. Kimball says differently.*[38]
>
> If you are told by your leader to do a thing, DO IT! None of your business if it is right or wrong.[39]

LDS Prophet (from 1985 to 1994), Ezra T. Benson proclaimed:

a. The Prophet rightly should be in politics…after all, we do need God in Government.
b. The Prophet is above all humanity, above all scripture, above all the other prophets, above scientific knowledge and Must Be Obeyed.

Sometimes, in American politics, we are asked to focus more on the platform than the candidate, because we can trust the party and the candidate's advisors to keep the candidate on the "straight and narrow" as best they can.

In Mitt Romney's case, his oath of office has already been sworn in a sacred LDS Temple ceremony. That oath is to the Mormon Plan for America, and it will supersede any oath of office as President.

And it doesn't really matter in the LDS scheme of things if Mitt Romney does not make it to the Oval Office, or even the office of Vice President. This Mormon Plan for America has been in the shadows for over 160 years. The Brethren believe it is their birthright, their purpose, their destiny to usher in the purification of the earth for Christ's return.

They did not give up on the plan when Joseph Smith failed in his bid for the Presidency, nor did they give up when George Romney withdrew his bid. They will rejoice if Mitt makes it, but if not, they will merely look ahead to the one who *will* usher in the "Kingdom of God" in the soon coming future. Meanwhile, they will continue to prompt their people to file for every level of public office, to be ready when the wonderful fulfillment of prophecy comes.

CHAPTER THIRTEEN

The Cash-Cow Kingdom

The "Kingdom of God" has become a cash-cow kingdom. The where and the why of the great wealth.

Among the closely guarded mysteries about the LDS Church are its finances and its involvement in the secular business world. Though it is not well known, the fact is that the Church is among the wealthiest institutions in America. It has become a Cash-Cow Kingdom. The money just pours into the coffers of the men who are the *only true prophets and apostles of God*. The mandatory tithes of 10 percent of the faithfuls' gross incomes are just the tip of an immense iceberg.

Just how wealthy was a matter of conjecture until the 1985 publication of *The Mormon Corporate Empire* by John Heinerman (a prolific Mormon author) and Anson Shupe, an American sociologist who studies religious groups and the anti-cult movement. The book's information was not only credible, but staggering. The information was updated six years later by a series of four major articles in *The Arizona Republic* newspaper and again in an extensive featured article, "Kingdom Come," in *Time* magazine on August 4, 1997, and subtitled: "The Mormons' True Great Trek Has Been to Social Acceptance and a $30 Billion Church Empire."

A $30 Billion Church Empire

LDS leaders, who have not willingly released any financial data about their church's finances in decades, heavily opposed *The Arizona Republic* series' development. It is my understanding that as thorough as the articles were, they were still censored by pressure from The Brethren, and even the paper admits that there may be a great deal more to learn about some aspects of this ecclesiastical empire. *Time* magazine investigator David Van Biema met with similar reluctance to share any financial information regarding the sacred, inner empire of Mormonism.

The Arizona Republic series, "Mormon, Inc., Finances and Faith," provided a rare and very comprehensive breakdown of the Church's finances and acquisitions.

A Fortune 500 Church?

The articles conservatively estimated that at the time of the 1991 report, the LDS Church collected about 4.3 billion a year through tithing, plus $400 million from its many *ecclesiastical* (church-related) enterprises. That comes out in tithing receipts alone, to *$11,780,822 a day!*

According to the August 1997 *Time* article, "Kingdom Come," they had, by then, reached 5.2 billion, or over *14 million dollars a day.* I would assume that with the growth of the church, by 2007, it is now well over $16,000,000 a day.

A comparison of the 1991 Church's 4.7 billion tithing collections with the sales of publicly traded companies placed it 110th on the Fortune 500. Its revenues were larger than Maytag, Hershey Foods or Avon, and the church has a much lower "cost of sales" than any of the regular businesses. *It is selling personal exaltation and godhood.*

In 1991, the Church's *business* subsidiaries generated an additional $4 billion a year in sales which, if counted in the total, would make the LDS Church an $8.7 billion corporation, between 54th and 55th place on the Fortune 500 and larger than Honeywell, General Mills or Campbell Soup.

Time stated that in 1997:

> Its current assets total a minimum of $30 billion. If it were a corporation, its estimated gross income would place it midway through the FORTUNE 500,

a little below Union Carbide and the Paine Webber Group but bigger than Nike and the Gap.

...The top beef ranch in the world is not the King Ranch in Texas. It is the Deseret Cattle & Citrus Ranch outside Orlando, Fla. It covers 312,000 acres; its value as real estate alone is estimated at $858 million. It is owned entirely by the Mormons. The largest producer of nuts in America, AgReserves, Inc., in Salt Lake City, is Mormon-owned. So are the Bonneville International Corp., the country's 14th largest radio chain, and the Beneficial Life Insurance Co., with assets of $1.6 billion.[1]

The *Time* article went on to say:

So great is the tithe flow that scholars have suggested it constitutes practically the intermountain states' only local counterbalance in an economy otherwise dominated by capital from the East and West coasts.

...But where other churches spend most of what they receive in a given year, the Latter-day Saints employ vast amounts of money in investments that *TIME* estimated to be at least $6 billion strong. Even more unusual, most of this money is not in bonds or stock in other peoples' companies but is invested directly in church-owned, for-profit concerns, the largest of which are in agribusiness, media, insurance, travel and real estate.

Deseret Management Corp., the company through which the church holds almost all its commercial assets, is one of the largest owners of farm and ranchland in the country, including 49 for-profit parcels in addition to the Deseret Ranch. Besides the Bonneville International chain and Beneficial Life, the church owns a 52% holding in ZCMI, Utah's largest department-store chain. All told, *TIME* estimates that the Latter-day Saints farmland and financial investments total some $11 billion, and that the church's non-tithe income from its investments exceeds $600 million.[2]

In 1991, its income exceeded donations to the United Way, the United States' largest charity, and easily surpassed the national incomes of the YMCA, the Salvation Army and the Red Cross. Although not as wealthy as the much larger Catholic church, the articles noted that the LDS Church had a much better "bottom line," since most American Catholic dioceses are awash in red ink, while the Mormon Church operates with no debt load at all.

The LDS Church released a response to the articles, which, as might be expected, gave no specific corrections, but said that the articles' estimates of Mormon wealth were "grossly overstated."

The Arizona Republic reported that LDS officials refused its reporters' requests for access to tax returns. They released the information only when the paper stood firmly on IRS regulations that permit public inspection of such documents. The *Republic* admits that it was not able to get a complete, up-to-date listing, but it concluded that, in 1991, the LDS Church:

Controlled at least 100 companies that generated about 400 million a year for the church through contributions, dividends or trusts.

- Never borrowed money to finance its acquisitions. It paid cash, using portions of its members' tithing and its business income.
- Had become one of the nation's largest landowners.
- Had investments in excess of $1 billion.[3]

The articles served to squelch one of the most common rumors, even among Mormons. The paper claimed that it could find no record of the Church having ever owning part of Coca-Cola. The closest it could come was the apparent fact that Mormons sold sugar to Coke for use in its soft drinks at one time.

In pursuing this, it is also important to note two things: 1) *financial information about the LDS Church is certainly incomplete and always out of date;* and 2) there is a big difference between businesses or corporations owned by the LDS Church and businesses *owned by individual Mormons*.

For example, the Marriott enterprises are Mormon-owned, but not owned by the LDS Church, but rather by the LDS Marriott family. Even there, much of the Marriott stocks and bonds are out there in other hands. Yet, it is helpful to know if Mormons run such corporations, because if they are active Mormons, then you can assume that at least 10 cents of every dollar they earn *individually* is given as a tithe on their income.

According to *The Arizona Republic* article, the Church owns at least 699,000 acres of land in the US and Canada, almost half of which is located in Florida near Orlando. In fact, the Church may be Florida's largest single owner of undeveloped real estate. Other states with LDS-owned farmland are Iowa, Illinois, Nebraska, Indiana, Missouri and Oklahoma, plus an 88,000-acre ranch in Alberta, Canada.

This does not include other commercial properties, which amount to over $204 million worth of properties in just Utah and California. The church has amassed farm, ranch and real estate holdings that, at the time of the report, exceeded $1 billion, including an $18 million Security Pacific Bank Plaza in Tucson and a $10 million shopping mall in Orange County, CA.

The Corporation of the President

In the midst of this dizzying array of billions of dollars in assets and income, it is important to note that the LDS Church *technically* owns nothing. Rather, all of the assets are owned by one of two holding companies: *The Corporation of the Presiding Bishopric*, which is in charge of the church's "ecclesiastical" assets (like buildings and Beehive Clothing, which makes the temple garments), and its parent holding company, *The Corporation of the President of the Church of Jesus Christ of Latter-day Saints (CPC)*.

The CPC is essentially the President of the Church and his counselors! Thus, a handful of men have total control of this huge amount of economic power! A complete listing of the companies they control would be longer and more brain numbing than this book would permit. But, by way of example, at the time of *The Arizona Republic* report, the CPC ran large conglomerates [with a total value: of about $1.6 billion] of secular industry such as:

- Deseret Management ($1.3 billion in known assets)
- Deseret Trust of California ($17.8 million in assets managed)
- ZCMI Department stores ($124 million in assets)
- Property Reserve of Arizona ($117 million)
- Columbia (Washington) Ridge Farms ($26.7 million)

The paper stated that the Church appeared to spend about $2 billion a year to maintain its Temples and its 16,000 local church buildings. Training and fielding tens of thousands of missionaries in the field cost the church $550 million dollars a year! Today, with higher costs everywhere and more missionaries, that figure may be closer to a billion.

Media Control

Another area of power would be the extraordinary inroads the LDS Church has made into the media. The LDS Church's media arm is the Bonneville International Corporation, which has owned the following radio and TV affiliates around the nation. You can be certain the list has changed a number of times since the 1991 report.

>KAAM-AM, KZPS-FM Radio (Dallas, TX)
>KBIG-FM (Los Angeles)
>Keystone Communications (sales, $25 million)
>KIRO, Inc. (Seattle, WA) (sales, $32 million)
>KMBZ-AM, KMBR-FM (Kansas City, MO) (sales, $1.1 million)
>KMEO-AM/FM Radio (Phoenix, AZ) (sales, $2.3 million)
>KOIT-AM/FM Radio (San Francisco)
>KSL (Salt Lake City)

KTMX-FM Radio (Chicago)
WNSR-FM (New York City) (sales, $1.1 million)

Additionally, the LDS Church owns the two most powerful daily newspapers in Utah, *The Deseret News* and *The Salt Lake Tribune*, as well as its own publishing company, Deseret Books. *The radio, TV and newspaper outlets in Salt Lake can be counted on to virtually ignore any story which shows any unpleasant truths about the LDS Church.* Deseret Books owns a chain of stores which sell about $50 million in "faith promoting" products each year. Only the Sunday School Board of the Southern Baptist Convention sells more.

You can imagine that with that sort of media influence, when the Church talks (or forbids others from talking), the networks listen. I have often run into strong, unreasonable opposition in media against running any stories on the Church which place it in a negative light.

The casual visitor to Salt Lake City, Utah, cannot help but be overpowered by the granite-like strength and power of the Mormon empire. Standing among the towering fountains and gardens in front of the Church Office Building and looking down to Temple Square, you have to think that this is the way God's home office would look if "The Kingdom of God" was listed on the New York Stock Exchange.

The details of this vast financial core of the LDS Kingdom are known within the LDS Church by a very select few of the leaders, and even only on a need-to-know basis. The complex network of corporations within corporations has spread out the controls and lines of authority so that even most of the LDS Church's business managers can only see what The Brethren want them to see on a very tight need-to-know basis. Most employees within the LDS business empire would need a road map to get to the top. The Brethren want it that way.

No Accountability

Although elevated to the office of spiritual leaders, the majority of The Brethren were successful businessmen before they were called by "revelation" to join the ranks of the LDS hierarchy.

Unlike members of other churches, Latter-Day Saints, including those in lower levels of leadership (such as Bishops and Stake Presidents) who have faithfully and sacrificially contributed their tithes and offerings, their time and energies, and given their whole identities to the Church, are powerless to call for an accounting or participate on any regular corporate decision. They faithfully submit to every decision from the top.

For a Mormon to ask for a financial accounting from The Brethren would be unheard of, an incomprehensible act. In their minds, it would be a lack of faith in God to even question their divine judgment. To do so would be ruinous to an individual's testimony of the truthfulness of the Mormon Church and a fatal first step into the downhill spiral to apostasy!

John Heinerman, the Mormon author of the book, *The Mormon Corporate Empire,* was asked what he thought of the wealth and power base of Mormonism. His response was quite revealing:

I have always been fascinated with the great wealth and power the Church of Jesus Christ of Latter-day Saints wields nationally and internationally. The Mormon corporate empire, in terms of dollars and cents is rather impressive, for several reasons. Number one, in the book [*The Mormon Corporate Empire*], we take a conservative figure of about 8½ billion dollars that the empire is worth and we of course have footnotes in the back of the book showing how we arrived at those figures. But really, with all the research that we have done, the figure is closer to 11½ to 12 billion dollars, worldwide, [for] all of their investment and holding.

> Now, these investments and holdings primarily fall into real estate, such as temples, meeting houses, seminaries, religious institutes, which comprise close to half of the assets of the Church. Another percentage of about 25 percent would be in business holdings, agribusiness, their ranches, their business real estate holdings, and their investment portfolios. Through the research that we obtained, some

of it came from computer printouts from the Church Finance Department, that was given to me in 1982 and '83, which formed the heart and core of the book.[4]

As this man poured out this immense storehouse of data regarding the affluence and might of his church, there was no doubt in my mind that John Heinerman was a wellspring of hidden knowledge and enthusiasm. He continued:

> The one thing that I was amazed at, was that the ... LDS Church rolls over every year between 1½ and 2½ billion dollars just in its investment portfolios. They're into everything from agricultural futures like soybeans, pork bellies, to cattle. They've invested heavily into power companies. They have one portfolio called the Bond Substitute Portfolio. And they have a little over a quarter of a billion dollars just in that.
>
> Some of these investment portfolios bring huge dividends and returns, and others lose millions of dollars. For instance, in the Bond Substitute Portfolio, which has investments in a number of power companies around the country, in that two or three hundred thousand shares here and there, many of these power companies have been involved in nuclear reactors, nuclear facilities that have drained the power

companies to where now the power companies have invested in basically white dinosaurs. The result is, the stocks of many of these power companies have plummeted.

The Church has taken a pretty good beating in this direction. When there was the collapse of the stock market here last fall, someone asked me how much I thought the LDS Church had lost. And I said, just based on what I was familiar with in 1984 and '85, I said that it was probably in the neighborhood at 11 to 15 million dollars in that. And someone I talked with from the finance department some years ago said, "When we make investments, we don't pray to God, and we don't go by revelation, we do it just like the world does." And so of course, you win some, you lose some.

When he got down to the question of what the Mormon Church *does* with all this wealth and power, Heinerman was refreshingly candid about it.

The LDS Church uses this wealth to go and help increase its membership, to go and promote and proselytize the gospel that it is advocating worldwide. The church has been fortunate to have a number of its people in prominent positions around the country in political authority: senators, congressmen, people in the Reagan cabinet, people in the CIA and the FBI. At times the Church has called upon them to go and do a favor for the Church, get the church out of a jam, or use their political clout in behalf of the Church.

> One thing I think is important to point out, most people do not realize the full extent and power of the LDS Church. Two examples very quickly. One, when I was doing research for *The Mormon Corporate Empire*, I had a run-in with the LDS Church Security. To make a long story short... I was sitting in a Church office building, in July 1983, and ... the Church attorneys were being located. They wanted to interview me and try to find out how I had gotten my information.

Heinerman related his discovery of confidential police and FBI documents while waiting for his interview.

> I was sitting in the office alone, and I happened to notice on a particular desk in front of me, several documents. And so I looked around, and no one was there, and I turned them around, and on the first one there was a name of an individual that I've forgotten, but it said, "Salt Lake City Police Department, Police Record." I slid the document down, and it [the second document] said, "Federal Bureau of Investigation," and the name of an individual. And these were apparently reports about these individuals and their activities.

The secretary came back into the room, took the documents, put them in the top drawer of her desk, locked it, and then proceeded to give me a mild tongue lashing, saying, "You know, you shouldn't be snooping around in there." I said, "Well, you shouldn't be leaving documents laying around. You know," I said, "this a police report and an FBI report, and I thought those things were confidential." And she said, "Listen, we can get anything we want, on anyone we want, at any time we want."

John Heinerman added a little more about Church Security. He smiled proudly as he said,

Now the profile of LDS church security! The fellow that I had first run into was with Air Force Counter-intelligence for 26 years. Another fellow was with the Los Angeles County Sheriff's Department. The head of Church Security, who recently died, was a top FBI man under J. Edgar Hoover. They have retired CIA men working, they have people from the Navy counter-intelligence. And so the church has amassed an incredible amount of security personnel from different law professions and that gives it some of the best security of any religion on the face of the earth.[5]

Why would any Christian church require one of the country's largest, most highly trained security forces ever found in any portion of this country's private sector? Certainly, no other church has such a force in place. The concept staggers the mind, except when you realize that The Brethren have the security force there because it is needed.

Having said all this, I can only summarize by saying that the Mormon Church and the Brethren who control it have a huge, powerful money machine in their hands and will use every unit part within it to further their goals.

Their goals are not just limited to bringing the Mormon gospel to the "ends of the world," but include the implementation of the Mormon Plan for America, the end-times theocracy they will control to prepare the world for the return of Christ and His thousand-year reign managed by the LDS Brethren.

CHAPTER FOURTEEN

The Book of Mormon: Foundation of Faith

A quick summary of the root heresies of Mormonism and how we are to deal with them.

The first thing the Mormon missionaries are going to do when they knock at your door, and enter into a conversation with you is offer you a free copy of *The Book of Mormon, Another Testament of Christ*. Millions are given out every year in many languages across the world. Every person who accepts one is asked to read it and pray about it and are told that God will *spiritually* reveal the truth of it to you—by personal revelation. No one is asked to read it and compare it to Biblical doctrine or historicity.

Setting aside all the Mormon claims of divine illumination for the moment, let's seriously "consider" *The Book of Mormon* on its own merit. In an undated LDS tract, entitled,

"The Challenge The Book of Mormon Makes To The World," the last paragraph states: "The first thing to do in examining any ancient text is to consider it in the light of the origin and background that is claimed for it. If it fits into that background, there is no need to look any farther since historical forgery is virtually impossible." While this is not necessarily true, we can use it as a fair statement of the *Mormon position* with regard to *The Book of Mormon*. Does *The Book of Mormon* measure up to even this simple test?

Joseph Smith declared that *The Book of Mormon* was "the keystone of our religion, and a man would get nearer to God by abiding by its precepts than by any other book"[1]

Let's Start at the Very Beginning

There is no better starting point than the very first page of *The Book of Mormon*. In the First Book of Nephi, we read the account of Lehi, the key prophet of what Mormons call the second migration. It is through this man that the actual *Book of Mormon* story comes forth. In 1 Nephi 1:4, we are told:

For it came to pass in the commencement of the first year of the reign of Zedekiah, King of Judah, (my father, Lehi, having dwelt at Jerusalem in all his days); and in that same year there came many prophets, prophesying unto the people that they must repent, or the great city Jerusalem must be destroyed.

Throughout the rest of chapters 1 and 2 we see that Lehi is portrayed as a mighty prophet of the Lord, and after much danger, leaves the city of Jerusalem at the Lord's bidding. Let's assume that this is true for the time being and as encouraged by the LDS tract above, "consider it in the light of the origin and background that is claimed for it. If it fits into that background, there is no need to look any farther since historical forgery is virtually impossible."

Using the clue that we are dealing with the reign of Zedekiah, it is possible to go to the Bible and examine 2 Kings 24: 17-18. We see that Zedekiah reigned for 11 years, starting about 600 BC and ended his reign with the fourth and last siege of Jerusalem. This siege was conducted by Nebuchadnezzar and ended with the destruction of Jerusalem and the Babylonian captivity.

At that time, Daniel and Ezekiel had already been taken captive to Babylon—Daniel in the first siege and Ezekiel in the third siege. The only true prophet left in Jerusalem during Zedekiah's reign was Jeremiah, and he made it perfectly clear that he was the only prophet speaking for God in that city in that time:

Jeremiah 2:8 "...and the prophets prophesied by Baal."

Jeremiah 5:31 "...and the prophets prophesy falsely."

Jeremiah 6:13 "...and from the prophet even unto the priest every one dealeth falsely."

Jeremiah 8:10 "every one dealeth falsely."

Jeremiah 14:14 "the prophets prophesy lies in my name: I sent them not....They prophesy unto you a false vision and divination."

Jeremiah 23:16 "Hearken not unto the words of the prophets that prophesy unto you."

Jeremiah 23:21 "I have not sent these prophets, yet they ran: I have not spoken unto them yet they prophesied."

Jeremiah 27:14-17 "Therefore hearken not unto the words of the prophets that speak unto you, saying, ye shall serve not the King of Babylon: for they prophesy a lie unto you...hearken not to the words of your prophets that prophesy unto you...hearken not unto them; serve the King of Babylon and live."

Jeremiah 29:8-9 "Let not your prophets and your diviners, that be in the midst of you deceive you...for they prophesy falsely unto you in my name: I have not sent them, saith the Lord." (All Scriptures above KJV)

These passages clearly warn the people not to listen to any of the other prophets because they were all false and spoke lies. It is quite clear that the words Jeremiah spoke (especially Jeremiah 27:14-17) would certainly include the prophet, Lehi, whom *The Book of Mormon* claims was shouting a prophetic word that was in *direct* opposition to that of Jeremiah, in the *same* city at the *same* time.

Since God didn't deliver Ezekiel, Daniel, and Jeremiah from bondage, but wanted all the people to serve the King of Babylon, why would he favor a prophet who is not mentioned in the Bible with a message in total contradiction to the one given to Jeremiah for the whole nation of Israel? God gave absolutely no indication in the Bible that some had to serve in Babylon, but some would be spared. In fact, He gave some pretty severe warnings to those who would attempt to escape captivity. In Jeremiah 28:10-17, we read about the false prophet, Hananiah, who spoke falsely of victory over Babylon to the people in the name of the Lord. That act brought swift judgment and his death.

> *10 Then Hananiah the prophet took the yoke off the prophet Jeremiah's neck and broke it. 11 And Hananiah spoke in the presence of all the people, saying, "Thus says the Lord: 'Even so I will break the yoke of Nebuchadnezzar king of Babylon from the neck of all nations within the space of two full years.'" And the prophet Jeremiah went his way.*
>
> *12 Now the word of the Lord came to Jeremiah, after Hananiah the prophet had broken the yoke from the neck of the prophet Jeremiah, saying, 13 "Go and tell Hananiah, saying, 'Thus says the Lord: "You*

have broken the yokes of wood, but you have made in their place yokes of iron." 14 For thus says the Lord of hosts, the God of Israel: "I have put a yoke of iron on the neck of all these nations, that they may serve Nebuchadnezzar king of Babylon; and they shall serve him. I have given him the beasts of the field also."'"

15 Then the prophet Jeremiah said to Hananiah the prophet, "Hear now, Hananiah, the Lord has not sent you, but you make this people trust in a lie. 16 Therefore thus says the Lord: 'Behold, I will cast you from the face of the earth. This year you shall die, because you have taught rebellion against the Lord.'" 17 So Hananiah the prophet died the same year in the seventh month.

If the judgment of the Lord against Hananiah was death, why would God call and send forth another prophet, Lehi, with the same rebellious opposition to the Lord's message given through Jeremiah and have him speak this false thing to the very same people and have call him a true prophet? *Impossible!* If *The Book of Mormon* were true scripture, Lehi would have to be in direct disobedience to God in leaving Jerusalem to escape capture and bondage in Babylon.

So, coming back to page 1 of *The Book of Mormon*, it immediately fails the basic test. It does not fit into its time frame correctly as true scripture. One need not go a page further to know that we are dealing with a false prophet. Yes, Lehi does fit into the Biblical picture, but only as a false prophet! The wise reader would put down *The Book of Mormon* after reading just one page.

Out of the Dust

Let's look at it from another angle. The late LeGrand Richards was often called the Gentle Apostle. In his famous missionary book, *A Marvelous Work and Wonder*, which has been given away to investigators by the hundreds of thousands, he described the biblical prophecies fulfilled by *The Book of Mormon*. He uses Isaiah 29:4 as a proof text for the coming forth of *The Book of Mormon*:

And thou shalt be brought down, and shalt speak out of the ground, and thy speech shall be low out of the dust, and thy voice shall be, as one that hath a familiar spirit, out of the ground, and thy speech shall whisper out of the dust.

Richards's comments:

Now, obviously, the only way a dead people could speak "out of the ground" or "out of the dust" would be by the written word and this was done through *The Book of Mormon*. Truly, it has a familiar spirit, for it contains the words of the prophets of the God of Israel.[2]

Unfortunately for *Book of Mormon* scholarship, the Hebrew word for "familiar spirit" in this passage of Isaiah is the word, *Ob,* which is translated in the King James Bible as *Familiar Spirit.* In the Hebrew, the word means *necromancer,* or *a spirit of witchcraft.* There are 15 Old Testament references to familiar spirits, and all of them deal with *witchcraft.*

The apostle LeGrand Richards and the hundreds of thousands of Mormons who have used his words as evidence that *The Book of Mormon* has this same "familiar spirit" tie their scripture solidly to witchcraft. They are heartily welcome to the label. Again, without raving shouts, *The Book of Mormon* fails its own challenge.

Sticks and Scrolls

Of the several other biblical prophecies used to substantiate *The Book of Mormon,* one other stands out as the most common of all LDS "proof" scriptures. It is used almost every time the missionaries teach on *The Book of Mormon.* Ezekiel 37:15-17 reads:

> The Word of the Lord came again unto me, saying, moreover, thou son of man, take thee one stick, and write upon it, For Judah, and for the children of Israel his companions: then take another stick, and write upon it, For Joseph, the stick of Ephraim, and for all the house of Israel his companions: and join them one to another into one stick; and they shall become one in thine hand.

The Mormon Church teaches that the sticks mentioned in this prophecy are two books that would become one witness as they are joined together by the Mormon Church. Mormon leaders say this scripture speaks of the Bible and *The Book of Mormon*! This is made clearly evident in the LDS scripture: "...and with Moroni, whom I have sent unto to you to reveal the Book of Mormon, containing the fullness of my everlasting gospel, to whom I have committed the keys of the record of the stick of Ephraim...." (*Doctrine and Covenants* 27:5)

In actuality, the Hebrew word used here for stick is *es*, or *ets*, meaning wood, tree or stick. The Hebrew words for scroll, roll, book, or writing, include *sepher, dabar, sephar,* and *siphrah*. The Old Testament talks about sticks, rolls, books, writings, scrolls and so on. Yet, in no case has God ever used the word for stick to mean anything but a piece of wood, certainly not a scroll of scripture. He never interchanged these words. The LDS church has applied the wrong meaning to the words.

What was happening in this scripture? If you read the very next few verses, the people ask Ezekiel what he meant by what he said, and he explains that the sticks represent the two kingdoms of Israel which shall be joined together just as the sticks were in his hands (verses 18-22). Unfortunately for the cause of reasonable scholarship, it is evident that Mormon theologians have missed those later verses for over 175 years.

Further, it was Ezekiel who wrote on both sticks. He obviously did not write both the Bible and *The Book of Mormon*. Again, the point is that the evidence of the Mormon interpretation for this prophecy just does not exist. Ezekiel clearly defined the exact conditions and scope of the prophecy, and we have concrete historical evidence of its fulfillment.

There is no evidence from the Bible of any future set of scriptures such as the Mormons claim. The LDS effort to fit *The Book of Mormon* into Biblical context has no point of reference, except the one which they have contrived.

The People Who Weren't There

Let's look at the history found in *The Book of Mormon*. God is not obtuse. If this great Nephite society described in *The Book of Mormon* really existed in the Americas, the evidences would have to be there. Sandra Tanner, one researcher on the Mormon question, commented:

The Book of Mormon claims to be an actual historical record translated from real plates that Joseph Smith unearthed in a hill in New York. Now, if this were a genuine history, one would assume you could study this, just as you would study any historical book.

When I study the Bible, I can approach it as a total atheist or as a believer in Christ, but either way I can study the book historically. It does not require a "testimony." You can determine where Jerusalem is; you can determine that there was a Hebrew language. *When we turn to The Book of Mormon we have nothing.* There is no Nephite language; there are no Nephite cities; there is not a map in any book of Mormon; you cannot locate any sites. *There is no evidence for the book and yet it's supposed to be an historical record.*[3]

When asked about this during the filming of a segment of "The God Makers" in London, LDS Mission President, Harold Goodman, commented:

> Many people do not understand *The Book of Mormon*. This is a history of the people that inhabited the American Continent—North, South and Central America, from about 600 BC to about 420 AD, and we have much evidence, of course, of people having lived there.[4]

We all know that a large, complex society *did* exist there during those years of Book of Mormon history. But, were they the descendants of Jewish immigrants? The question is still, "Does *The Book of Mormon* fit the time frame?" We do not think it does. Yet, with fervent zeal and that same burning testimony, the Mormons claim it does.

President Goodman is aware that Mormon missionaries throughout the world are converting people to the Mormon Church by explaining to them that archaeology has proved *The Book of Mormon* to be true. Slide presentations, special fireside meetings, and filmstrips are used along with volumes of specialty books on the subject, available wherever Mormon books are sold.

Where *are* all these so called "evidences" so readily available as proof? Either they exist as presented by the Mormons or they don't. We can't play games with historical facts.

In LDS Visitors Centers throughout the world, a painting by the artist John Scott is displayed. Copies are available in great abundance wherever LDS materials are sold. The painting is called, *The Resurrected Christ in America.* What is so important about this painting? It represents Christ standing before the multitudes in front of several of the temples in Meso-America, graphically tying in, for the millions who have viewed this painting of Jesus, *The Book of Mormon* and the temples of these early civilizations. *What is wrong?* Neither temple depicted in the painting existed until about 1000 AD, almost ten centuries after the supposed appearance of the Mormon Christ in the Americas!

The two temples are actually very well known; they are El Castillo and El Caracol. They are also used in one of the well-known LDS proof works, *The Trial of the Stick of Joseph*, by LDS Bishop Jack West. In both representations, their use can only be out of blind ignorance or blatant deception.

The fact that the painting is an artist's rendition is not important. It *is* important that the church as an expression of implied fact publishes it widely. The same painting is used, in part, as the cover of an LDS pamphlet, "Christ in America," written by Apostle Mark. E. Petersen and published in 1983. Jack West's representation may be waved away as the work of an individual, yet it is used widely to convert people out of the Christian body through the use of open deception.

Could the church and people like Jack West be just blind to the facts? We think not. A friend, Jack Sande, wrote to John L. Sorenson, Chairman of the Department of Anthropology at Brigham Young University, and asked him about this problem after receiving a copy of the West book from a Mormon Bishop.

LDS Problems with Their Own Professionals

In a letter to Jack, dated October 5, 1981, John Sorenson replied:

I understand that people who have not had educational experiences concerning archaeology could be enthusiastic about books like these of West or Farnsworth when they see these as supporting the Book of Mormon in which they strongly believe. I presume the Bishop who gave you the West volume would fall into that class—overcome by zeal. Nevertheless, the fact remains that those books are worse than useless, because they are not reasonably close to the truth. I wish the zealous had other options open to them in the way of truthful books, but at the moment, that is a problem.

John Sorenson sounded like a pretty up-front scholar. We went to a book of his, dated 1980, and found that he had made a couple of very significant observations. First, regarding the Bible, Sorenson said:

Learning about context seems unimportant to some readers of the book [*The Book of Mormon*]; others consider it impossible. To me the Bible is a model in this regard. Biblical scholarship has illuminated certain unobvious meanings of that scriptural text showing the complex interplay between human and divine influences and establishing the Bible as a record all the more profound, because it is anchored in a complex reality of time, space and behavior. I have wanted that same illumination for Lehi's people and their book.

And what of that book, *The Book of Mormon*? He made no evasive apologies, but hit directly home with his point:

After nearly 150 years since the Nephite record was first published by Joseph Smith, we Mormons have been unable confidently to pin down the location of a single city, identify even one route they traversed, or sketch an accurate picture of any segment of the life they lived in their American promised land. In many respects, *The Book of Mormon* remains a sealed book to us because we have been incapable of placing it in its specific setting.[5]

John Sorenson is not the only Mormon scholar who is a realist in this matter. Dr. Ross T. Christensen, BYU professor and head of the Society for Early Historic Archeology, stands by his side. Over twenty years earlier, in an article for the University Archaeological Society, Dr. Christensen wrote:

> In the first place, the statement that *The Book of Mormon* has already been proved by archaeology is misleading. The truth of the matter is that we are only beginning to see even the outlines of the archaeological time-periods which could compare with those of *The Book of Mormon*. How, then, can the matter have been settled once and for all?

Christensen continued:

> That such an idea could exist indicates the ignorance of many of our people with regard to what is going on in the historical and anthropological sciences. With the exception of Latter-day Saint archaeologists, members of the archaeological profession do not [espouse] and never have espoused *The Book of Mormon* in any sense of which I am aware.

He added:

As for the notion that *The Book of Mormon* has already been proved by archaeology, I must say with Shakespeare, "Lay not that flattering unction to your soul." (*Hamlet* III, iv)[6]

Another honest Mormon scholar, Dee F. Green, asserts, "The first myth we need to eliminate is that Book of Mormon archaeology exists." He has termed the Church's current approach to Mormon archaeology as a back-door one, and he is right.[7]

In the January/February 1981 *Sunstone Magazine*, Martin Raish, a doctoral candidate and teacher of art history at BYU, wrote one of the best scholarly reports we have read on this subject of amateur attempts to prove *The Book of Mormon* through historic evidence.

He goes through the works of such well-known Mormon men as Jack West, Dewey Farnsworth, Paul Cheeseman and Wayne Hamby, showing the exact manner in which the reader of their works is manipulated with sweeping assumptions, questionable artifacts, misdated archaeology and mismatched scriptures and pictures, all designed to assure the reader that *The Book of Mormon* is fact. Raish cautions the LDS community that these pseudo-scholarly tactics thwart the best efforts of the LDS professionals. He concludes:

I do not think that we will ever prove the Book of Mormon to be true through archaeological evidences any more than we can yet prove the date of the Creation through scientific means alone.[8]

A Leap of Faith

So we fall back again on the pamphlet, "Challenge the Book of Mormon Makes to the World," which we spoke of earlier. Its premise was that an authentic historical text has to fit the time frame of which it speaks. This is not only reasonable, but also imperative. Yet, while it is the proven standard for the Bible, it appears to be impossible for *The Book of Mormon*.

Dr. Charles Crane has spent most of his lifetime studying the Bible and also the LDS scriptures. He is an active student of both Bible and Mormon Archaeology. He emphasized the differences to us. "The simple facts," he said, "are that the truth does not match the LDS stories. While the accuracy of the Bible has been vindicated time and again, we have yet to find the first Book of Mormon City. Not one city as named in *The Book of Mormon* has ever been found...not one."[9]

The Mormon non-scholars keep trying to "associate" Book of Mormon archaeology with the historic evidences of the Aztec and Mayan temple builders. Yet at every corner, warning flags leap up. On March 26, 1982, the Utah Museum of Natural History held a presentation by Nicholas M.

Hellmuth. His subject: "The Human Sacrificial Practices of the Maya." If the Mormons want to associate with butchers who killed innocent people in their religious ceremonies, they are free to do that, but then to say that "restored" Christianity sprang from that well is ludicrous!

In the May 25, 1980 *Salt Lake Tribune*, an article authored by *New York Times* writer, Boyce Rensberger, listed archaeological findings that push back the Mayan origins to 9000 BC Lehi and his people supposedly arrived in Meso-America around 600 BC, over 8,000 years off schedule. That certainly stretches that *Book of Mormon* time frame.

Jesus, the Feathered Serpent

In his book, *Christ in Ancient America, Volume II*, Dr. Milton R. Hunter, then a member of the First Council of the Seventy, described Quetzalcoatl, god of the Aztecs and the Olmecs as Jesus. He states:

> Quetzalcoatl could have been none other than Jesus the Christ, the Lord and God of this earth, and the Savior of the human family. Thus Jesus Christ and Quetzalcoatl are identical.

He further quotes LDS President and Prophet John Taylor, who in 1882 stated:

The story of the life of the Mexican divinity, Quetzalcoatl, closely resembles that of the Savior; so closely, indeed, that we can come to no other conclusion than that Quetzalcoatl and Christ are the same being.[10]

Dr. Hunter explains that Quetzalcoatl was represented as the "Feathered Serpent," which has its identification with the "Plumed Serpent" of Egyptian origin, and the serpent in the Garden of Eden [or Satan]. He says, "The serpent, in early times was also identified with the Crucifixion, and hence was also a symbol of the Son of Man." He goes on to explain, "In this Chapter and throughout the book, the serpent will be presented as a symbol of Quetzalcoatl or Jesus and no further reference will be made to its identification with the Prince of Darkness, or Lucifer."[11]

This is absolute, utter nonsense. Quetzalcoatl dates back into the far distance long before *The Book of Mormon* era began. He was the god of learning and civilization, and he appeared in the Olmec religion around 2000 BC The Feathered Serpent was a pagan idol requiring blood sacrifice. From this point and all through the temple building eras surrounding *The Book of Mormon* dating, the Feathered Serpent God Cult began to take over and the once beneficent Quetzalcoatl was incarnated into the bloodthirsty Feathered Serpent. Untold hundreds of thousands of innocent victims died to offer up their still-beating hearts to this bloody idol during the so-called "Book of Mormon" years. That serpent is a bloodthirsty demon, not the Jesus Christ of the Bible.

It wasn't until many hundreds of years beyond *The Book of Mormon* era that a Toltec king named *Ce Acatal Topiltzin* ascended the throne and took the name of Quetzalcoatl and sought to re-establish the gentle theology of the original god as the principle deity of the Toltec nation. This took place in AD 968. The bloodthirsty priests disgraced and banished him from the nation. This gentle king promised to return in a "one reed year" (according to the Mayan Calendar), and hence the legend of the return of Quetzalcoatl. By the way, the Spanish explorer, Cortez landed in 1519, a "one reed year," which is one of the reasons the native people accepted him with such open arms.[12]

Returning again to the difficult task of trying to fit *The Book of Mormon* into its own background and time frame, let's look at another of literally hundreds of conditions that make it impossible. Remember our earlier test: to examine *The Book of Mormon* in the light of the origin and background that is claimed for it. If it fits into that background, "there is no need to look any farther since historical forgery is virtually impossible" and if it doesn't fit in, it is simply a forgery.

Assuming that Lehi was right and Jeremiah wrong, and assuming that these travelers truly did land on the western shores of the Americas somewhere, then let's evaluate one of the major activities of this group in light of this test of history and fact.

In *The Book of Mormon*, 2 Nephi, Chapter 5, Nephi separates himself and his family from his very difficult brother, Laman. He takes several other of his family groups and all those who would go with him. These people become the foundation of the Nephite nation. Bear in mind that this whole story takes place before 30 years have passed since they left Jerusalem. Just getting to the boat took enough time that Jacob and Joseph, sons of Lehi, were born, so we can't be talking about much more than 20-25 years at best.

In all, we can't be talking about more than a half dozen grown men, some young boys and a very small number of women and children. You can't build a nation of much size in one single generation, starting from the travelers on the tiny vessel that supposedly brought them from Jerusalem, especially when that nation is split away from the whole. Yet, in 2 Nephi 5:15-17, Nephi describes how they built a mighty temple constructed after the manner of the Temple of Solomon.

Just try to envision at best a few dozen able-bodied people building a temple "like unto Solomon's." The Bible says that Solomon's Temple was built of stone, precious metals and enough cedar to keep 80,000 hewers of wood busy (1 Kings 5:13-15). It took Solomon over 7 years (1 Kings 6:38), and well over 150,000 full-time workers (2 Chronicles 2:18).

In verse 15, Nephi claims to have taught his people to build with all manner of wood, iron, steel (not found in the

Americas for over another 1500 years), gold, silver and precious ores which "were in great abundance." Then, in the very next verse, he states that they could not use these things since they were not to be found upon the land.

At the completion of this great temple, and still within the 30 years since leaving Jerusalem, Nephi reports that the people desired that he should be made king. Remember, this is a small clan of only about two dozen people—men, women and children included. Where is this mighty temple today? Has God taken it away as he supposedly has done with the gold plates? He must have, to hide such a temple from the plundering hands (and records) of the Spanish explorers.

Again, the Book of Mormon cannot fit into its background and time frame. It cannot be what it pretends to be.

Jewish Distinctions

There is another item of significance that is totally outside anything we have read about the Book of Mormon or any of its promoters' claims or its critics' challenges.

If we were to gather together 4 or 5 families and leave for an unknown land to be able to worship in our own manner, we would probably take our scriptures and our form of worship and develop our religious practices in a very fundamentalist manner—a form of worship that would have a lasting effect upon our new society. This is easily seen in the arrival in North America of the Pilgrims and the Puritans.

Likewise, if the Book of Mormon were true, we would see this same determination in the Jewish people of *The Book of Mormon*.

One thing for which the Jewish people are noted is their tenacity over centuries of time to maintain their own identity. Yet, this is not represented by a single shred of evidence anywhere in the Americas of a Jewish influx as described in *The Book of Mormon*. Another unmovable Jewish trait is the utter inability of anyone to destroy the Hebrew language throughout centuries of time. We are asked to believe that devout Jewish scholars would transcribe their most sacred scriptures in "reformed Egyptian." Bear in mind that the Hebrew people were forbidden to deal with anything Egyptian. To do so would defile the priesthood of God! (Nehemiah 13:23-31)

Check the Calendar

Lastly, if we were to embark on such a journey, we would take our calendar! This is the final flaw in their mimicry. Jewish people who fled across a perilous ocean rather than submit to a Babylonian King who would not let them worship as Jews are not going to give up their calendar and holy days. They would die first.

What about the Book of Mormon people? Did the people who lived in the Americas between 600 BC and AD 420 have anything even remotely resembling the Jewish 360-

day calendar? Did their months and holidays bear any name resemblance? *If not, they could not have been Jewish!*

In actuality, approximately three thousand years ago, on the coastal plain of southern Mexico, a priest received a revelation from the Sun God that not only determined the course of history for Meso-America, but also destroyed the remotest possibility of the Book of Mormon being a true history of these people.

"At precisely noon on the date we call August 13, probably in the year 1358 BC, the priest noticed that no tree, pillar or post cast a shadow." Counting the days to the next such experience, he finally was rewarded 260 days later, and again after another 105 days, on the next August 13th, it occurred again.

These events took place at Izapa, a ceremonial center on the Mexico-Guatemalan border. And here began a sacred calendar of a 13-unit cycle with 20 day names, known as the "Tzolkin" or "Tonalamatl." Once in place, this almanac became the basis of all religions, art and science in the civilizations that followed on this part of the continent.

The Izapans used the sacred calendar names to name their chiefs and nobles. These names were designated by "one of 20 animals important to the local mythology, such as Alligator, Buzzard, Eagle, Jaguar, Snake, Deer, etc." Each 52 years, they would recycle the whole process.

This 365-day solar calendar tied together the nations and religions of this entire part of the world. Under no circumstance could such a complex calendar exist and extend its influence out across the many centuries if the advanced civilization of the 1000-year Book of Mormon era ever existed.[13]

The Truth and Proof is in the DNA

Are *The Book of Mormon* Lamanites, the American, Meso-American and South American Indians really the descendants of Israelites who came to the Americas? The LDS Church claims they are, and the validity of *The Book of Mormon* requires that they must be Israelites to make the book correct in any regard.

Now, finally, incontrovertible scientific evidence has arisen that proves that *The Book of Mormon*, the foundation of the LDS faith, is a fabricated tale and the claims of Mormonism false. After over six years of interviews and studies, the issue of DNA and *The Book of Mormon* has finally proven conclusively that the People of Lehi, the Nephites, and Lamanites have absolutely no Jewish DNA in their system and the whole *Book of Mormon* story is a fraud and Mormonism is a faith built upon one fraud after another.

You would expect public confessions and apologies from its leaders and mass exodus from the pews, but the leaders have spoken and said that they must trust in them, and need only to pray about its validity, not look at any scientific evidence.

Some years ago, when the scientific validity of DNA research proved to be unassailable, I sent an open letter to the LDS Presidency and asked them to settle the matter by taking DNA samples of native people groups in Meso-America, Peru, and North America and compare them to native Israelites and to native groups in Eastern Asia. My letter received no response.

You would think that if the LDS Leaders actually believed what they taught about the origins of *The Book of Mormon* peoples, they would have their scientists racing to take this golden opportunity to finally prove, without any doubt, that Mormonism was everything it claimed to be. But apparently they already knew the answer or secretly did the research but did not like the results and have kept them hidden from their own people.

Then a small church congregation in Brigham City, Utah, took up the cause and did the work necessary to either prove or disprove the authenticity of *The Book of Mormon* and the whole base line of Mormonism.

Before this project came to its practical conclusion, I pled with the Leaders of the LDS church to, at long last, deal in reality and set aside the many warm, fuzzy faith-building stories and get down to the scientific facts that can put an end to 175 years of controversy. The facts are in, but I wanted you to read part of a letter I received at the beginning of the project. Everything this pastor researched proved that the

DNA of the Meso-American People could not match *The Book of Mormon* story.

In a 2002 letter from Joel Kramer, Pastor of Living Hope Christian Fellowship in Brigham City, Utah, he wrote, in part:

> Our heart for Mormons is perfectly reflected by Paul's heart for his fellow Israelites*: "My hearts desire and prayer to God for the Israelites is that they may be saved. For I can testify about them that they are zealous for God, but their zeal is not based on knowledge." Rom 10:1.* In light of this, we have begun a DNA study on the claim of Hebrew origin for Native Americans taught in the Book of Mormon.
>
> I would like to emphasize that this is a church project that every member is aware of and in some degree involved with. It was thoroughly discussed with the congregation and agreed upon through a series of meetings before we committed to doing it.
>
> You can go to www.mormonchallenge.com and download the video clip that we have produced so far [now the finished product]. This explains what *The Book of Mormon* teaches in regards to Native Americans having a Hebrew origin and it shares the first interview we conducted with DNA Anthropologist, Dr. Stephen L. Whittington at the

University of Maine. His area of expertise is DNA testing ancient skeletons from the Maya civilization, which of course is where Lehi's family is said to have landed. We have four more interviews with DNA specialists coming up, three in August and one in October. Two are involved with studying mummies and skeletons of Native Americans before the coming of the Europeans in 1492. One is involved with DNA testing of living Native Americans. To date over 5,000 Native Americans from more than 140 tribes from Alaska to the tip of South America have been DNA tested. The research shows that 96.5% of them show an Asian origin, having migrated to the American continents across the Bering Strait. The 3.5% discrepancy shows a European origin (mostly Spanish) that emerged after Columbus opened up the Americas to European trade and colonization. Researchers know this because the discrepancy occurs most frequently in areas that had high post-Columbus activity. Also, all ancient bones tested show a 100% Asian origin for pre-Columbus Indians. **To date, a Hebrew origin has not been linked to even one Native American.**

The fourth interview we have scheduled for October is with Senior DNA Scientist Dr. Simon Southerton. He was a Mormon Bishop when he discovered through his work the DNA evidence against *The Book of Mormon.*

We have reserved mormonchallenge.com for professional scientists only, separated from this site is our own site www.livinghopeministries.info. We are developing the gospel message and links to websites such as Saints Alive.

The goal of our project is first and foremost a local desire to actively defend the Bible and proclaim the gospel to Mormons. So far God has blessed us as we have openly announced in Newspapers that we are actively involved in this project. By association with Living Hope, God has opened the doors for witnessing and having to answer many people's questions. It is a great relief and benefit to be active in ministering to Mormons as it brings the intended purpose of the church to us. Our goal is to keep the pressure on the Mormons to defend *The Book of Mormon* in the hopes that some might turn to the truth and be saved. We need prayer support as we have already experienced many attacks from the enemy.... More than anything we need prayer that God would move by His Spirit to redeem the lost in Utah. We fully believe and expect Him to do just that!

Keep in mind that we are at the very beginning of this project and are involved with a major learning curve. For this reason our sites are still under construction and being organized better.

Now, I sent the above article to Pastor Kramer for his review prior to publishing it, and he wrote back, in part:

> On Monday afternoon [August 5, 2002] we received an e-mail from an LDS anthropologist. He found out about us through the DNA scientist who we will be interviewing this Tuesday in California. We did an hour and forty-minute interview with this Mormon anthropologist yesterday [August 7, 2002]. It was amazing! God completely delivered this man to us as we had no idea he was out there. His name is Tom Murphy; he has a BS and MA degree in anthropology and is currently writing his doctoral thesis on the DNA issue and Mormonism.
>
> He openly admitted on camera that the recent genetic evidence proves that *The Book of Mormon* is a false document written by Joseph Smith in the 19th Century. He also admitted that it proves that Joseph Smith openly and knowingly deceived people. With authority and sound reason he refutes every argument that Mormon scholars have attempted to explain the DNA problems they face. He refutes them both as a scientist and a Mormon. He also pleads with the LDS people and leadership to come clean in these areas. The interview was discovered, arranged and conducted in such a way that there is nothing that we can take credit for. It was all God! Praise Jesus!

What More Can We Say?

What more can we say? *The Book of Mormon* has had over 4,000 changes to it, and yet, it is supposed to the "most perfect book in the world," according to its translator. Eleven men bore witness to its reality, yet eight of these left the Mormon Church as apostates. There has never been a gold plate found of such type as was described by Joseph Smith, nor brass plates such as the ones described as containing the Jewish scriptures taken from Jerusalem. Not one exists anywhere in the Jewish world. The people who were supposed to be Jews aren't even close—Lie after Lie after Lie....

Further, why would God speak to Joseph Smith, a nineteenth century American, in archaic, seventeenth-century English? Would he speak that way to a Peruvian? Is God limited to King James English as His official language? Where do we stop and call the Mormon Church to account for what has been said? The Bible talks about people who mock the truth: "And for this cause God shall send them strong delusion, that they should believe a lie" (2 Thessalonians 2:11), but it comes at a steep price:

For the leaders of this people cause them to err,
And those who are led by them are destroyed. Isaiah 9:16

CHAPTER FIFTEEN

Finally, Brethren

The basic doctrinal core belief of Mormonism has been summed up in the religion's key theological position regarding God and Man. It is called "The Law of Eternal Progression." This doctrine is the center of the Mormon faith. It teaches that *"as Man is, God once was and as God is, Man may become."*[1] It is the Mormon quest for Godhood. It is the great secret of the Mormon faith, that they can become gods and goddesses, rulers over their very own kingdoms.

The Law of Eternal Progression teaches that you and we, all of the human race, were sent here from that place to gain physical bodies like the Mormon god Elohim did, and to go through a time of testing and learning as Elohim did before us.

As the story unfolds, when it was time for Elohim to prepare the earth for occupancy, the head of the gods called a council of the gods, and there the gods concocted the plan for earth. Elohim asked his two eldest sons—brothers (probably from Elohim's number-one wife), to prepare plans for the council to review. These brothers were Jesus and Lucifer!

Upon review of the plans, the Council chose the plan of Jesus, and he was raised to the position of godhood. Apparently, the vote was a close one, for Lucifer became angry over the decision. He led one-third of the children of Elohim into an open rebellion over the decision. They battled against one-third of the children who were in agreement with the Council decision. The other third of Elohim's children were obedient to the council, but didn't want to get involved in the battle. They were not valiant in defending the decision.[2]

It is hard to imagine how the spirit children of a physical god fought without physical bodies, or why Elohim was unable to control his own children, but at the end of the fighting, those who fought for Jesus won. Lucifer and his third of the spirit children were cast out from Kolob, and arrived here on earth as Satan and the demons.

Those who fought valiantly with Jesus would come to earth as "white and delightsome" people—the more valiant we were, the blonder our hair; the whiter our skin. The less valiant we were, the darker our complexion and hair. That third who did not want to get involved became the black race, born under the curse of Cain. There were no neutrals in Kolob!

The Mormon god, Elohim, apparently forgave black people on June 9, 1978. Now they too go to the LDS temple and take out their "endowments" when they are "worthy," and worthy black men can become members of the Mormon Melchizedek priesthood and eventually become polygamous Mormon gods (and become white).

When it came time for Jesus to take on flesh, Elohim came to earth physically, and had sexual relations with Mary, one of his daughters from Kolob, to beget Jesus. Remember, Elohim is an exalted man—totally *physical* in nature.[4]

The Mormon Jesus was married to at least three identified women: the two sisters of Lazarus, and Mary Magdalene. He converted water into wine at one of his own weddings at Cana. One Mormon apostle taught that the reason Jesus was so persecuted was because he had so many wives and concubines. Other teachers taught that Jesus was a father of many children.[5]

The Mormon Jesus died on a cross to atone for Adam's transgression which was an actual *blessing* that allowed us to gain physical bodies and mortality. Without this transgression we could not gain the physical attributes we needed in our own journey to godhood, because it was through the transgression that we knew how to procreate and become gods.

Adam's act brought mortality and physical death into the world. Jesus' death on Calvary brought us only physical resurrection and immortality. This atonement assured *all mankind* of only physical resurrection; after that we will each be judged according to our works, and blessed for our own works or punished for our own sins.[6]

The Mormon doctrine teaches that the Christian emphasis on the Cross is pagan and of the devil. There is no cross displayed in any Mormon building anywhere. Even its use in the home or as a piece of jewelry is forbidden! The Cross, as the place where Jesus became our sin offering, is vehemently labeled as heresy.

Likewise, the doctrine of His shed blood is rejected. The Mormons use only bread and water in their Sacrament. The true doctrine, according to Mormonism, is that Jesus sweat blood for our sins in Gethsemane, on the condition that we are obedient to all the laws and ordinances of the Mormon gospel.[7] The blood and the cross only give the world physical resurrection so that each person who has ever lived on earth can be judged for his or her works.

The Real Story behind the Sacrament Bread

We need to take a moment and think about the Mormon form of Communion. They don't call it *Communion*. They call it *The Sacrament*. It doesn't fit the normal definition for sacrament, which is the term for a formal church ritual frequently described as an outward and visible sign of an internal and spiritual grace. Most Protestant denominations only recognize two: Baptism and Communion. Some include

Ordination. The Mormons baptize and ordain, but they call Communion "The Sacrament."

As I said earlier, Mormon "Sacrament" consists of water and regular white bread, such as Wonder Bread. Since I became a born-again Christian and began taking "Communion," I clearly felt that the LDS Sacrament had, in my LDS life, washed away the reality of Christ's shed blood on Calvary with water, diluting His gift of true salvation for every believer, his shed blood leaving me with just works in its place.

While most churches use unleavened wafer types of bread, the Mormons use leavened bread. While I don't think it's necessarily wrong if you have used leavened bread for your communion, I realize that the Biblical warnings about leavened bread were tied to false teachers and false doctrines.

In Matthew, Jesus warned his disciples to beware the leaven of the Pharisees (Matthew 16:6-12). They finally understood that He did not tell them to beware of the leaven of bread, but of the doctrine of the Pharisees and Sadducees (verse 12).

In Mark 8:15, He charged them, saying, "Take heed, beware of the leaven of the Pharisees and the leaven of Herod." In Luke 12:1, He began to say to His disciples first of all, "Beware of the leaven of the Pharisees, which is hypocrisy."

In First Corinthians 5:7, we are told to "purge out the old leaven, that you may be a new lump, since you truly are unleavened. For indeed Christ, our Passover, was sacrificed for us." A study of Exodus shows that there was a purpose for the Feast of Unleavened Bread that sanctified the people, as an Everlasting Ordinance (Exodus 12:17).

It is no wonder the Mormon leaders removed the Biblical reasoning behind the use of unleavened bread and replaced it with regular white bread. It is the representation of their false doctrines that continues, in every way, to shut their people way from the simple act of Christ's death on the Cross for the lost, for them. The Mormons will not find it in the Cross, because it has been removed from their sight, and they will never find it in their sacrament of water and Wonder Bread.

Becoming Gods and Goddesses

If we are thus committed and also go through the Mormon Temple Ceremony, if we are obedient to the end, and if the judgment on our personal works of obedience are sufficient to cover the personal sin in our lives, we can be judged worthy to enter into the Celestial Kingdom, the highest degree of glory, be exalted and become gods and goddesses![8]

Each exalted man will be given many wives to take to his new kingdom, and will be sent out to some outer galaxy, some new planet to prepare for his new earth, even as Elohim was sent out before him! There the process will begin anew. Finally, in order to go into the Celestial glory, we must each "pass by brother Joseph" and receive his final approval![9]

While the Mormon Church teaches that we will go forth in the family unit, with all our worthy family members, the actual doctrine is that when the worthy man goes forth, only his wife will accompany him, and she only as the first wife of many. Each worthy son will go forth as a god over his own kingdom. Each worthy daughter will be given as a wife to some worthy god elsewhere.

Whatever else you may think about that neighbor, friend or loved one who is a Mormon, you need to remember that each and every Mormon you know is committed to this great plan and is struggling somewhere on the rung of a ladder in their own personal progression, their own personal Kingdom of God.

To challenge their belief in this doctrine would be to reinforce their teaching that the True Faith will be persecuted. Mormons must be approached with prayer and love. Your attitude is most important. Scripture says that Jesus told the foolish and blind of His day that they would not see Him until they say, "Blessed is he that cometh in the name of the Lord" (Matthew 23:39). It is likewise true that the Mormon people will open their blinded eyes and see the Lord when they truly feel that you are there, with love, in His Holy name.

The Antidote for Falsehood

The many times that Jesus was confronted with false doctrine, He spoke of the True Word of God. In every area of false doctrine with Mormonism, the True Word of God can be given as the antidote. Let's compare the Mormon doctrine of "The Law of Eternal Progression" with the Word of God.

First, let's explore the doctrine that god/Elohim is a part of a multi-generation family of gods. The Biblical God of Christianity says:

>...*before me there was no God formed; neither shall there be after me.* (Isaiah 43:10)
>
>*I am the first, and I am the last; and beside me there is no God!* (Isaiah 44:6)
>
>*Ye are my witnesses. Is there a God beside me? Yea, there is no God; I know not any!* (Isaiah 44:8)

Our God says that He had no father or mother, or gods above Him. He has no brothers or sisters who are gods, and there will never be any god after him. It is pretty clear that God knew what He was talking about! When He blessed Abraham, He swore by Himself, because He knew none greater (Hebrews 6:13). The Scripture says that it is impossible for God to lie (Hebrews 6:18). Let's believe God! Who would dare take Joseph Smith's word over the very Word of God?

Our God denies that He grew up on another planet. He denies that He became a god through the judgment of some other God. He inhabits eternity (Isaiah 57:15). He does not change (Malachi 3:6); In Him there is no variableness or shadow of turning (James 1:17). He was always God even before time even existed (John 1:2).

The Mormon doctrine has turned people away from the Living God into a fable of vain imagination. Their foolish hearts have been darkened. Professing themselves to be wise, they have become fools! Why?

> *[They] have changed the glory of the incorruptible God into an image made like corruptible man! [They have] changed the truth of God into a lie and worshiped and served the creature more than the Creator, who is blessed forever!* (Romans 1:21-25)

Unlikely Brothers

Digging through the fable that men will become gods, have goddesses for wives, propagate societies of "spirit children," I must pause at another startling heresy: the doctrine that Jesus and Lucifer are brothers!

We are told in Scripture that the great Son of the Morning, Lucifer, was cut to the ground and brought down to hell, because he sought to exalt his throne above the stars of God (Isaiah 14:12). He was an anointed cherub or angel of God, but was a *created* being (Ezekiel 28:14-15). Yet it was Jesus who created the very angel the Mormons claim was His physical brother (Hebrews 2:11). Finally, Christ's position, and that of any angel is made crystal clear. Jesus was always

God—far better than the angels: "Unto which of the angels said he [God] at any time, 'Thou art my Son; this day have I begotten Thee'" (Hebrews 1:4-5). None!

Begotten or Elected?

According to the Mormon gospel, Jesus became our Savior through a vote of a "council of gods," because he had a better plan than Lucifer. The Scripture again declares that Jesus always was God and was with God from before time existed (John 1:1-5). In the Greek, John 1:18 declares that He is the "only begotten *Theos*" or, the *only begotten God without beginning*. His goings forth have been from of old, from everlasting (Micah 5:2). He told the world that "before Abraham was, I AM" (John 8:58). Our Jesus is the Alpha and Omega, the beginning and the end, the first and the last (Revelation 22:13). To reduce Him to anything less is to deny His very divinity, the very reason only He could be the sin-offering to end all sin-offerings! (Hebrews 9:12-14)

A Physical Act of Sex

Since the Mormon god is a physical man, preoccupied at Kolob with the work of procreation, it must also be that he had physical relations with Mary, to purposely "beget" Jesus. The prophet Brigham Young said that the Holy Ghost could not be involved; otherwise it would not be safe to lay hands on the young women of the church for the receiving of the Holy Ghost because the Holy Ghost would make them pregnant, and bring great shame to the Elders of the Church.[10]

The Word of God clearly destroys this blasphemy. Mary was with child of the Holy Ghost (Matthew 1:18; Luke 1:34-35). It was prophesied that He would be born of the seed of woman (Genesis 3:15) and He would be born of a virgin (Isaiah 7:14).

The Gravest Heresy of All

The gravest heresy among so many is the Mormon doctrine of Jesus Christ, a son of one god of many gods, our elder brother and a polygamist, whose death on Calvary gives all mankind physical resurrection so that we can be judged for our sins and pay the penalties for all sin not covered by our works! To believe this would require the removal of the major portion of the New Testament and a good amount of the Old Testament. It would need a latter-day prophet whose words would even supersede the Mighty Word of God. It would need a Joseph Smith and a people who would believe the lie the Mormons call The Law of Eternal Progression.

The Way of Escape

The Mormon must come to understand that we all sin and come short of God's best for us (Romans 3:23). But God loved us, even though we separated ourselves from Him so very long ago. He sent His Son to reconcile us with Him. He became sin for us (2 Corinthians 5:21). He became our Passover Lamb (1 Corinthians 5:7). For while we were enemies of God, we were restored through Calvary (Romans 5:8-10). We, in Christ, are redeemed from the curse of the law (Galatians 3:13). Through the shedding of His blood, we have the forgiveness of sin (Ephesians 1:6-7) and have been accepted by God, raised up, and seated together with Christ in Heavenly places (Ephesians 2:6).

This reconciliation is not of our works of righteousness, but through His death at Calvary. It is our acceptance of this fact that makes us holy and unblameable and unreprovable in His sight. (Colossians 1:21-22)

The laws and ordinances that were against us (and still against the Mormon people) were moved out of the way 2000 years ago by Christ, who nailed them to the Cross (Colossians 2:14).

The Mormon leaders have removed the one true sin offering—the only one possible! *What a grievous error!* They have taken God's perfect gift—His perfect love—and replaced Calvary with their own judgment, their own version of the first covenant. They have taken the shed blood of Calvary away from Jesus.

The doctrines of Mormonism cannot stand the test of the Word of God. We are told that false teachers will come, fleeing from sound doctrine, they shall turn away their followers from the Truth, unto fables (2 Timothy 4:4). How true that is of the Mormon leaders. *"For the leaders of them shall cause them to err and they that are led of them are destroyed."* (Isaiah 9:16)

The tragedy of all this is that such beautiful, hardworking, and committed people are spiritually blinded people, with the light of the glorious gospel of Christ hid from them by Satan (2Corinthians 4:3-4). The Mormon people are not the enemies of God, but victims of a horrible and wicked hoax fed to them by evil teachers, who are of their father, the devil.

Only those sent by God, with the knowledge of God, using the Word of God can set them free. Are you one who can reach out to them and bring them the living light? We pray that you can and that you will!

A Warning to Christians

With the constant barrage of Mormon advertising and proselytizing, the Christian church must again be warned in the strongest way to stay true to sound biblical teaching. Do not buy the lie. Mitt Romney's run for the Oval Office and the alignment of so many "Christian" leaders will have this subject at the forefront of American society through the soon-coming General elections and for years to come if Mitt Romney is elected and if the present Hate Crimes Bill before Congress gets past, when speaking unkindly of a Mormon President's religion may land one in jail.

Christians must realize that the Mormon hope of outwardly appearing Christian is not reflected in their foundational teaching. Mormons still believe that all Christian pastors are part of the great whore of all the earth. They still have the hope of becoming gods and goddesses. The Mormon Jesus is still the brother of Lucifer. They still teach that our holy God was once a man, and has a body. Their Jesus was still begotten thorough a sexual relationship between the Father and Mary. They still believe that the Garden of Eden was in Missouri. They still believe the Bible is missing many plain and precious parts—that *The Book of Mormon* is still the most correct of any book on earth. They still believe plural marriage is a holy principle.

They still follow the teachings of a false prophet. They still usurp the holy priesthood of Christ. They still baptize for the dead. They still wear occult underwear with Masonic markings. They still believe they must offer up secret handshakes and secret names to enter into God's presence. They still teach that all the Christian creeds are an abomination in God's sight.

But God's Word is still reliable, and it doesn't vacilate, and Mormonism is still in direct violation of the Word of

God. One cannot revise Mormonism enough; one has to repent of it.

A Spiritual Battle

There is no basic difference between being led to hell through the doctrines and gods of Mormonism and being led there through the gods and doctrines of the pagan New Age Movement, Hinduism or Buddhism.

I had this point strongly brought home while speaking at a church. I was sitting quietly in the back row of the church as I waited for the congregation to file in for the service. I have always marveled at the speed with which a church can be filled in those last few moments before the start of a service. It's as though every family has worked out the very minutes and seconds it takes to rise, shower, dress, eat and drive to church, and walk in from the parking lot to their favorite pews. It is an amazing example of human engineering.

Looking about me, I noticed a magazine sitting on the pew next to me. Its front cover and lead story caught my eye. The headline read: *BUDDHISM: Golden Temples, Empty Hearts*. I picked up the magazine and turned to the article inside.[11]

The author, Robert Houlihan, shared his dismay as he visited the Buddhist Shwedagon Pagoda in Yangon, Myanmar.

Why would anyone worship such idols? Why would people pay money to pour water over stone gods that are eroded from years of usage? Why would they teach their children to bow before gods that look like devils, show no compassion and have the vile nature of humanity?

In his article, Houlihan shared his zeal for bringing the glorious message of Jesus Christ to the 300 million souls in over 1000 people groups who are bound by the power of Buddhism.

In a follow-up article titled "Warfare in the Temple," an unidentified missionary speaks of the spiritual battle for souls lost to the demonic powers of Buddhism:

> I stood in the temple doorway and stared at the Buddha. All around me pilgrims prostrated themselves before the idol. Only oil lamps lighted the temple. Hot air, laden with the stench of sweaty bodies and rancid oil, hung over me. In my spirit I felt the heavy bondage of the worshippers. This temple was a stronghold of the devil, and these people were his captives. "I come here in the name of Jesus," I declared aloud. "He is going to tear down this stronghold. He is going to set the captives free."[12]

My own heart raced as I read those words. Just getting a church to even agree to hear a message on the tragedy of the millions of people lost to the spiritual darkness of Mormonism is in itself a victory these days.

People in churches like the one I was sitting in easily understood the mighty battle when it came to Buddhism, but experience had taught me that I was going to have a difficult time stirring their hearts to engage in spiritual battle for the souls of their friends and neighbors lost in Mormonism.

Something Special in the Air

The church had miraculously filled by now, and I went forward to sit with the pastor, saying my hellos as I worked my way to the front and climbed the few stairs to sit at his side in front of the choir. The service quickly got underway, but my own thoughts drifted back to a time when my good friend, Dr. Ron Carlson and I spoke at a series of meetings throughout the Philippine Islands.

One morning our host took us to a Buddhist temple outside the city we were visiting. I remembered the ornate structure, the giant statue of Buddha, and the prostrate pilgrims. The smells of the place had been burned indelibly in my mind, and they returned to me in the middle of this church service as fresh as though I had just experienced them. I remembered how Ron and I both felt the intense heaviness of spiritual darkness in the air of that place and how it remained with us until we stepped outside the gardens surrounding the property and returned to the street. Our hearts had been broken for those souls lost in that terrible darkness. There was no doubt in either of our minds that this temple was truly a stronghold of the devil.

I preached that day on God's broken heart for those lost in false faiths like Buddhism and Mormonism. No one wept, and the church emptied as swiftly as it had filled up. I walked outside and took in a deep breath of clean air and wondered what I was doing there.

Not long after my return to the United States, I went to Salt Lake City, Utah, for a conference. One weekday morning I took advantage of a break in the schedule to take a solitary walk around downtown Salt Lake City to reflect on the ministry in which I was involved and to pray for the Mormon people. Like most walks through downtown Salt Lake, mine ended at Temple Square. I walked through the gates and felt the same intense heaviness of spiritual darkness that I remembered from our visit to the Buddhist temple.

I determined to go quietly through both the North and South Visitor Centers and pray for the Mormon people held in bondage to that demonic power I felt in such control of the place. Much like the missionary in the magazine article, I kept praying that God would break the spiritual stranglehold the devil held over these people, in the mighty name of Jesus!

I walked through every display area, entered presentation rooms that were largely empty at that hour of the workday, and continued through each level of each building and along every pathway between.

Finally I made my way down to the lower level of the Visitor Center nearest the Assembly Hall, which housed the famous baptismal font, a great basin that stands on the backs of 12 bronze oxen, representing the twelve tribes and is a replica of the ones used in Mormon Temples for the baptisms for the dead. The place was deserted. I went into a little theater area and by some automatic mechanism or the hidden hand of an attendant, I watched an animated *Book of Mormon* presentation.

When it was over I sat there, alone in that dark and quiet place, asking God what to do, how to reach these lost people with His message of freedom. I saw clearly that the Mormon people were not the enemies of God, but victims who had fallen prey to the wiles of the devil. I saw clearly that Lucifer was the god of this place, blinding even those who loved God and sought only to serve Him. They were bond slaves to the prince of darkness. I wept that morning for the Mormon people, with groanings from deep within my soul. I knew that the battle was "not against flesh and blood, but against principalities, against powers, against the rulers of the darkness of this world, against spiritual wickedness in high places" (Ephesians 6:12).

I finally stepped back into the hallway and, rounding a corner, headed for an escalator that would return me to the main floor. As I neared the escalator, I startled a small, elderly lady who was apparently asleep on a comfortable bench against the wall. She jumped up and brushed her clothes back, straightening her white hair and her hostess badge, a bit embarrassed to be caught sleeping at her post. She smiled sweetly at me, and as I stepped onto the escalator, said:

> **My, My! Isn't this the most peaceful place on earth? Don't you feel that special something in the air, smell that holy aroma? Have you ever experienced anything like that before?**

I already knew about that special heaviness she was describing, but I didn't have the heart to tell this sweet dear lady. I smiled back at her and kept my lips closed, letting her comment slip into the air. But God had other plans. The escalator stopped in its tracks. There I stood and there she stood, waiting for my response to her inquiry. Our eyes locked. Seconds seemed like minutes.

Finally, I spoke:

> Yes, I recognize it. It is the very same heavy air of spiritual darkness that I found in a Buddhist temple in the Philippines. It has the same weight, the same aroma. My heart broke for those lost in *that* terrible darkness because there was not a shred of doubt in my mind that temple was truly a stronghold of the

devil. I am sorry, but I am convinced that it holds true of this place as well.

Looking down at the dead escalator, I added, "I think the Lord wanted you to know that and that he loves you as a precious daughter." The lady looked at me for a moment, and then I saw the silent tears falling from her eyes. The escalator mysteriously started again at just that moment, and I silently rose away from her view.

Footnotes:

Chapter One:

1. *Mormon Doctrine*, Apostle Bruce R. McConkie, [abbreviated *MD*], p.321
2. *History of the Church* [HC] Vol.6, Joseph Smith, p.306
3. Achieving Celestial Marriage Manual [abbreviated *ACCM*], p.3
4. Ibid, p.203
5. *Doctrine & Covenants* [abbreviated *D&C*] 124:28-36 (considered LDS scripture)
6. Ibid, 128:15
7. Ibid, 131: 1-3
8. Joseph Smith, *The Pearl of Great Price*: Moses 1:39 (considered LDS scripture)
9. *D&C* 76:53-58, 70
10. Ibid, 132:19-20
11. *ACMM*, pp.131-132
12. *D&C*, 132:1-6; 61-64
13. *MD*, pp.529-530

[14] http://en.wikipedia.org/wiki/Heavenly_Mother_(Latter_Day_Saints)

Chapter Two

[1] *Encyclopedia of Mormonism*, Vol. 3, pp.1363-1364
[2] Ibid
[3] Chuck Sackett, *What's Going On In There?*, p.62. Letter rescinding oath, Apostle George. F. Richards, February 15, 1927
[4] Ibid
[5] *MD*, p.538
[6] *The Encyclopedia of Mormonism*, Vol. 1, p.423
[7] Joseph Smith, *History of The Church*, Vol. 5, pp.218-219
[8] Brigham Young, *Journal of Discourses*, Vol. 7, pp.290-291
[9] Ibid, Vol. 10, p.110
[10] John Taylor, *Journal of Discourses*, Vol. 22, p.304
[11] Joseph Fielding Smith, *The Way To Perfection*, pp.101-102
[12] Joseph Fielding Smith, *Look Magazine*, October 22, 1963
[13] *MD*, 10th printing, pp.527-528
[14] *MD*, p.616
[15] *MD*, p.109
[16] *MD*, p.343
[17] *MD*, p.114
[18] John Heinerman and Anson Shupe, The Mormon Corporate Empire, *The Mormon Public Relations Quest*, pp.70-71
[19] Ibid, pp.71-72
[20] *US News and World Report*, Sept. 28, 1992 Science and Society, "Latter-day struggles"

[21] Ibid, p.77

[22] *US News and World Report*, May 14, 1990, p.14

[23] Vern Anderson, "Historian explores LDS women and priesthood," *Provo Daily Herald*, Utah News section Friday, December 25, 1992. p.A11

[24] Ibid

[25] Elder Boyd K. Packer, of the Council of the Twelve Apostles, during a Priesthood Restoration fireside, May 1989. *Provo Daily Herald*, December 25, 1992, p.A11

[26] Ezra Taft Benson, "Don't Limit Family Size," *Salt Lake Tribune*, February 23, 1987

[27] Ezra Taft Benson, Church News, February 28, 1987, "Benson affirms home is heart of gospel," p.3

[28] *Rocky Mountain News*, May 26, 1990, p.32

Chapter Three

[1] Joseph Smith, *Pearl of Great Price*, 2:14-20

[2] Ibid, Joseph Smith 2:30-35

[3] *D&C,* Section 135

[4] David Breese, video interview, 1992, on file, Jeremiah Films

[5] *No Man Knows My History, The Life of Joseph Smith*, Fawn M. Brodie, Alfred Knopf Publishers, 1971 p.457

[6] *Nauvoo Expositor*, June 7, 1844

[7] *History of the Church*, Vol. 6, pp.616-619

[8] Ibid, Vol. 6, p.408

[9] *The First Vision: The Pearl of Great Price,* Joseph Smith – History – Chapter 1, Verses 14-20

[10] *D&C* 130:22 (Joseph)

[11] *PGP: JS 2:20*

Chapter Four

[1] *The Evangel*, May -June 1992, p.10, quoting *The Salt Lake Tribune*, February 13, 1992

[2] Bill Schnoebelen, Video interview, on file, Jeremiah Films

[3] John Heinerman, Video interview, February 27, 1988, on file, Jeremiah Films

[4] Ibid

[5] Huffaker, Homosexuality at BYU a two Part Series, *Seventh East Press*, Provo, Utah, March 27, 1982, April 12, 1982, p.1, both issues

[6] Ibid

[7] http://www.pinknews.co.uk/news/articles/2005-5226.html

[8] Dawn House, "Evergreen Holds Private Meet for LDS Bishops, Gays," *Salt Lake Tribune*, May 7, 1990, page 2B

[9] Saints Alive Newsletter Update Report, "Utah Divorce Rate Still High," February 1990, p.4, cites *Salt Lake Tribune*, January 11, 1990

[10] Saints Alive Newsletter Update Report, "Concern about Domestic Violence Increases," March 1992, p.3 cites *Salt Lake Tribune* January 4, 1992)

[11] The Inner Circle. Vol. IX. JULY 1992 #7. Child Abuse and Neglect Jump 20%, pg 1 cites the Utah Division of Family Service's Report 1991

12. Saints Alive Newsletter Update Report, "Zion Going Downhill," June-July 1992, p.3, cites Salt Lake Rape Crisis Center
13. Saints Alive Newsletter Update Report, May 1990, "Utah High in Child Labor-law Violations" cites *The Salt Lake Tribune*, April 24, 1990
14. Saints Alive Newsletter Update Report, January 1991, p.4, "Unwed Teen Pregnancies Reaching Crisis" referencing a *Utah Holiday Magazine* article dated November 1990
15. *Provo Herald*, May 24, 1990 "Utah ranks fourth for its prison population"
16. Utah Criminal Code # 76-5-406.5
17. Saints Alive Newsletter Update Report, February 1990, p.2, "Utah Child Abuse rises 44% in two years," reporting on article on Child Abuse increases, *Salt Lake Tribune*, January 24, 1990
18. *The Salt Lake Tribune*, February 16, 1989
19. Utah Criminal Code 76-5-406.5, Circumstances required for probation or suspension of sentence for sex offense against a child, Section 1.h.
20. Paul Rolly, "Did God Influence Jury?," *Salt Lake Tribune*, March 17, 1988, p.4B
21. FAX on file at Saints Alive
22. Peggy Fletcher Stack, "Attacking LDS Church Is Way of Life For Some," *Salt Lake Tribune*, December 7, 1992, Section d, p.1
23. Jorgensen/Stack, "Its Judgment Day for Far Right: LDS Church Purges Survivalists," *Salt Lake City Tribune*, November 29, 1992, pp.A1, A2
24. "Hero turned Heretic? Gritz May Be Leading LDS Flock into Wilderness," *The Salt Lake Tribune*, November 29, 1992, p.A5

25 "Ultraconservative Gritz Remains As Bold As Ever," *The Salt Lake Tribune*, December 7, 1992, p.B1

26 http://en.wikipedia.org/wiki/Bo_Gri

27 Transcription of KTVX (Channel 4) 10 PM News, December 11, 1993, Salt Lake City, UT "LDS Pro Lifers Being Excommunicated"

28 Peggy Stack, "LDS Apostasy Investigation Launched Against Historian," *The Salt Lake Tribune*, February 13, 1993, pp.A6-A7

29 Ibid

30 Vern Anderson, AP, "BYU Bans Students Who Quit LDS Church," *The Salt Lake Tribune*, March 20, 1993, p.C1

31 *"Historian: LDS church wants 'cookie-cutter' members,"* *The Salt Lake Tribune* Utah, Sunday, December 6, 1992, p.C3

32 http://en.wikipedia.org/wiki/Bo_Gri

Chapter Five:

1 Sackett, *What's Going On In There?*, Sword of The Shepherd Ministries, Inc., Thousand Oaks, CA. 1982

2 Spencer & Schnoebelen, *Mormonism's Temple Of Doom*, 1987, Through The Maze Ministries, PO Box 8656, Boise, ID 83707

3 Sackett, *Shocking News Of The Secret Renovation of The LDS Temple Ritual,* Sword Of The Shepherd Ministries, Inc. Thousand Oaks, CA, April 15, 1990

4 Sandra Tanner, *Evolution of The Mormon Temple Ceremony: 1842-1990*, Utah Lighthouse, SLC, UT., 1990

5 Sackett, *Shocking News...*

[6] Sackett, *What's going On in There?*, Sword of The Shepherd Ministries, Inc., Thousand Oaks, CA, 1982, p.33

[7] Kim Sue Lia Perkes, "Mormon Temple Rite gets Major Revision" *The Arizona Republic*, April 28, 1990 (Kim is Religion Editor.)

[8] John Dart, "Mormons Summon Those Who Spoke to Media of Temple Rites," *L.A. Times*, June 2.1990 (Dart is Times Religion Writer)

Chapter Six:

[1] Joseph Smith made this statement at the conclusion of a speech in the public square at Far West, Missouri on October 14, 1838. This particular quote is documented in Fawn M. Brodie, *No Man Knows My History*, second edition, 1971, pp.230–231

[2] John Ankerberg & John Weldon, *The Facts on Islam*, Harvest House Publishers, 1998, pp.8–9 and Eric Johnson, *Joseph Smith & Muhammed*, Mormonism Research Ministry, 1998, pp.6–7

[3] Joseph Smith, *Documentary History of the* [Mormon] *Church*, Vol.4, pp.461

[4] Joseph Smith, *History of the Church*, Vol. 6, pp.408-409

Chapter Seven:

[1] Billy Graham, column, *Seattle Post Intelligencer*, circa 1985

[2] Gordon R. Lewis. *Confronting the Cults*, Presbyterian and Reformed Publishing Co., Philipsburg NJ, 1966, p.3

[3] Concerned Christians & Former Mormons newsletter, July 1992, p.3

4 "A Baptist ward each week," *The Latter-Day Sentinel* April 2, 1988, Church Digest Section

5 Erickson, "Mormon Tries To Reach Out To Other Faiths," *Journal American*, Bellevue, WA, May 21, 1988, Religion Page

6 Decker, "Peril To Churches," *Journal American*, Bellevue, WA, June 4, 1988, Letter To Editor Column

7 Anderson, *Soft Answers To Hard Questions,* self-published, 1987, available In LDS bookstores

8 *LDS Sentinel*, Phoenix, AZ, August 10, 1986

9 "Missionaries to Zion," *The Inner Circle*, Marlow, OK, September 1992, p.7

10 Don and Brennan Kingsland, Dear Pastor, Platen Publications form letter, August 11, 1987

11 http://blog.beliefnet.com/blogalogue/2007/06/who-gets-to-define-christian.html

12 http://blog.beliefnet.com/blogalogue/2007/07/the-church-of-the-devil.html

13 David Briggs, "Mormons smooth relations with other denominations," *Journal American*, June 16, 1990, Religion page

14 Ed Decker, letter to Rev. Harry Applewhite, Pastor, First Congregational Church, Bellevue, WA, January 19, 1989

15 *The Inner Circle*, Marlow, OK, July 1992, p.1

16 *The Book of Mormon*, I Nephi 14:10

17 Robert McKay, *The Evangel*, July-August 1992, p.6

18 "Mormons forge links with other faiths" *The Orange County Register*, October 20, 1990, p.E11 Religion

19 Ibid

[20] Chuck Sackett, video Interview, November 7, 1991, on file, Jeremiah Films

[21] Ibid

Chapter Eight:

[1] *Vine's Expository Dictionary*, p.904

[2] *History of the Church*, Deseret Books, Salt Lake City, UT., 1978, 2:380-81

[3] See ibid, 2:187 for a list of the Twelve Apostles chosen

[4] Ibid, 2:528

[5] Ibid, 3:20

[6] Ibid, pp. 31-32

[7] Ibid, pp. 166-167

[8] Ibid, 7:483

[9] *Doctrine & Covenants*, Official Declaration-1, pp.291-92, 1981 edition

[10] Larry S. Jonas, *Mormonism Claims Examined*, Baker Books, Grand Rapids, MI., 1961, p.52

[11] *The Evening and Morning Star*, Vol. 1, issue 8

[12] Letter from Dick & Patty Baer, dated October 10, 1981, p.9

[13] *History of the Church*, Deseret Books, Salt Lake City, UT., 1978, 1:315-16

[14] *History of the Church*, Deseret Books, Salt Lake City, UT., 1978, 5:336.

[15] Ibid, p. 394

[16] *Documentary History of the [Mormon] Church*, Vol. 6, pp.408-409

17. *Doctrine & Covenants*, Chapter 135: 1-2
18. *Teachings of the Prophet Joseph Smith*, compiled by Joseph Fielding Smith, Deseret Books, 1972, p.368 #46
19. Ibid, Vol.6, p.350
20. Mormon Ward Teachers' Message, *Deseret News*, May 26, 1945, #47
21. S. Dilworth Young, BYU Stake fireside meeting on May 5, 1974
22. "President Benson Pleads, 'Follow the Prophet!'" Brigham Young University TODAY Speech, delivered February 26, 1980, in Marriott Center
23. Neal A. Maxwell, *Scriptures for the Modern World*, ed. Paul R. Cheesman and C. Wilfred Griggs, Provo, Utah: Religious Studies Center, 1984, p.1
24. *A New Witness for the Articles of Faith*, Salt Lake City: Deseret Book Co., 1985, pp.348-50
25. Brigitte Greenberg, "As membership grows, Mormon president wanes," *Journal American*, Bellevue, WA, February 20, 1993, p.B1
26. Wendy Ogata, "Benson too frail to attend [General Conference]" See picture accompanying article, *Ogden Standard Examiner*, Religion page, October 4, 1992
27. "LDS Apostle wrote of 'Revelations'" *The Salt Lake Tribune*, Sunday, December 4, 1988, p.B15

Chapter Nine

1. Joseph Smith, *Pearl of Great Price*, p.60
2. Orson Pratt, *The Bible Alone an Insufficient Guide*, Early LDS Pamphlet, pp.44-47

[3] Joseph F. Smith, *The Teachings of the Prophet Joseph Smith*, 1938, p.327

[4] *D&C*, Section 9: 8-9

[5] *Ensign Magazine*, October 1979, p.18

[6] Edvalson & Smith, *Plain and Precious Parts*, published by the Seventy's Mission Bookstore, Provo, Utah, 1977, pp.62-63

[7] Richard A. Parker, "The Joseph Smith Papyri, A Preliminary Report," *Dialogue Journal*, Summer 1968, p.86

[8] Klaus Baer, "The Breathing Permit of Hor," *Dialogue Journal*, Summer 1968, pp.109-110, 119

[9] Dr. Edward H. Ashment, "The Facsimiles of the Book of Abraham," *Sunstone*, Vol. 4, Numbers 5 and 6, pp.33-48

Chapter Ten

[1] *D&C*, Chapter 135: 1-4

[2] Ibid, verses 20, 21

[3] Fawn M. Brodie, *No Man Knows My History,* 1945, pp.335-336

[4] Ibid, pp.458-459

[5] Brigham Young, *Journal of Discourses,* Vol. 11, p.269

[6] *D&C*, Official Declaration 1. Also, see Heinerman, Mormon Corporate Empire, p.10

[7] Jane Zhang, "Polygamy, a way of life in small Utah, Arizona," *The Desert Sun,* May 23, 2003, p.A32

[8] Margaretta Spencer, "The God Makers II" Video [abbreviated GMII] interview, July 22, 1988, on file, Jeremiah Films

[9] James Spencer, GMII Video interview, July 22, 1988, on file, Jeremiah Films

[10] Harold Schindler, "Leaders, Descendents to Dedicate Monument at Mountain Meadows," *Salt Lake Tribune,* September 9, 1990, p.B3

[11] Thelma Geer, GMII interview, September 7, 1988, on file, Jeremiah Films

[12] Art Buella, GMII Video interview, Oct. 14, 1988, on file, Jeremiah Films

[13] Lillian Chynoweth, Video interview, September 25, 1988, on file, Jeremiah Films

[14] Evan Moore, "Dead Cult Leader's doctrine still leaving trail blood," *Hustone Chronical,* June 28, 1988, section 1, p.11. Also see "Hanson/Liebrum, Four Killings tied to LeBaron cultists," same paper and day, section 1, p.1

[15] President J. M. Grant, *Journal of Discourses,* Vol. 4, p.51

[16] President Brigham Young, *Journal of Discourses,* Vol. 4, p.220

[17] AP Report, Blood Atonement concerns church, *Daily Herald,* Provo, Utah, April 30, 1989, p.A5

[18] Lillian Chynoweth, Video interview, September 25, 2988, on file, Jeremiah Films

[19] *D&C,* Section 132

[20] Come Unto Christ, Melchizedek Priesthood Personal study Guide, 1984/1988, 1986 Edition, Lesson 20, Joseph Smith, *The Prophet of the Restoration,* pp.139-145

[21] EYEWITNESS NEWS report, June 27, 1988, Video copy, on file, Jeremiah Films

[22] AP Report, Houston, Texas, January 21, 1993

23 Bruce R. McConkie, *Mormon Doctrine*, p.92

24 Art Buella, GMII Video interview, October 14, 1988, on file, Jeremiah Films

25 Thelma Geer, Video interview #2, September 17, 1991, on file, Jeremiah Films. Also see Thelma Geer, *Mormonism, Mama and Me*, 1983, Calvary Missionary Press, Tucson, AZ, pp.119-123

26 Art Buella, GMII Video interview, October 14, 1988, on file, Jeremiah Films

27 Letter to Ed Decker November 25, 2003, on file at Saints alive office

28 *Salt Lake Tribune*, December 14, 1997, p.A1. The above article by Greg Burton is copied, as published from http://www.mazeministry.com/mormonism/women/teenbrides.htm

29 Associated Press, Salt Lake City, August 20, 2006

30 www.azcentral.com, originally published August 1, 2004

31 Wade Goodwyn, Howard Berkes and Amy Walters For National Public Radio, from http://www.npr.org/templates/story/story.php?storyId=4629320

32 John Dougherty & Kirk Johnson, "Sect Leader Is Convicted as an Accomplice to Rape" *New York Times*, September 26, 2007

33 http://en.wikipedia.org/wiki/Fundamentalist_Church_of_Jesus_Christ_of_Latter_Day_Saints

Chapter Eleven

1 Bishop Glenn L. Pace, Memorandum: July 19, 1990, Strengthening Church Members Committee: Ritualistic Child Abuse, pp.1, 5

2. Ed Decker, "The Sure Sign of the Nail," *Saints Alive Journal*, Spring, 1987, pp.9-10
3. William J. Schnoebelen & James R. Spencer, *Mormonism's Temple of Doom* (1987) and *Whited Sepulchers: The Hidden Language of the Mormon Temple* (1990) from Triple J Publications, Box 8656, Boise, ID. 83707
4. Chuck Sackett, *What's Going on in There?*, p.57
5. Lucy Mack Smith, HISTORY. Manuscript trans. by Martha Jane Coray in 1845. Photocopy, Special Collections in the J. Willard Marriott Library, University of Utah, Salt Lake City, UT., p.46
6. Sworn affidavit by Rev. Wesley P. Walters, October 28, 1971
7. D. Michael Quinn, *Early Mormonism and the Magic World View*, Signature Books, 1987, pp.118-132
8. Guinn Williams, "A Necromantic Incident in Palmyra, N.Y.," *Saints Alive Journal*, 1989, pp.2-12
9. C.R. Stafford, *The Naked Truth About Mormonism*, January 1888, p.3
10. William Stafford, sworn affidavit; and Francis W. Kirkham, *A New Witness for Christ in America*, 1959, Vol. 2, p.367
11. Reed C. Durham, *Is There No Help for the Widow's Son?*, Martin Publishing, Nauvoo, IL, 1980, pp.22ff
12. William J. Schnoebelen & James R. Spencer, *Mormonism's Temple of Doom* (1987) and *Whited Sepulchers: The Hidden Language of the Mormon Temple* (1990)
13. Bishop Glenn L. Pace, Memorandum: July 19, 1990, Strengthening Church Members Committee: Ritualistic Child Abuse, p.5
14. Ibid, p.4

[15] Ibid

[16] Ed Decker, "Temple of the God Makers," Saints Alive in Jesus, 1985. Tanner, The Lucifer God Doctrine, November, 1987

[17] Bill Schnoebelen, "Joseph Smith and the Temple of Doom," Saints Alive tapes, Capstone 1986. Tanner, "Covering Up Syn," Utah Lighthouse, SLC, UT, April, 1988. See also, Spencer, RE: "Attack on Mormonism's Temple of Doom," Through the Maze Ministries, 38 page response

[18] Decker, Schnoebelen, "Lucifer God Doctrine, Shadow or Reality?," Saints Alive, December 20, 1987, [60 pages plus, response]

[19] Dr. David Breese, Video interview, 1992, on file, Jeremiah Films

Chapter Twelve

[1] http://en.wikipedia.org/wiki/George_W._Romney

[2] Harvest House Publishers; Revised, Updated edition, November 15, 1997

[3] http://www.saintsalive.com/mormonism/temple_ritual.htm

[4] Ibid

[5] Klaus J. Hansen, *Quest for Empire, The Political Kingdom of God and the Council of Fifty in Mormon History*, pp.55-56

[6] John J. Stewart, op. cit., p. 204

[7] *Los Angeles Times*, April 5, 1980, Part 1:1, p.1

[8] Kostman et al, op. cit

[9] *Salt Lake City Tribune*, October 1, 1981

[10] Ibid

[11] Kostman et al, op. cit

12. *The Wall Street Journal*, November 9, 1983, p. 16
13. *Journal of Discourses*, Vol. 7, p. 15
14. Hyrum L. Andrus, *Joseph Smith, the Man and Seer*, p.5
15. John J. Stewart, op. cit., p.209; Hyrum L. Andrus, *Joseph Smith and World Government*, op. cit., p.54
16. *The Ensign*, January 1979, "To Prepare a People," p.18
17. Brigham Young, *Journal of Discourses*, Vol. 1, p.230
18. End of quote from *The God Makers*, Chapter 16
19. Brigham Young, *Journal of Discourses* [JOD] Vol. 7, p.150
20. Brigham Young, *Journal of Discourses*, Vol. 2, p.317
21. George Q. Cannon, JOD, Vol. 23, p.104
22. George Q. Cannon, JOD, Vol. 23, p.104
23. Brigham Young JOD, Vol. 2, p.317
24. *D&C* 104, verse 1
25. *D&C* 104:14-16
26. *D&C* 42
27. *D&C* 42:30
28. *D&C* 51:3
29. Documentary History of the Church, Vol. 7, pp.412-413 30UPI Staff, United Press International, February 19, 2007 WASHINGTON 31"Romney's Campaign Of Transformation," J. Pinkerton, *Newsday*, February 15, 2007
32. Posted: August 2, 2007 by Aaron Klein © 2007 WorldNetDaily.com
33. *Improvement Era* (Official LDS church magazine), June 1945, p.345
34. LDS Stake Bulletin, Renton Washington Stake, Fall, 1976
35. President N. Eldon Tanner [1st Counselor to the Prophet, "The Debate is over," *The Ensign*, August 1979, First presidency Message

36 *Ensign*, May 1978, p.64

37 Elder Wilford Woodruff, *Journal of Discourses*, Vol. 5, p.83

38 Elder S. Dilworth Young, BYU Fireside, May 5, 1974

39 President Heber C. Kimball, *Journal of Discourses*, Vol. 6, p.32

Chapter Thirteen

1 David Biema, "Kingdom Come," *TIME* Magazine, August 1997

2 Ibid

3 "Mormon, Inc., Finances and Faith" a 4 part series, *Arizona Republic Newspaper*, Phoenix, AZ, beginning on June 30, 1991

4 John Heinerman, video interview, February 27, 1988, on file, Jeremiah Films

5 Ibid

Chapter Fourteen

1 Joseph Fielding Smith, *Teachings of the Prophet Joseph Smith*, p.194

2 LeGrand Richards, *A Marvelous Work and Wonder*, p.69

3 Sandra Tanner, "The God Makers," video, 1982, Jeremiah Films

4 Harold Goodman, "The God Makers" video, 1982 Jeremiah films

5 John L. Sorenson, *An Ancient American Setting For The Book of Mormon*, 1980, pp.0/2-0/3

6 Dr. Ross T. Christensen, The University Archaeological Society Report, Number 19, December, 1960, pp.8-9

7 Michael Coe, "Mormons and Archaeology, An Outside View," Dialogue, *A Journal of Mormon Thought*, pp.40-48

8. Martin Raish, "All That Glitters: Uncovering Fool's Gold in Book of Mormon Archaeology," *Sunstone*, Vol. Six, Number One, pp.10-15
9. Dr. Charles Crane, "A Comparison of The Bible and The Book Of Mormon," a paper, Caldwell ID, 1982, pp.9-11
10. Milton R. Hunter, *Christ in Ancient America*, Vol. II, pp.51-53
11. Ibid, p.121
12. James Witham, "Archaeology and the Book of Mormon," a Slide presentation with notes, p.5-8, Saints Alive Ministries.
13. Vincent H. Malmstrom, "Where Time Began," *Science Digest*, December 1981, pp.56-59, 112-113

Chapter Fifteen

1. *Ensign*, May 1977, p.49
2. *Mormon Doctrine*, by LDS Apostle Bruce R. McConkie, p.828; D&C 29:36-41
3. *Mormon Doctrine*, McConkie, pp.526-528; *The Pearl of Great Price*, Moses 5:16-41, 7: 8-22
4. *Mormon Doctrine*, McConkie; pp.547-742
5. *Journal of Discourses*, Vol. 2, p.82
6. *History of Church* Vol. 4, pp.535-541
7. LDS pamphlet, "What the Mormons Think of Christ," p.22
8. *Mormon Doctrine*, McConkie, p.321, *Attaining Celestial Marriage Manual*, pp.3, 203
9. LDS pamphlet, "What the Mormons Think of Christ," p.22
10. *Journal of Discourses*, Vol. 1: 51-52, *Answers to Gospel Questions*, Joseph Fielding Smith, Vol. 5 p.128

[11] Robert Houlihan, *Mountain Movers*, November, 1992, Assemblies of God Missions magazine, Springfield, MO. pp.7-9

[12] Ibid

CPSIA information can be obtained at www.ICGtesting.com
Printed in the USA
LVOW100244020512

279982LV00001B/53/A